A. Lev,
privat

Materialien zum ausländischen und internationalen Privatrecht

44

Herausgegeben vom

Max-Planck-Institut für ausländisches
und internationales Privatrecht

Direktoren:

Jürgen Basedow, Klaus J. Hopt und Reinhard Zimmermann

Intellectual Property in the Conflict of Laws

Edited by

Jürgen Basedow, Josef Drexl,
Annette Kur & Axel Metzger

Preface by

Stig Strömholm

Mohr Siebeck

Jürgen Basedow is Professor at the Law Faculty of the University of Hamburg and since 1997 Director of the Max Planck Institute for Foreign Private and Private International Law in Hamburg.

Josef Drexl is Professor at the Law Faculty of the University of Munich and since 2001 Director of the Max Planck Institute for Intellectual Property, Competition and Tax Law in Munich.

Annette Kur is Head of Department at the Max Planck Institute for Intellectual Property, Competition and Tax Law (Nordic countries) and Associate Professor at the Law Faculty of the University of Stockholm.

Axel Metzger is Research Fellow at the Max Planck Institute for Foreign Private and Private International Law in Hamburg and Lecturer at the Law Faculty of the University of Hamburg.

ISBN 3-16-148513-0
ISSN 0543-0194 (Materialien zum ausländischen und internationalen Privatrecht)

Die Deutsche Bibliothek lists this publication in the Deutsche Nationalbibliographie; detailed bibliographic data is available in the Internet at *http://dnb.ddb.de*.

Printed in Germany.

Preface

It is a frequently made statement in legal writing that the rights which are known under the common name of intellectual property are highly international in character. National frontiers, it is often said, are not able to stop the productions which these particular rights protect, both in their capacity as "goods" – literary or artistic works, inventions, or trade marks – with a greater or smaller economic value, and in their capacity as expressions of the author's, inventor's or business man's personality. These productions are by definition ubiquitous, or at least capable of being made accessible in one form or another irrespective of political and legal frontiers.

It is also frequently stated, however, – and this is true particularly about writers in the field of private international law – that intellectual property has for a long time been an area neglected by conflict lawyers. This statement is usually made with regret, as a kind of excuse, or as an expression of criticism or self-criticism. The reasons put forward to explain this state of affairs vary considerably from one time to another and from one country to another.

The fact that industrial inventions like literary and artistic works are independent of physical links with any territory but at the same time represent great values, which are increasing rapidly with the enormous investments continuously made in these intellectual productions, creates an urgent need for such solutions as can provide an adequate international protection against infringements of the rights related to them. In most European countries intellectual property came into existence through a successive development of systems of individual *ad hoc* privileges strictly limited to the territory of the state granting them. These historical roots may well be described as a sort of original sin, which this field of law dragged with it, like heavy intellectual chains, into the modern era. The difficulty of solving the legal problems involved by applying the normal methods of private international law resulted, at the end of the 19th century, in a solution *sui generis*, viz. the creation of international conventions, which do not lay down rules for the choice of the applicable law but embody substantial rules, based upon the solutions given by the national laws concerned even where the provisions of the conventions deal exclusively with international relations. One consequence of this has been that private international law in the strict sense of that term has been slow in developing in this field and – it has to be admitted – that both conflict lawyers and intellectual property lawyers have looked upon the area where they meet each other as a disputed and dangerous legal borderland. The conspicuous lack of monographs in the leading countries before the 1990's illlustrates the situation eloquently.

There is no point in finding fault with the other side. Having worked for a long time in both fields, the present writer considers himself entitled to assure that the problems are important and interesting enough to deserve – indeed to need urgently – being discussed in peaceful cooperation by experts bringing knowledge and experience from both sides. It is in the first place what may be called "*the digital revolution*" – the new electronic means of communication – that makes it imperative to examine closely the private international law problems raised by the exercise of intellectual property rights on an international level. The main principle, which has so far been considered self-evident, at least for practical purposes – the tenet that international property is *territorially limited* and that protection beyond national frontiers is granted only by virtue of agreements between the jurisdictions concerned – is now under attack, or at least under serious critical discussion. In a report commissioned by an international organization in 1998, a leading American expert summarizes: "Now that digital media make possible the instantaneous, worldwide communication of works of authorship, the territorially discrete approach to international copyright has come under considerable strain."

It should be added, by way of precaution that a realistic analysis of the present situation does not make knowledge of the historically given and still largely prevailing traditional view of intellectual property rights as territorially limited rights unnecessary. There are strong reasons to believe that the time-honoured solutions will remain valid for substantial sectors of law even if other sectors call for new methods; there is no point in throwing the egg away with the shell. It must also be remembered that inertia is one of the most powerful actors in all legal and legislative development, not least on the international level. If and when the representatives of the strong political and financial interests involved succeed in designing and formulating such solutions as are deemed necessary to master the growing problems on a global level, it will certainly take a long time before such solutions are adopted by the international community at large, and even longer time before a system embodying them can be made operative. Meanwhile, the traditional rules cannot be neglected.

Against this background, the meeting organized in Hamburg on 2 and 3 March 2004, by two internationally leading centres of study in the fields of law concerned, acting in common – the Max Planck Institute for Foreign Private and Private International Law in Hamburg and the Max Planck Institute for Intellectual Property, Competition and Tax Law in Munich – is an initiative of great value and an encouraging sign of the times.

The papers published in the present volume constitute an impressive *florilegium* of studies concerning many essential aspects of the problems facing conflict lawyers and intellectual property lawyers and calling for their cooperation. The first section deals with topics rightly described as items on the current political agenda; it presents important recent initiatives in the fields of legislation and international conventions taken by the European Commission, the

American Law Institute and the Hague Conference on Private International Law. In a second section, a number of questions are discussed which concern the choice of law problems arising within the framework of contractual obligations, where recent developments – notably the emergence of so-called internationally mandatory rules – have contributed to create a new situation as compared with traditional conflict law. Lawyers familiar with the two fields discussed in the volume will not be astonished to note that the greatest number of contributions are found in the section headed "Non-contractual obligations"; here, competition law, patent law, copyright and trademarks are discussed separately, and particular attention is paid to the relation between community rights and the conflict of laws.

By bringing together a panel of experts as distinguished as those participating in the Hamburg symposium and by selecting a number of subjects as essential as those dealt with in the present volume, the organizers of this meeting have rendered a most important service to the development of a field of law that calls urgently for solutions based upon active, strong and lasting support by the international community of legal experts in the areas concerned. It is not the first time that members of the family of Max Planck Institutes take initiatives of this kind.

Uppsala, September 2004 *Stig Strömholm*

Table of Contents

Contributors

Jürgen Basedow, Dr. iur., Dr. h.c., LL.M. (Harvard), is Professor at the Law Faculty of the University of Hamburg, Director of the Max Planck Institute for Foreign Private and Private International Law in Hamburg, and Chairman of the German Monopoly Commission

Friedrich Wenzel Bulst, LL.M. (Yale), is Research Associate at the Max Planck Institute for Foreign Private and Private International Law in Hamburg

Graeme B. Dinwoodie, Dr. iur., LL.M. (Harvard), is Professor of Law at the Chicago-Kent College of Law and Director of the Program in Intellectual Property Law

Josef Drexl, Dr. iur., LL.M. (Berkeley), is Professor at the Law Faculty of the University of Munich and Director of the Max Planck Institute for Intellectual Property, Competition and Tax Law in Munich

Claudia Hahn, is Administrator at the Directorate-General Justice and Home Affairs of the European Commission in Brussels

Christian A. Heinze, LL.M. (Cambridge), is Research Associate at the Max Planck Institute for Foreign Private and Private International Law in Hamburg

Catherine Kessedjian, Dr. iur., is Professor at the Law Faculty of the Université Panthéon-Assas Paris II and Hauser Global Visiting Professor at the New York University School of Law

Annette Kur, Dr. iur., is Head of Department (Nordic Countries) at the Max Planck Institute for Intellectual Property, Competition and Tax Law in Munich and Associate Professor at the Law Faculty of the University of Stockholm

Matthias Leistner, Dr. iur., LL.M. (Cambridge), is Scholar of the "Bayerischer Habilitationsförderpreis" (Postdoc Scholarship) at the Max Planck Institute for Intellectual Property, Competition and Tax Law in Munich

Axel Metzger, Dr. iur. (Munich and Paris), is Research Fellow at the Max Planck Institute for Foreign Private and Private International Law in Hamburg and Lecturer at the Law Faculty of the University of Hamburg

M. Pertegás Sender, Dr. iur., LL.M. (Leuven), is Professor at the Law Faculty of the University of Antwerp and Off counsel at the Law firm Nauta Dutilh (Brussels)

Haimo Schack, Dr. iur., LL.M. (Berkeley), is Professor at the University of Kiel and Director of the Institute for European and International Private and Procedural Law in Kiel

Andrea Schulz, Dr. iur., LL.M. (Florence), is First Secretary at the Hague Conference on Private International Law and responsible for the Judgments Project

Stig Strömholm, Dr. iur., Dr. iur., Dr. h.c. mult., is Professor emeritus at the Law Faculty and former Rector of the University of Uppsala

Olivier Tell, is Principal Administrator at the Directorate-General Justice and Home Affairs of the European Commission in Brussels

Winfried Tilmann, Dr. iur., is Partner at the law firm Lovells (Düsseldorf) and Professor at the Law Faculty of the University of Heidelberg

Abbreviations

AC	Law Reports, Appeal Cases
AIPPI	Association Internationale pour la Protection de la Propriété Intellectuelle
ALAI	Association Littéraire et Artistique Internationale
ALI	American Law Institute
All ER, All E.R.	All England Law Reports
Am. J. Comp. L., AmJCompL	American Journal of Comparative Law
Anh.	Anhang
Art., Artt., Arts., art., arts.	Article(s), article(s)
AS	Amtliche Sammlung der Bundesgesetze und Verordnungen (Official Collection of Federal Laws and Regulations, Switzerland)
ASA	Advertising Standards Authority
ATF	Recueil officiel des arrêts du Tribunal fédéral suisse
B.I.E.	Bijblad bij De Industriële Eigendom
B2B	business-to-business
BBl.	Bundesblatt (Bulletin of Laws of Switzerland)
Berkeley Tech. L.J.	Berkeley Technology Law Journal
BERTT	Block Exemption Regulation on Transfer of Technology
BEUC	Bureau of European Consumer Organisations
BGB	Bürgerliches Gesetzbuch (German Civil Code)
BGBl.	Bundesgesetzblatt (Bulletin of Federal Laws of Germany)
BGBl.	Bundesgesetzblatt (Bulletin of Laws of the Federal Republic of Germany)
BGE	Amtliche Sammlung der Entscheidungen des Schweizerischen Bundesgerichtes (Decisions of the Swiss Federal Supreme Court)
BGH	Bundesgerichtshof (German Federal Supreme Court)
BGHZ	Entscheidungen des Bundesgerichtshofes in Zivilsachen (Decisions of the German Federal Supreme Court in Civil Law Disputes)
BTDr.	Drucksache des Deutschen Bundestags (official documentation of the German Parliament)
CAP	Committee of Advertising Practices
CD	Community Design
CDPA	(British) Copyright, Designs and Patents Act
ch.	chapter
COD	Codecision
Colum. L. Rev.	Columbia Law Review
Colum.-VLA J.L. & Arts	Columbia-VLA Journal of Law and the Arts
COM	European Commission
CP	Community Patent
CPBR	Community Plant Breeders' Rights
CPI	Code de la Propriété Intellectuelle (French Copyright Act)
CR	Computer und Recht

CRi	Computer und Recht international
CTM	Community Trademark
CTMR	Community Trademark Regulation
D.	Recueil Dalloz
D.C. Cir.	United States Court of Appeals, District of Columbia Circuit
DHJC	Draft Hague Jurisdiction Convention
DMCA	(United States) Digital Millennium Copyright Act
e.g.	exempli gratia
E.I.P.R.	European Intellectual Property Review
EC	European Community
ECJ	European Court of Justice
ECR	European Court Reports
ed., eds.	edition, editor, editors
EEA	European Economic Area
EEC	European Economic Community
EGBGB	Einführungsgesetz zum Bürgerlichen Gesetzbuch (Introductory Law of the Civil Code)
EMOTA	European Mail Order and Distance Selling Trade Association
EPA	Europäisches Patentamt (European Patent Office)
EPC	European Patent Convention
et seq., et seqq., s., ss.	and the following
EU	European Union
EuGVO	Europäische Gerichtsstands- und Vollstreckungsverordnung (Council Regulation on jurisdiction and enforcement of judgments in civil and commercial matters)
EuroISPA	European Internet Service Providers Association
EWS	Europäisches Wirtschafts- und Steuerrecht
F. Supp.	Federal Supplement
f., ff.	and the following
F.3d	Federal Reporter, Third Series
F.S.R., FSR	Fleet Street Reports
FCA	Federal Court of Australia
GESAC	Groupement Européen des Sociétés d'Auteurs et Compositeurs
GRUR	Gewerblicher Rechtsschutz und Urheberrecht
GRUR Int.	Gewerblicher Rechtsschutz und Urheberrecht Internationaler Teil
Harv. L. Rev.	Harvard Law Review
HL	House of Lords
Hous. L. Rev.	Houston Law Review
i.e.	id est
I.E.R.	Intellectuele Eigendom en Reclamerecht
I.I.C.	International Review of Industrial Property and Copyright Law
I.L.M.	International Legal Materials
I.P.Q.	Intellectual Property Quaterly
Ind. J. Global Legal Stud.	Indiana Journal of Global Legal Studies
IP	Intellectual Property
IPRax	Praxis des internationalen Privat- und Verfahrensrechts
IPRs	Intellectual Property Rights
ISP	Internet Service Provider
ITRB	IT-Rechtsberater
J. Copyr. Soc.	Journal of the Copyright Society of the USA

JCP	Jurisclasseur périodique (Semaine juridique)
JZ	Juristenzeitung
K&R	Kommunikation und Recht
KG	Kammergericht (Court of Appeals of Berlin, Germany)
Law & Contemp. Prob.	Law and Contemporary Problems
Law Q.Rev.	Law Quaterly Review
MMR	MultiMedia und Recht
MPI	Max Planck Institute
n., nn.	note, notes
N.I.P.R.	Nederlands Internationaal Privaatrecht
NILR	Netherlands International Law Review
NJW	Neue Juristische Wochenschrift
no., nr., nos.	number(s)
OECD	Organisation for Economic Co-operation and Development
Ohio St. L. J.	Ohio State Law Journal
OJ, O.J.	Official Journal
OLG	Oberlandesgericht (Court of Appeals, Germany)
p., pp.	page, pages
para., paras.	paragraph(s)
PCT	Patent Cooperation Treaty
PIL	Private International Law
PIPC	Paris Industrial Property Convention
Prel. Doc.	Preliminary Document
RabelsZ	Rabels Zeitschrift für ausländisches und internationales Privatrecht
Rev. crit. DIP	Revue critique de droit international privé
RIDA	Revue internationale du droit d'auteur
RIW	Recht der internationalen Wirtschaft
RPC	Reports of Patent Cases
S.D.N.Y.	United States District Court for the Southern District of New York
SCT	(WIPO) Standing Committee on the Law of Trademarks, Industrial Design and Geographical Indications
Sec.	Section
Slg.	Sammlung der Entscheidungen des EuGH (Collection of ECJ Decisions)
SLT	Scots Law Times
SME	small and medium-sized enterprises
Stan. L. Rev.	Stanford Law Review
TLD	Top Level Domain
TRIPS	Agreement on Trade-Related Aspects of Intellectual Property Rights
U. Pa. L. Rev.	University of Pennsylvania Law Review
U.N.T.S.	United Nations Treaty Series
U.S.	United States
U.S.C.	United States Codes
U.S.P.Q.	United States Patents Quarterly
UDRP	Uniform Domain Name Dispute Resolution Policy
UFITA	Archiv für Archiv für Urheber- und Medienrecht (bis 2000 Archiv für Urheber-, Film-, Funk- und Theaterrecht)
UK	United Kingdom
UNIDROIT	International Institute for the Unification of Private Law
UrhG	Urheberrechtsgesetz (German Copyright Act)

US	United States Reports
USPTO	United States Patent and Trademark Office
v.	versus
Virginia J. Int'l L.	Virginia Journal of International Law
vol.	volume
WIPO	World Intellectual Property Organization
Wm. & Mary L. Rev.	William and Mary Law Review
WRP	Wettbewerb in Recht und Praxis
WuW	Wirtschaft und Wettbewerb
ZUM	Zeitschrift für Urheber- und Medienrecht
ZWeR	Zeitschrift für Wettbewerbsrecht

Introduction

JÜRGEN BASEDOW

An academic conference organized by two Max Planck Institutes is a rare occurrence. The Max Planck Institute for Foreign Private and Private International Law and the Max Planck Institute for Intellectual Property Rights, Competition, and Tax Law have convened this conference in view of the synergies that can be expected from a cooperation in a field which has been considered marginal to both of our respective areas for many years, but which has gained increasing importance recently. Let me explain this from my own experience as a scholar of private international law.

When I joined the academic staff of this institute as a full-time researcher twenty-five years ago, my first job was to review two papers written for the International Encyclopedia of Comparative Law that dealt with the law applicable to liability sounding in tort. One of these chapters was entitled Enterprise Liability, the other Intentional Torts. The first had been written by the late Professor Albert Ehrenzweig,[1] the second by Professor Stig Strömholm,[2] whom we have the pleasure to welcome among us today. The basic message of both papers was that the traditional discussion of the private international law of torts under the sole heading of the *lex loci delicti* has to be criticized. Drawing from the rich experience of American case law, Professor Ehrenzweig in particular favored a differentiation of the relevant conflict rules depending on the type of delict in question: he advocated special conflict rules for road accidents, airplane crashes, product liability, etc. Despite this elaborate program, the two aforementioned chapters of the Encyclopedia do not cover liability arising from the infringement of intellectual property rights. Instead, the editors of the Encyclopedia considered this area to be so specialized that it was left to special chapters authored by two Swiss experts of this discipline, Kamen and Alois Troller.[3]

---

[1] *Albert A. Ehrenzweig*, Enterprise Liability, in: International Encyclopedia of Comparative Law vol. 3 ch. 32 (1980).

[2] *Stig Strömholm*, International Torts, in: International Encyclopedia of Comparative Law vol. 3 ch. 33 (1980).

[3] *Kamen Troller*, Industrial and Intellectual Property, in: International Encyclopedia of Comparative Law vol. 3 ch. 22 (1994); *Alois Troller*, Unfair Competition, in: International Encyclopedia of Comparative Law of vol. 3 ch. 34 (1980).

Looking at the matter from the other side of intellectual property law, it appears that the issue of the applicable law has never been the main concern of international law in this area. Instead, intellectual property law has focused, from its very beginning, on two central issues: first, the recognition by a legal system of intellectual property rights as such; and second, the equal protection of nationals and foreigners. By their nature, intellectual property rights are legal artifacts created by a given state as monopolies limited in time and designed to determine the competitive conditions in the relevant markets of that country. This perspective implies a territorial limitation of those rights[4] which has been more or less automatically transferred from the issues relating to their existence and reach to the issues of their protection, including sanctions flowing from private law.

The different approaches of intellectual property law and private international law did not contradict each other as long as the *lex loci delicti* was generally applied, as it was in most countries. In cases relating to the infringement of intellectual property rights, the *lex loci delicti* could be interpreted as referring to the law of the country for whose territory protection was granted.[5] But things started to change when private international law began to handle the *lex loci delicti* in a more flexible way, allowing the application of a law which was definitely more closely connected to the case at hand than the place of acting or the place of injury. This could be, for example, the law of the country of the common habitual residence of the parties, which may clearly differ from the country where an intellectual property right is registered and for which protection is sought. Moreover, the rapid growth of international exchange and commerce brought about an increase in situations where the place of acting and the place of injury diverge in different states, and where one and the same act may generate injury in various other states. Thus, the *lex loci delicti*, as the starting point of every debate in this area, gives rise to increasing doubts as to its appropriateness. The least that can be said is that it is incomplete in various situations.

Moreover, the economic development of society has triggered changes in the substantive law of torts. While that law started as an annex to criminal law designed to make good the harm caused by the perpetrator, it acquired new functions in the course of the twentieth century. In the first place, the law of torts is one of the legal tools that allows society to deal with the losses which are inevitably connected with technical and industrial innovations; in this area, the distribution of loss – i.e., the central theme of insurance – is gaining

[4] See, e.g., *Wolfgang Fikentscher*, Wirtschaftsrecht vol. I (München 1983) pp. 274-276; *Heinrich Hubmann/Horst-Peter Götting*, Gewerblicher Rechtsschutz (6th ed. München 1998) p. 92.

[5] See *Bernd von Hoffmann* in Staudinger, Kommentar zum Bürgerlichen Gesetzbuch mit Einführungsgesetz und Nebengesetzen (13th ed., Neubearbeitung, Berlin 2001) Art. 40 EGBGB no. 390; *Karl Kreuzer* in Münchener Kommentar zum Bürgerlichen Gesetzbuch vol. 10 (3rd ed. München 1998) nach Art. 38 Anh. II, no. 26.

importance next to the traditional objectives of compensation and loss prevention. In other areas, the law of torts increasingly determines the risk exposure of economic activities affecting third parties. Thus, the profitability of the production of goods certainly depends inter alia on the risk of environmental or product liability. And the liability for the infringement of privacy has a strong impact on the risk exposure, and thereby on the profitability of press and media undertakings. Given the alternation of innovation and imitation in economic competition, the risk of exposure to sanctions for the infringement of intellectual property rights determines the success of business strategies to a large extent. The growing economic significance of tort law has drawn the attention of business to the issue of the applicable law in international markets. While the different interests of the various economic sectors put the *lex loci delicti* under pressure, a progressive disintegration of the conflict rules for non-contractual liability can be observed. Professor Ehrenzweig's and Professor Strömholm's predictions have come true.

This evolution is evidenced by a number of national codifications of private international law. They either maintain the traditional ideal of a sole conflict rule of non-contractual liability – which, however, has to be framed in very general and flexible terms in order to allow for an adjustment to the different fact situations; this is the path followed by the German codification of 1999.[6] Or in the alternative, national legislators try to keep track with the outlined development; thus, the Swiss law on private international law has hammered out a number of different conflict rules for the various types of tort.[7] The European Commission has made the same choice. The proposal for a regulation on the law applicable to non-contractual obligations of July 2003 (often simply called "Rome II") contains, next to the general rule of Article 3, no less than five specific conflict rules.[8] They cover product liability, unfair competition, violations of privacy and rights relating to the personality, damage to the environment, and the infringement of intellectual property rights. The proposal for the latter subject contained in Article 8 has recently been matched by the second preliminary draft of a working group of the American Law Institute dealing with intellectual property, in particular principles governing jurisdiction, choice of law, and judgments in transnational disputes.[9] The following

[6] See Arts. 40-41 of the Introductory Law of the Civil Code (EGBGB), added by the Law of May 21, 1999, BGBl. I, p. 1026.

[7] See Arts. 129-142 and Art. 110 of the federal law on private international law of December 18, 1987, BBl. 1988 I, 5, AS 1988, 1776; English translation in Am. J. Comp. L. 37 (1989) 193.

[8] Proposal for a Regulation of the European Parliament and the Council on the Law Applicable to Non-Contractual Obligations ("Rome II"), COM (2003) 427 final of 22 July 2003; see also the comments on the preceding preliminary draft: *Hamburg Group for Private International Law*, Comments on the European Commission's Draft Proposal for a Council Regulation on the Law Applicable to Non-Contractual Obligations: RabelsZ 67 (2003) 1 seq.

[9] Principles Governing the Jurisdiction, Choice of Law and Judgments in Transnational Disputes, Preliminary Draft N° 2 of 20 January 2004, see below, annex 2.

surveys of the American and European drafts and the subsequent more detailed contributions on the Rome II proposal will allow for a first comparative discussion of these texts that will frame the future competition between the U.S. and the EU in this area.

The infringement of intellectual property rights cannot be discussed without a closer look at license agreements. In the field of conflict of laws, such a look is suggested in particular by another activity of the European Commission. By the publication of a "Green paper on the conversion of the Rome Convention of 1980 on the law applicable to contractual obligations of 1980 into a Community instrument,"[10] the Commission has indicated its intention to adjust, insofar as necessary, the rules of Rome I to the changing needs of the business community. Our conference therefore provides a timely platform to discuss such needs; this will be done in the second block of this conference.

[10] COM (2002) 654 final of 14 January 2003.

Part 1: Current Political Agenda

The European Commission's Agenda: The Future "Rome I and II" Regulations

CLAUDIA HAHN and OLIVIER TELL*

I. Introduction

The following contribution elucidates the current European Agenda on private international law and its impact on intellectual property rights. First, it will be demonstrated that the Rome Convention of 1980[1] is already applicable for intellectual property issues; there seems to be no need for further clarification in a future Rome I Regulation (II). Second, it will be asked if a rule for infringements of intellectual property rights should be provided in a future Community instrument for non-contractual obligations (III).

* The opinions expressed by the authors of this document are purely those of the writers and may not in any circumstances be regarded as stating an official position of the European Commission.

[1] Rome Convention of 1980 on the law applicable to contractual obligations (consolidated version), OJ EC, C 27, 26.01.1998, 34.

II. Intellectual Property and Rome I

1. The Green Paper Adopted by the Commission on 14 January 2003

On 14 January 2003, the Commission published the so-called Rome I Green Paper.[2] In addition, a public hearing was organised on 27 January 2004 in Brussels.

The general objectives of the Rome I project:

- improve uniform application of the rules contained in the Convention, mainly by giving competence to the European Court of Justice; thus also improving coherence with the interpretation of the rules on jurisdiction contained in the Brussels-I-Regulation;[3]
- facilitate extension of the standardised conflict rules of the Rome Convention of 1980 to acceding countries;
- modernise some of its rules, mainly the rule on consumer contracts which does not seem adapted any more in the digital era.

Until now, the Commission received about 90 answers to this Green Paper. A summary of the contributions as well as most of the contributions are available on the Directorate-General Justice and Home Affair's website.[4]

2. The Absence of Intellectual Property Rights in the Comments Received by the Commission

The Rome Convention of 1980 does not contain one single reference to intellectual property rights. However, its different rules on contractual obligations nevertheless apply to the different contractual obligations arising in this context. These matters are discussed in other contributions.[5]

Nevertheless, in the framework of the Green Paper, the Commission did not receive one single comment on the application of the rules of the Rome Convention of 1980 to contracts related to intellectual property. There are two possible conclusions: either the present rules work perfectly well for this matter and there is no reason to modify the text. Or, the specialists of intellectual property did not realise that the Rome I Green Paper presented an occasion to comment on these specific issues. It is true that the Green Paper did not

---

[2] Green Paper on the conversion of the Rome Convention of 1980 on the law applicable to contractual obligations into a Community instrument and its modernisation, COM (2002) 654 final of 14.01.2003.

[3] Council Regulation (EC) No 44/2001 of 22.12.2000 on jurisdiction and the recognition and enforcement of judgments in civil and commercial matters, OJ EC, L 12, 16.01.2001, 1.

[4] <www.europa.eu.int/comm/justice_home/news/consulting_public/rome_i/news_summary_rome1_en.htm>.

[5] See the contributions of *Josef Drexl* (p. 79 et seq.), *Axel Metzger* (p. 61 et seq.) and *Haimo Schack* (p. 107 et seq.) in this volume.

specifically address the question whether the rules of the Convention work well in the context of intellectual property.

3. *Timetable*

The Commission intends to submit a proposal for a Rome I Regulation in the near future. In the meantime it will continue the consultation process on more specific questions. Everybody is invited to send comments to the Commission.

III. Intellectual Property and Rome II

1. *Existing Community Instruments: No Clear Conflict of Laws' Rules*

Although the harmonisation at European Community level on substantive intellectual property law is quite complete by now, experts generally agree that European Community legislation does not yet contain a complete set of rules on civil law dealing with all aspects of intellectual property infringements. For instance, although the Directive 2004/48/EC on the enforcement of intellectual property rights[6] aims at harmonising, among others, the level of damages, nevertheless does this not lead to full harmonisation of all related aspects of civil law and this for different reasons: (i) following the "minimum harmonisation approach", the directive leaves a margin of flexibility to the Member States when transposing the text into national law; thus the effective degree of harmonisation is still uncertain; (ii) claims for damages are often linked to a lot of questions concerning general private law such as contributory negligence, duty to pay interest and vicarious liability, sharing of liability between co-tortfeasors; liability for employees. These topics are not dealt with in the directive. The question of the applicable national law thus remains important.

However, the relevant Community instruments in this field lack clarification on the question regarding the applicable law.

It is true that some specific Community instruments contain choice of law rules (e.g. the Community Trademark Regulation,[7] or the Community Design Regulation.[8] However, this is not the case for all Community instruments relating to intellectual property.

Furthermore, the conflict of laws' rules contained in the above mentioned Community instruments are drafted as follows: "on all matters not covered by this Regulation a (…) court shall apply its national law, including its private

[6] Directive 2004/48/EC of the European Parliament and of the Council of 2904.2004 on the enforcement of intellectual property rights, OJ EC, L 157, 30.04.2004, 45.

[7] Council Regulation (EC) No 40/94 of 20.12.1993 on the Community trade mark, OJ EC, L 11, 14.01.1994, 1.

[8] Council Regulation (EC) No 6/2002 of 12.12.2001 on Community designs, OJ EC, L 3, 05.01.2002, 1.

international law".[9] Given the reference to the national conflict of laws' rules, it is clear that these instruments do not provide for harmonisation of these rules at European Community level, each Member State applying its own rules.

2. *General Architecture of the Rome II Proposal*[10]

a) Civil and Commercial Matters

Like the Rome Convention of 1980 and the Brussels-I-Regulation, the future Rome II instrument will apply to non contractual obligations in "civil and commercial matters". Intellectual property rights are not excluded from its scope of application. Thus the instrument will apply to claims for damages following the infringement of an intellectual property right.

b) Universal Scope of Application

The instrument also applies when the law designed by the conflict rule is not that of a Member State. Thus, like for the Rome Convention of 1980, the rules of the future Rome II instrument will completely replace the national conflict of laws' rules for non contractual matters.

c) General Rule (Art. 3-1)

Article 3 applies for all matters for which the following Articles 4 to 9 do not give a specific rule. The general rule states the application of the law of the place where the direct damage arises (in German "Erfolgsort", which is different from "Schadensort") or is likely to arise. Thus the law of the place where the harmful act was committed is not longer relevant; neither is the place where the indirect consequences of the damage arise (e.g. financial loss following an accident).

d) Common Habitual Residence (Art. 3-2)

If the parties have their common habitual residence in the same country, the law of that country applies (§ 2).

---

[9] Art. 97 para. 2 of the Community Trademark Regulation; Art. 88 para. 2 of the Community Design Right Regulation contains a similar rule.

[10] Proposal for a Regulation of the European Parliament and the Council on the law applicable to non-contractual obligations, COM (2003) 427 final of 22.7.2003.

e) General Exception Clause (Art. 3-3)

The Rome II proposal also provides for a general exception clause, authorising the judge to apply a different law if the situation presents a manifestly closer link with the law of another country. Such close connection particularly exists in the case of a pre-existing relation between the parties, such as a contract ("accessory choice of law in respect of pre-existing relationships").

f) Conflict of Laws' Rules for Specific Torts (Article 4 to 9)

The instrument contains specific rules for specific torts. Thus you might be the most interested in the specific rule for unfair competition (Art. 5) which provides for the application of the law of the country in which the competitive relations were affected (so called "market place principle"). The other specific rule interesting for intellectual property rights infringements, at least in some Member States, is Article 9 on quasi-contracts, especially the one on unjust enrichment. Article 9 provides that the applicable law is that of the country in which the enrichment took place. However, rules on accessory choice of law in respect of pre-existing relationships, common habitual residence as well as the general exception clause also apply.

g) Freedom of Choice

Art. 10 of the proposal allows the parties to chose the law applicable to their non contractual obligation, but only after the dispute arose.

3. *Intellectual Property Rights in the Preliminary Draft Proposal of May 2002 and the Comments Received by the Commission*

a) Intellectual Property Rights in the Preliminary Draft Proposal

In the preliminary draft proposal[11] there was no specific article on intellectual property rights, neither was the matter excluded. Comments thus concentrated on the question whether the general rules of the Rome II proposal such as described hereabove should also apply to intellectual property infringement.

The Commission received about 10 comments on the intellectual property rights aspects of its proposal[12] and this matter was also intensively discussed

---

[11] See "Consultation on a Preliminary Draft Proposal for a Council Regulation on the Law Applicable to Non-Contractual Obligations", <www.europa.eu.int/comm/justice_home/unit/civil/consultation/index_en.htm>.

[12] See the summary at <www.europa.eu.int/comm/justice_home/news/consulting_public/rome_ii/news_summary_rome2_en.htm>.

during the public hearing organised in Brussels on 7 January 2003. At the hearing of 7 January, the Commission asked whether a provision drafted in line with Article 5 of the Berne Convention[13] would be satisfactory.

b) Comments Against Inclusion of Intellectual Property Rights

Most comments recalled that Article 3 – providing for the application of the law of the country in which the direct damage took place – is not compatible with the universally accepted principle of territoriality, written down in different international treaties (Paris Convention, Berne Convention). This principle – and the closely linked rule that the law of the country for which protection is sought is applicable – provides in case of infringement of an intellectual property right for the application of the law of the country which has granted the industrial property right (which has registered a patent or trademark). For copyright, this principle leads to the application of the law of the country in which the infringement took place. This solution leads to the "Mosaik-principle" – application of different laws to the rights which the owner of an intellectual property right holds in different countries.

Some comments suggested that priority should be given to a solution at WIPO level. *GESAC (European Grouping of societies of authors and composers)* recalled that the interpretation of Article 5.2 of the Berne Convention is not clear when it comes to locating a delict which took place via Internet. They called for a clarification of Article 5.2 of the Berne Convention in the digital context, favouring the location of the delict in the country of reception, i.e. in the country in which the protected work or object is accessible to users. This clarification should be dealt within the framework of WIPO regarding a problem raised at worldwide level. Until the adoption of a new international Treaty or a clarification and a unanimous interpretation of Art. 5.2 Berne Convention, it would be advisable to exclude literary and artistic property from the scope of application of a Rome II instrument until work on this matter has permitted the emergence of consensus at international level.

It was agreed by nearly all comments on that matter that party autonomy is not suitable for claims relating to intellectual property rights infringements. It seems in fact self-evident that parties cannot be allowed to choose the law of a country in which the litigious right is not protected by the law of that country.

Finally some comments insisted that the rules provided for by a Rome II instrument would never allow answering all questions regarding the very complicated issue of applicable law to intellectual property rights and that the solution proposed by the Rome II proposal would thus remain an incomplete one.

---

[13] Berne Convention for the Protection of Literary and Artistic Works of 09.09.1886, last revised in Paris on 24.07.1971.

c) Comments Favouring the Inclusion of Intellectual Property Rights

There was of course the proposal of the Hamburg Group on Private International Law[14] which favoured the inclusion of a specific rule on intellectual property right and which directly inspired the Commission's proposal. We will come back to it later.

Other comments were in favour of the inclusion of the matter into the scope of Rome II instrument, but suggested a redrafting of Article 24 relating to the priority of choice of laws' rules contained in existing international treaties in order to make sure that the principle of territoriality and the *lex loci protectionis* principle are preserved. However, in the view of the Commission this solution could not be sufficient since this could perhaps work for Article 5-2 of the Berne Convention; there are other international instruments (e.g. the "International Convention for the Protection of Performers, Producers of Phonograms and Broadcasting Organizations on related rights" ["Rome Convention" of 1961][15]) which do not contain choice of law rules.

4. Intellectual Property Aspects in the Rome II Proposal

a) Motivation for the Solution Finally Adopted by the Commission

- At WIPO level, work has been delayed for a long time, saying that this matter is too complicated; the Rome II proposal could be a good occasion to discuss this matter. The Hamburg conference was a good illustration of this.
- Despite large degree of harmonisation of material law, many questions will still be governed by national law. As already mentioned before, a conflict of law rule is thus needed.
- Some academics still contest that Art. 5.2 of the Berne Convention contains a conflict of laws' rule (although this academic debate does not concern judges who apply this article as if it was a bilateral conflict rule).
- Although the "territoriality principle" seems to be universally recognised, some Member State still seem to have a different approach. We were told that two Member States, for instance, apply the law of the place where the infringement took place for copyright infringements. The Rome II proposal could thus lead to greater harmony at EC-level.
- There is a close link with unjust enrichment in certain Member States when, in the case of an intellectual property infringement procedure, the

---

[14] See *Basedow et al.* („Hamburg Group for Private International law"), RabelsZ (67) 2003, 1, 11.

[15] International Convention for the Protection of Performers, Producers of Phonograms and Broadcasting Organizations of 26.10.1961.

claimant also requests damages on the basis of unjust enrichment (which happens very often in Germany).

In its Rome II proposal, which was directly inspired by the proposal of the Hamburg Group for Private International Law, the Commission finally chose to introduce a specific rule on intellectual property rights.

Following the explanatory memorandum, intellectual property rights in the sense of this proposal are copyright, related rights, databases and industrial property rights (patents, trademarks, design rights).

The Rome II proposal contains 2 different rules on intellectual property rights:

Article 8-1:

"The law applicable to a non-contractual obligation arising from an infringement of an intellectual property right shall be the law of the country for which protection is sought".

The current German translation of this rule is not correct.[16] Instead of "Land, in dem" it should be drafted "Land, für das". We will try to correct this during the negotiations in the Council.

Art. 8.1 confirms the principle of territoriality and the *lex loci protectionis* principle such as they results from the international conventions. To make sure that there is no doubt about this Recital 14 again recalls that "the universally acknowledged principle of lex loci protectionis should be preserved."

Article 8-2:

"In the case of a non contractual obligation arising from an infringement of a unitary Community industrial property right, the relevant Community instruments shall apply. For any question that is not governed by that instrument, the applicable law shall be the law of the Member State in which the act of infringement is committed".

This Article confirms the application of the relevant European Community instruments. This somehow self-evident rule is completed by a genuine conflict of laws' rule: application of the law of the place where the infringement took place. This is really new.

Indeed, the *lex loci protectionis* is not sufficient for Community intellectual property rights, since the protection "country" is the whole Community with its very varying internal rules. After applying the lex loci protectionis rule it is still unclear, which Member State's law is applicable to the claim for damages. Therefore the principle of territoriality needs a supplementary rule for Community intellectual property rights with a unitary character. Following the suggestions of the Hamburg Group for Private International Law, the Rome II proposal introduces the application of the law of the Member State in which the

[16] See Vorschlag für eine Verordnung des Europäischen Parlaments und des Rates über das auf außervertragliche Schuldverhältnisse anzuwendende Recht („Rom II"), KOM (2003) 427 endgültig vom 22.07.2003.

act of infringement is committed. This rule is of course inspired by the general conflict rule of Article 3 of the Regulation.

b) Exclusion of Party Autonomy

Article 10-1 of the Rome II Proposal on the parties "freedom of choice on the applicable law" specifies that party autonomy does not apply for intellectual property rights. The Commission thus took into account an opinion which was expressed with unanimity during the written consultation of 2002.

c) Claims Based on Unjust Enrichment Linked to Intellectual Property

Article 9-6 of the Rome II proposal, relating to quasi contracts, specifies that all non-contractual obligations in the field of intellectual property shall be governed by Article 8. As a consequence, the specific rules on unjust enrichment will not apply. This rule aims at making sure that the entire claim regarding an intellectual property rights infringement is governed by one single law in to order avoid the application of two completely different conflict of laws' rules to one single claim.

d) Consequences for Negotiations at International Level

What happens if WIPO finally decides to elaborate a Protocol regarding the interpretation of Article 5.2 of the Berne Convention? Such an instrument would be a new international Treaty which would have priority over the Rome II conflict rule, provided that other conditions regarding accession are fulfilled, unless the Community asks for a disconnection clause. For the negotiation of this new instrument there will be a genuine Community competence and Member States will be obliged to adopt a coherent approach. The project of the American Law Institute tries to define rules on transnational intellectual property infringement.

We know that Art. 8 Rome II proposal does not solve all questions regarding the applicable law for intellectual property (question of validity or the existence of intellectual property rights). However, as of today, there are no plans at European Community level to definitively regulate this very complicated issue.

5. *Reactions to the Rome II Proposal*

a) Negotiations in the Council

Our first impression was that Member States tend to be in favour of the inclusion of intellectual property rights into the scope of application of the future Rome II instrument, mainly in order to have a certain parallelism with the scope of application of the Rome Convention of 1980 and the Brussels-I-Regulation. Most delegations stressed however that internal consultations with administrations in charge of intellectual property rights are still ongoing.

However, as usual in this debate, there is one general problem: you have either specialists of private international law or specialists of intellectual property rights. In the Council working group on the future Rome II instrument, at this stage, there are but specialists on private international law. They raised a lot of questions within mere questions of comprehension, beginning with the question for explanation of the territoriality principle.

The following examples may illustrate that not all questions raised by the delegations are simple questions of comprehension:

- Art. 8.2 concentrates on the place where the infringement took place, whereas Art. 3 and more generally most of the rules of the proposal concentrate on the place where the damage took place. One might question here, why the place of damage is not relevant for intellectual property rights.
- The interplay between Art. 8 on intellectual property and Article 5 on unfair competition is not very clear. What happens if an act of unfair competition consists of the violation of an intellectual property right (e.g. passing off)? The Commission explained that this is not a problem. Art. 8 is a *lex specialis* which excludes the application of Art. 5 insofar as an intellectual property right is affected. However, some concern was expressed on how this would work for passing off and it was stressed that judges would have difficulties to know what rule to apply.
- A general question of transparency was also raised. A part of conflict of laws rules for intellectual property rights is stated in specific European Community instruments on intellectual property rights. In addition, the general rule of Art. 8 of the Rome II proposal is to be applied; this could lead to a lack of awareness that there is a specific rule in Rome II.

b) Questions Raised by Academics

Although most academics seem to agree with Article 8-1 Rome II proposal, some seem to suggest improvements regarding the rule on the infringement of a Community intellectual property right.

Thus *Rainer Hausmann* questioned[17] why there is a need to exclude party autonomy for Community intellectual property rights. The argument against party autonomy in national rights – parties cannot be allowed to choose the law of a country which does not grant protection for the litigious right – does not seem relevant for Community intellectual property rights, since, by definition, all Member States provide for this protection. E.g. in case of multi state infringement of a community trademark in different Member States, the present solution leads – for the questions which are not harmonised in the relevant EC-regulation – to distributive application of the laws of the different Member States involved. Why not allow the parties to choose the law of one single Member State to resolve these questions (e.g. application of one single law for the quantification of damages) in order to facilitate an agreement or to speed up judicial procedures?

More generally, *Axel Metzger*, seems to suggest[18] that the general rules of the Rome II Regulation (including party autonomy, accessory choice of law relating to a pre-existing relationship, exception clause, etc.) should apply for Community industrial property rights as long as the law of a Member State is applicable under this rule. He even seems to favour a specific rule to avoid the application of different laws in the case of a multi-state infringement.

These are of course very interesting approaches and we were very happy to have the occasion, together with our colleagues from the Directorate-General Internal Market (*Sami Sunila* and *Johannes Karcher*), to discuss those with specialists during the Hamburg conference.

6. Timetable and Conclusion

Negotiations within the "Internal Market" Committee of the European Parliament have not started yet. Thus, an opinion is not to be expected under the present Parliament, which is likely to delay the discussions on the future Rome II Regulation. Indeed, it is not likely that there will be an opinion of the European Parliament before the beginning or even the middle of 2005. Given the high interest from some private groups on this proposal (mainly on defamation, e-commerce and unfair competition), a certain number of amendments are expected.

We thus think that it is still time to improve the rules proposed by the Commission if we discover that improvement is possible. The Hamburg seminar was an excellent occasion to discuss this highly complicated matter and we thank the organisers for their efforts to bring together both specialists of intellectual property and specialists of private international law.

---

[17] *Hausmann*, European Legal Forum 2003, 278, 287.

[18] See *Metzger* in *Drexl/Kur (ed.)*, IP and Private International Law: Heading for the Future (forthcoming).

Current International Developments in Choice of Law: An Analysis of the ALI Draft*

CATHERINE KESSEDJIAN

« L'industrie cherche l'utile, la philosophie cherche le vrai, la littérature cherche le beau. L'utile, le vrai, le beau, voilà le triple but de tout l'effort humain... »
Victor Hugo, Discours inaugural à la Société des gens de lettres de France A l'occasion du Congrès littéraire international de Paris, 1878, Comptes-rendus, 1879, p. 105

I. Introduction

Being conscious that the organizers have limited this conference to conflict of laws, namely choice of law or applicable law,[1] it is nonetheless necessary to say at the outset that current international efforts started with jurisdiction and enforcement of judgments,[2] and it is only recently that applicable law has been added to the list of private international law issues for intellectual property rights.[3]

* In the interest of full disclosure, I should mention here that I serve as one of the advisers to the ALI project. Rochelle Dreyfuss, Thomas Dreier, Richard Garnett, Hélène Gaudemet-Tallon, Jane Ginsburg, and André Lucas have been kind enough to comment on an earlier draft of this paper. All errors, misguided conceptions, or unrealistic proposals remain the author's only.

[1] In the United States, the preferred expression is "jurisdiction to prescribe." I do not use this expression, since I prefer to reserve the word "jurisdiction" for court jurisdiction.

[2] The effort at the Hague Conference on Private International Law for a worldwide convention on jurisdiction and foreign judgments, including intellectual property matters, first triggered the attention.

[3] This was done by Jane Ginsburg and Rochelle Dreyfuss on the occasion of a colloquium organized by WIPO in Geneva in January of 2001, at a time when it was still unclear whether the Hague effort was to be continued as is.

It is quite new[4] for intellectual property specialists to be concerned with applicable law theories and issues because, traditionally, the famous so-called "territoriality" principle prevented any real question of applicable law from arising. Also, most intellectual property specialists were satisfied that the majority of issues[5] had been unified by international substantive norms such as the Berne Convention and other major international instruments in the field.[6] Since then, however, the world has evolved and the free circulation of persons and rights, as well as goods and services in a globalized economy, has transformed issues that initially could be circumscribed to one country into multi-jurisdictional issues. Some disagree on the exact significance of international substantive norms. Others argue that some gaps exist in those norms. Yet others are of the opinion that it is about time to think in terms of universality and get away from the territoriality principle. This discussion, of course, is not new for the private international law specialists. We have it in the area of bankruptcy, where the tension between both principles has always been felt. We have it also in areas such as tort (for example, defamation or unfair competition) or family law (for example, as to the validity of a marriage or adoption). Private international law decided a long time ago that rights legally acquired in a foreign country could be recognized outside the country where they were acquired and thus be exercised extra-territorially.

At present, and without considering the EC regional context since other speakers have been charged with EC issues,[7] there are mainly two venues in which applicable law is presently discussed.[8] For some time, WIPO has been trying to adopt a Convention on Protection of Audiovisual Performances; the

---

[4] In copyright, for example, it was not until 1986 that ALAI, on the occasion of its centenary conference, started to study applicable law. See André Lucas, "La loi applicable au droit d'auteur," communication au Congrès de l'ALAI à Neuchâtel, September 2002.

[5] Even though one may argue that the most difficult issues (ownership, transferability, moral right, or open-ended defenses, notably) were not unified through substantive rules.

[6] Lucas (*supra* note 4), puts it very nicely when he says that, for many, "national treatment" meant that conflict of laws analysis was not necessary: "Joue dans le même sens l'idée reçue que la question de la loi applicable est commandée par le principe du 'traitement national' énoncé par l'article 5.1 de la Convention de Berne et qu'elle est donc sans objet en tant que telle. Traiter l'étranger comme le national, cela voudrait dire qu'on doit forcement lui appliquer la loi locale. Le tour, ainsi, serait joué: on ferait l'économie du conflit de lois." For an in-depth analysis of this question, see Mireille van Eechoud, *Choice of law in copyright and related rights – Alternatives to the Lex Protectionis*, The Hague, Kluwer Law International, 2003, pp. 95-127.

[7] Having excluded EC questions, we should nonetheless call the attention of non-EC specialists to the fact that solutions adopted within Europe may not be exported in a transnational context. Indeed, for example, the law of the country of origin principle, as adopted in the satellite and the e-commerce directives, is justified by the internal market obligations imposed on EC Member States. Outside this special context, the rule loses most of its rationale.

[8] There are more than two venues – notably think tanks such as ALAI, AIPPI, the Max Planck Institute, and others – that have established working groups which reflect on the same issues and make proposals that are a useful contribution to the debate.

diplomatic session[9] called to negotiate and adopt such a text was unable to reach agreement on a conflict of laws rule in lieu of a substantive rule which could not be agreed upon either.[10] Thereafter and in coordination with the Hague Conference on Private International Law, WIPO organized a two-day conference on issues of private international law mostly devoted to jurisdiction and judgments, but with some discussion on applicable law. Until now, WIPO has been considering what to do in this matter and has commissioned two law professors to prepare a study.[11] While the efforts in the Hague were slowly going down the drain on the larger project, two law professors, intellectual property specialists, decided that it would be a pity to lose momentum and expertise; they decided to take the ball in their own court and prepare a project in their field on private international law issues. As a result, their project included not only jurisdiction and judgments but also applicable law. At that time, the American Law Institute was looking for a good intellectual property project to launch. And since the American Law Institute is trying to become more and more "international," it accepted the two professors' project as an ALI project.[12] This is the second venue in which applicable law is discussed in the context of IP law.

The discussion offered in this paper draws from the experience I gained at the Hague during WIPO negotiations and studies and as an adviser to the ALI project. As mentioned earlier, I will discuss only the applicable law issues. I will do that by considering in sequence the following issues: The issue of *dépeçage*, namely, should we consider applying one law to all issues or should we consider each issue separately and create a conflict of laws analysis for each

[9] The diplomatic session was held in Geneva from December 7 to 20, 2000.

[10] This is not specific to intellectual property matters. When strong conflicting policies are behind substantive rules, international efforts for unification may fail. There is very little reason why a conflict of laws rule would more easily inspire consensus. For a general discussion on this question, see C. Kessedjian, "Codification du droit commercial international et droit international privé – De la gouvernance normative pour les relations économiques transnationales", *Collection of courses, Hague Academy of International Law*, Volume 300, 2004, pp. 83-308.

[11] The study of April 30, 2003, by Jane Ginsburg (Columbia Law School in New York City) and André Lucas (Université de Nantes in France) is available on WIPO's website under the title: "Study on transfer of the rights of performers to producers of audiovisual fixations."

[12] The project is called: "Intellectual Property: Principles governing jurisdiction, choice of law, and judgments in transnational disputes." The reporters are Rochelle Dreyfuss, Jane Ginsburg, and François Dessemontet. A preliminary draft #2 was issued for discussion on January 20, 2004. It was discussed at an advisors' meeting in Philadelphia on February 6, 2004. The reporters will amend the texts as they deem necessary after that meeting. In this paper, any quote to the ALI draft will refer to the 2004 preliminary draft #2.

one of them (II.)? What role, if any, should party autonomy play (III.)? and What default rule(s) could be proposed (IV.)?[13]

II. The Issue of Dépeçage

There are in fact two issues of dépeçage with which we should be concerned: the first is linked with the subject matter of the situation for which a conflict of laws analysis should be conducted; the second has to do with the issue of territoriality versus universality, namely with the question of whether a situation should be solved for all territories in which it is posed, or whether it can be solved on a country-to-country basis.[14] The second issue is better dealt with at the stage of the conflict of laws analysis because it really goes to the core of the connecting factor to be chosen for the default rules; hence, it will be discussed later in Chapter III of this paper. This is why the present chapter will only discuss the subject matter of dépeçage.

It is obviously difficult to discuss the question of dépeçage in the abstract. Indeed, some would argue that the idea of dépeçage may only be discussed in conjunction with the conflict of laws rule chosen. In other words, it may be acceptable to apply only one system of law to all issues if, for example, it is the *lex fori* but not if another law is held applicable. There is also the other way to look at the question of dépeçage: depending on which law is chosen, that law may cover only a number of issues, others being covered by another law. Hence, in the latter sense,[15] the issue is one of scope of application of the law held applicable. Even if we agree that there is a strong link between the two issues, I am of the opinion that the issue of dépeçage is indeed a preliminary question since it goes to the heart of the conflict of laws analysis. Thus, it must be clarified first whether an intellectual property right is to be considered as one matter for which a single general conflict of laws analysis must be con-

---

[13] In the following developments I will not always use the term "author" or "title owner" unless I clearly address comments to one or the other, because for us non-specialists in intellectual property, these concepts seem to assume an answer to a question which, very often, is at the center of the applicable law discussion. Whenever appropriate, I will use the expression "person who claims the right."

[14] For an absolute plea of territoriality, see Nicolas Bouche, *Le principe de territorialité de la propriété intellectuelle*, Paris, L'Harmattan, coll. Logiques juridiques, 2002. A less absolute plea – in the sense that the author allows some room for party autonomy – is made by Tristan Azzi for neighboring rights in his doctoral dissertation entitled *Recherche sur la loi applicable aux droits voisins du droit d'auteur*, Thèse Paris II, November 2000, direction H. Gaudemet-Tallon.

[15] Some commentators have seen a contradiction between the thrust of the argument in this chapter and what I say later on, when discussing infringement (see Section IV.4.), about the separation of the issue of liability and damages. I would like to clarify here that I am not, in principle, opposed to dépeçage. I am hopefully making a clear argument for a strong rationale behind dépeçage if it is considered necessary for a better solution of the issues at stake. In other words, if dépeçage is deemed necessary, it should be justified.

ducted, or whether the right must be divided into specific issues for which different conflict of laws analysis apply.[16]

The ALI project covers a wide range of matters, namely copyright, neighboring rights, patents, trade secrets, trademarks, domain names and other intellectual property rights, together with unfair competition.[17] When reading the draft, it is clear that the reporters have tried to find common ground, if possible, to all these rights. But the issue of dépeçage has been resolved in the affirmative as far as applicable law is concerned. Therefore, the reporters propose several rules covering the following issues: (a) existence and scope of rights and remedies; (b) scope of rights and remedies in exceptional cases; (c) initial title, which is further divided into registered rights, non-registered trademark rights, and other rights; (d) transferability; (e) transfers of title and grants of licenses; and (e) transfers by operation of law.[18]

The first comment one may have is that the draft provides for a fairly comprehensive set of issues. However, it is striking that the drafters have not deemed it necessary to propose a rule for the determination of who is the author. It may be that the author is always the one who holds the initial title or the initial owner of the rights. But this may not always be true. Sometimes, and in some legal systems, the initial owner and the author may be two different persons/entities. If we understand correctly how, for example, the concept of "work for hire" functions, in some jurisdictions at least, the person who holds the initial title is not the author but the person who pays. Whether the author (in the strict sense) in such a case does hold some rights nonetheless is probably an issue by itself which must be addressed separately from the others if the idea of dépeçage is accepted.

The second comment goes to the rationale of dépeçage. In the ALI project, the reporters say very little about that rationale. The reporters declare that the overall goal of the project is to "balance civil and common law approaches,"[19] enhance "procedural and substantive fairness,"[20] and help "create an efficient method for adjudicating international disputes."[21] But I have not seen any comment addressed directly to the justification of dépeçage.

The first (and perhaps only) reason for dépeçage may be that nobody seems to be able to agree on a single law applicable to all issues.[22] Thus, as a move

[16] For the conclusion that intellectual property rights must be divided into several issues for choice of law purposes, see van Eechoud (supra. note 6), at pp. 225-232.

[17] Section 101. See also the comment to Section 101 which clarifies that the reporters placed their project within the very broad ambit of the TRIPS Agreement as incorporating the Paris Convention.

[18] See Part III of the project from p. 104 to 137.

[19] *Supra* note 12, p. 19.

[20] Ibidem.

[21] Ibidem at p. 21.

[22] I also realize that all matters may not be regulated by the same law as we will see in Chapter III. However, the point is that there should be a strong rationale behind a policy which advocates dépeçage.

toward consensus, there is an attempt to slice up the right and give to each of the potentially conflicting laws a little to decide. It is argued that positive domestic laws do not have the same characterization of the rights, and therefore dépeçage is necessary because of that. The answer in private international law is that conflict of characterization happens all the time, and it is a pretty much settled rule that characterization is made by the forum state. In case there is no forum so to speak, as in arbitration, the characterization will be made freely by the arbitral tribunal. Consequently, dépeçage is not justified if the only reason is a difference in characterization among the legal systems interested by the relation at stake.

In my opinion, the extent of dépeçage in the ALI draft seems to be a misguided conception of the evolution of conflict of laws versus substantive law as it may apply to intellectual property rights.[23] Let us first face the reality that conflict of laws exists for only two reasons: (1) the laws which may wish to regulate a situation are in conflict, i.e., they decide in opposite ways on the same issue; or (2) no international consensus or convergence may be found on substantive solutions. WIPO negotiations on the protection of audiovisual performances[24] are the paradigm of this two-fold test. It is because the negotiators could not reach an agreement on a proposed substantive rule that would give the producers all the rights of the performer subject only to contractual provisions to the contrary[25] that an attempt was made to reach a solution through conflict of laws. However, as stated above,[26] chances are not great to see parties reach an agreement on a conflict of laws rule when there are strong policies behind the substantive rules in conflict. As one could expect, negotiators at WIPO could come to an agreement on neither a conflict of laws rule nor on the substantive rule.

Second, for practitioners – and in general the subject of the rule of law – conflict of laws analysis is a complicated one. It does not serve them to complicate matters even further with an over-sophisticated refinement of the applicable law analysis as dépeçage does. Hence, it seems that one of the goals lawyers in general, and international lawyers in particular, should keep in mind is to resort to dépeçage only when it is absolutely necessary and there is no possibility to deal with an issue as a whole. In other words, I would argue that

---

[23] This paper's proposals do not take into consideration positive law solutions that have been defined in the application of long-existing international instruments or in domestic practice. I am essentially concerned with a *de lege ferenda* analysis, which may very well be received as pure anathema to all members of the intellectual property milieu.

[24] See above, and note 9.

[25] The proposal was, in substance, the following: "Once a performer has consented to the incorporation of his performance in an audiovisual fixation, he shall be deemed to have transferred all exclusive rights of authorization provided for in this Treaty with respect to that particular fixation to its producer, subject to written contractual clauses to the contrary."

[26] See note 10 and related text.

dépeçage must be specifically justified and backed by strong policy rationale when the unitary vision would be the preferred route.

It is sometimes argued that dépeçage is necessary because of public policy reasons. This argument seems to fall short of the goals it wishes to achieve. Indeed, in traditional private international law analysis, public policy is always understood to be an accepted and even expected exception. Whether it takes the form of *a priori* mandatory rules (*lois de police)* or *a posteriori* exception,[27] it is always available to the forum state. It is true that, at least in the United States, the so-called "revolution" in conflict of laws analysis which took place between the first and the second restatements built a policy reasoning into the analysis, rendering a public policy exception mostly – or even entirely – moot. However, even in the United States, this has not induced a dépeçage of the matters. Consequently, one cannot craft conflict of laws rules by taking each substantive mandatory norm and trying to accommodate the applicability of that norm by choosing a different connecting factor, ending up with as many conflict rules as there are substantive public policy issues. Doing so would almost invariably come back to a pure territoriality mechanism.

As a final comment on this issue, I should clarify that when a field is unified by substantive law and the conflict of laws rules are only necessary for a few remaining questions, dépeçage may follow, but with a different meaning than an *a priori* dépeçage such as the one proposed in the ALI draft, for example. Indeed, when the conflict of laws rules are adopted as a complement to substantive rules, they do not pretend to deal with a subject matter in its entirety, but only if there is a gap in substantive norms. A classic example of this is the 1980 Vienna Convention on international sales of goods, which leaves a number of issues unresolved, causing these issues to be regulated by national law as defined by choice of law rules. But even then, the same conflict of laws rule may be used for all the remaining issues. For this reason, it may be important in a field such as intellectual property to ascertain whether rules are proposed as a complement to existing uniform substantive norms or as a substitute to these norms. The following developments are an attempt to break free from existing international norms and propose a fresh look at the issues in the hope that it may help new thinking in the area.

III. A Role for Party Autonomy?

In the world in which we live, party autonomy and even self-regulation has become the most common request (if not demand) made by strong actors in a field. This is not specific to intellectual property, and it is hardly surprising that

[27] The difference between *lois de police* and the public policy exception is also one of *instrumentum*; a *loi de police* is mostly embodied in a statute, while the public policy exception is usually defined by case law. Having said that, however, it is not uncommon for the public policy exception applied by courts to have its roots in a statute.

this trend is presently reaching intellectual property areas of interest. This trend may be identified, for example, by the European Green Paper on authorship and neighboring rights of 1995, which tends to give a very large area of application to contract law, leaving only a few limited issues to the law of the state where the exploitation of the work occurs.[28] This trend nowadays goes to areas which have been traditionally hermetic to freedom of contract, as was until recently the law applicable to real rights.[29] But with the new Hague Convention on the Law Applicable to Certain Rights in Respect of Securities Held with an Intermediary,[30] one may argue that no area of the law is now exempt from party autonomy. This means that in areas where state public policy does not impose mandatory rules, parties are free to decide not only on the substantive rules which will govern their relations – for example, by applying any usage developed in the profession or any general principles of law from practice – but also on governing rules of law.

There are several limits to freedom of contract. The first was already identified in the preceding paragraph. Parties may contract out only for rights that are not covered by public policy or *lois de police* (mandatory rules). This issue is a recurring one and does not need to be further discussed at this stage. However, one example directly imported from intellectual property may be proposed here. It deals with the transferability of rights. It is clear that it is not for the law of the contract only to say what can be the subject of a contract. Public policy will dictate which rights are non-transferable. Now, it is important to know which public policy we are talking about. First, in a very classic manner, public policy of the *lex fori* may dictate the outcome on this issue.[31]

[28] See Com (95) 382 final, July 1995. For an approval, see A. Strowel and J.P. Triaille, *Le droit d'auteur, du logiciel au multimedia,* Story-Scientia et Bruylant, Bruxelles, 1997, notably at n. 514. For a critic, see Lucas (*supra* note 4), at p. 5-6. However, later in the same article, André Lucas seems to be willing to give a fairly large area of application to the law of contract: "La méthode pourrait consister à poser le principe que cette loi a vocation à régir toutes les hypothèses où la nature et le contenu du droit ne sont pas en cause, sauf à établir une liste limitative d'exceptions dans lesquelles retour serait fait à la loi du droit et sous réserve des cas, également exceptionnels, dans lesquels les Etats seraient libres de faire jouer la réserve des lois de police ou celle de l'ordre public international."

[29] I must also mention here that tort law is nowadays no longer insulated from freedom to choose the law. Obviously, in tort law the choice will be made after the tort has occurred. For a step in that direction, see the proposal for a European Regulation on the law applicable to non-contractual obligations.

[30] The draft Convention was adopted in December 2002. It has not yet been signed by any state, although the United States is presently considering it. For an analysis of that Convention and the role of party autonomy, see M. Germain and C. Kessedjian, "La loi applicable à certains droits sur les titres détenus auprès d'un intermédiaire – Le projet de convention de La Haye de décembre 2002", *Revue critique de droit international privé*, 2004, p. 80.

[31] This would not apply if the matter was to be decided by an arbitral tribunal for the obvious reason that an arbitral tribunal has no forum. However, in this instance, the law of the place of arbitration may impose its public policy at the recognition and enforcement level as will certainly any other state in which the award has to be enforced. The latter would also be true for the enforcement of a court decision. A good example of public policy in this context is

This is why it is so important that jurisdictional rules also be well drafted at the same time as the applicable law rules. But it is probably not only the public policy rules that may be applicable. It seems safe to say that the law which created the right[32] also has a role in saying what part(s) of that right is not transferable.[33] Finally, it would not be uncommon to see the state where the rights are exercised imposing its public policy. For this to happen, however, one does not need to create a conflict of laws rule.

The second limit deals with the fact that party autonomy has a role to play only in cases where parties have equal bargaining power. Thus, in each area of business, it is important to know whether some actors need to be protected or whether the general public policy rules are sufficient to provide for the protection needed. It is also a matter of policy for the states to decide whether to act *a posteriori* (only when the freedom of contract resulted in an unacceptable outcome) or *a priori* in deciding once and for all that a certain category of actors is excluded from party autonomy. This traditional way of thinking, however, is slowly being replaced by one which focuses not on the nature of the parties at stake but on the way the contract was entered into. In other words, what matters is whether the contract was fully negotiated or not. This trend has been identified in France in the consumer protection area, where there is a trend toward not being concerned with who is a "consumer" but whether the contract was actually negotiated or not. Whether this renders the analysis easier is not entirely proven.[34]

The third limit is actually a double preliminary question that cannot be solved by the law applicable to the contract. Indeed, it is important to know whether the parties who entered into the contract were the right owner/holder and whether the rights are transferable.[35] Asking this question of the law applicable to the contract is actually somewhat of a vicious circle. This is why, even if there is a policy toward refusing dépeçage, as demonstrated in part I of

---

that embodied in the proposed European Regulation on the Community patent (draft of September 4, 2003) which provides in Article 53 that "a Community patent may not be declared invalid or be invalidated in arbitration proceedings."

[32] I use the expression "law which created the right" in a neutral, descriptive sense, awaiting the discussion of which is the law which does create the right. I do understand that, under the Berne Convention, the law which creates the right is that of the country of exercise; hence, rights arise simultaneously in each and every country where they are exercised. I do not use the expression with that meaning.

[33] In Section IV below, we will study the conflict of laws rule to define which law is applicable to the creation of the intellectual property right.

[34] For a similar trend in Internet law, see Sylvette Guillemard, *Le droit international privé face au contrat de vente cyberspatial*, Thèse, Université Panthéon-Assas, Paris II, décembre 2002, pp. 432 to 446. Sylvette Guillemard presents a fresh look at the same analysis in an article entitled "Le cyberconsommateur est mort, vive l'adhérent" *Journal du droit international*, 2004, p. 7 to 62. In domestic law, see Marie-Stéphanie Payet, *Droit de la concurrence et droit de la consommation*, Paris, Dalloz, 2001.

[35] This text provides: "The law governing the right to which the assignment is related shall determine its assignability... ."

this paper, at least as far as the determination of who is the right owner and whether the rights are transferable, a law other than the law applicable to the contract must apply. As far as the second part of the question is concerned, this is exactly what Article 12.2 of the Rome Convention on the law applicable to contractual obligations does.

Finally, there are acts which clearly do not fall under a contractual analysis, such as infringement by third parties. This is not to say that party autonomy is completely excluded from tort. Indeed, it is more common these days to accept that once the tort has been committed, the victim could agree on which law would apply to liability and compensation.[36]

Obviously, party autonomy is good as long as the parties to a contract use the freedom granted to them. If they do not and thus remain silent on the law applicable to their agreement, there must be a default conflict of laws rule available to fill the gap. This will be studied in the following chapter.

IV. Which Default Rules?

1. Nationality

The matter of nationality is probably no longer a matter of controversy, but for the sake of clarity I would like to briefly explain why nationality is not a pertinent criterion, particularly in intellectual property matters. Does a work protected by intellectual property rights have a "nationality"? Very often, discourses on intellectual property rights use a language that seems to suggest nationality: a U.S. patent, a French book, a Japanese trademark, an Argentinean film. In fact, each of these expressions covers a different reality. In the case of a patent, trademark, or any other registered right, it probably means that the right has been registered in that country. In the case of a book, it may mean either that it was published in France or in the French language. In the case of a movie, it may mean that it was shot in Argentina, is in the Spanish language, the director was Argentinean, or the production was completely or mostly from Argentina. This shows that speaking in terms of "nationality" is at best loose, non-conclusive language that can be very damaging because it is completely misguided and confusing. It is even worse when it comes to domain names and websites. The generic TLDs do not give any information on the supposed "nationality" of the website. This is also true of the countries' TLDs, which at first sight may seem to give an indication but in reality do not. The first reason is that most registrars accept registration of country domain names by non-resident aliens. Second, there is an international convergence on the principle that a domain name (and the website attached to it) is not an establishment for

[36] See, for example, the proposal for a European Regulation on the law applicable to non-contractual obligations (Rome II), Com (2003) 427 final, July 22, 2003, 2003/0168 (COD).

any legal purpose.[37] Hence, unless we accept the legal fiction that a domain name is a *rem* situated at the place where the registrar is situated,[38] no inference may be taken from a domain name for private international law purposes.

In addition, one must realize that private international law theories and practice have evolved from a nationality-centered analysis to one centered around habitual residence. This is true for individuals, of course. For legal entities it is a little more complicated because several concepts are still used depending on the legal system in which one is situated. In common law countries, it is the place of incorporation which works as a functional equivalent of habitual residence. In civil law countries, in contrast, the main place of business is the criterion used in this respect. There is now a third concept which has already been used in bankruptcy, that of center of activities. It is easily understandable why in bankruptcy a more concrete concept must be used. It remains to be seen whether this concept will indeed replace the two traditional criteria mentioned above, in general private international law, but it certainly works as a good functional equivalent of habitual residence, hence unifying the criteria used for legal persons or corporate bodies with that used for individuals.

Consequently, I would conclude that the criterion of nationality should be avoided in any attempt to draft conflict of laws rules in the area of intellectual property because it has been slowly but surely abandoned in other areas of private international law.

2. *Place of Registration*

From all the discussions I have heard and participated in, it seems that the place of registration has a great – and possibly exclusive – role to play when it comes to registered rights.[39] At least in patent law, I have been convinced by argu-

---

[37] See, for example, the European Directive 2000/31 on Electronic Commerce of 8 June 2000, OJEC L 178 of 17 July 2000, p.1, and the OECD resolution of 2000 on the interpretation of Article 5 of the model tax treaty.

[38] This is what the U.S. Anticybersquatting Consumer Protection Act does, particularly against foreign defendants against whom no *in personam* jurisdiction may be found in the United States. See, for example, Porsche Cars North America, Inc. v. Porsche.net, 302 F3d 248, 259-260 (4th Cir. 2002). Some authors argue that such an application of the *in rem* jurisdictional provision violates due process. See Catherine T. Struve & R. Polk Wagner, "Realspace sovereigns in cyberspace: Problems with the Anticybersquatting Consumer Protection Act," 17 *Berkeley Tech. L.J.* 989, at 998-1018 (2002).

[39] Section 301 (1) of the ALI draft provides that "as a general rule, with respect to rights that arise out of registration, the law applicable to determine the existence, validity and scope of those rights and remedies for their infringement is the law of each country of registration." For registered rights, the reporters accept no exception to the rule (see Sections 311 (1), 314 both alternatives, 316 (1)) even in exceptional circumstances (see Section 302), apart from the application of the law of the contract for the conditions of the transfer and the grant of licenses (see Section 315) and if the subject matter of the registered right was created by contract

ments claiming that even though two registered patents – let's say one in the U.S. and one in the UK – are very close and tend to cover the same innovation, they are still two different patents and should be dealt with separately. Whether or not a consolidation mechanism is put into place at the jurisdictional level,[40] the judge must apply as many laws as there are patents at stake. There is an attraction of territoriality for all issues, including validity and infringement. This attraction seems to be dictated by the idiosyncrasy of patent law and its deep roots in the culture and economy of the country which grants it. Whether this is also true for other registered rights remains to be demonstrated. But the rationale should be discussed along the lines identified for patent.

3. *Desperately Seeking a Single Law for Non-Registered Rights*

According to the above conclusions on dépeçage and the need for a single law, I would argue that the same law would decide who is the right holder, what kind of rights he/she holds, whether those rights are transferable in all or in part, and, generally, how those rights may be exercised. Having said that, the difficulty is to know which law that should be. There are several possibilities: the law of the habitual residence/establishment of the person/entity who claims to be the right owner; the law of the habitual residence/establishment of the producer of the work; the law of the place of first availability to the public;[41] or the law of the place where the rights are exercised or claimed. Let's try to discuss the pros and cons for each of those laws.

The law of the habitual residence/establishment of the person/entity who claims to be the right owner seems to have the closest connection to the person who claims to be the right owner. It may be argued that intellectual property is concerned with favoring creativity and thus giving incentives to creators. If that's accepted as a major goal of IP laws, then it seems that the law of the place where a creator is situated has the greatest interest in providing the rules about whether that person is the title owner, the scope of the rights granted, whether these rights are transferable, and to what extent they may be exercised. It is also for that law to say in which ways the right owner should be protected and to what extent he/she may contract out of the system. At first glance, then, it is the law which has the most titles to apply, particularly if it contains strong policies toward the protection of the right owner. However, there is one major

(Section 311 (2)). As a minor comment on the ALI draft, it is a little unfortunate that the reporters have chosen to structure their work by issues, with the result that for each type of rights, one has to look up almost every section in order to have a clear and complete picture of the rules that cover them.

[40] See the ALI draft Section 225.

[41] It is on purpose that I avoid using the expression "first publication" so as not to crystallize the analysis around one of the core expressions in the Berne Convention which has not always been interpreted uniformely.

inconvenience for the application of this law, i.e., when one is confronted with joint work (multi-authored work). It is impracticable to apply at once all laws of all persons who claim a right in the joint work, particularly because, if there is a contradiction in the results, the concrete situation will result in chaos, with some countries saying that it is indeed a joint work and others saying that it is not.

The law of the habitual residence/establishment of the producer of the work is certainly an easy solution, at least for the producer, particularly when a joint work is at stake. Some argue that it has the advantage of predictability because the producer is always known as well as its location. However, if the producer is operating through a branch or other establishment, it would be necessary to provide for a rule defining whether the principal establishment or the branch location will be the connecting factor. The law of the producer also has the advantage of universality. However, it has the disadvantage of giving strong power to the person/entity that may be considered as the strongest in the relationship with the author/composer/actor. There is also a difficulty when a work is co-produced for it would then be necessary to either apply several laws simultaneously (which is totally impracticable, particularly when they conflict with each other) or to determine which producer is the main one, with a concrete impossibility when they have an equal share in the production. The main disadvantage is also due to the fact that the producer may fairly easily choose to locate itself in a country which offers no or little protection to the creator/author. Consequently, this law renders manipulations too easy to perform.

The law of the place of first availability to the public[42] has the advantage of universality.[43] Contrary to what is sometimes argued, it seems to me that the person who claims to be the right owner carefully chooses the place of first publication, which is not fortuitous.[44] If one writes a book in French, that person has the choice of publishing it in a number of countries. It is in that country that the publisher and the alleged right owner meet (at least intellectually). As far as a reasonable expectation of the parties, that law seems to

---

[42] For a strong advocate of the place of first publication, see J.S. Bergé, *La protection internationale et communautaire du droit d'auteur: essai d'une analyse conflictuelle*, Paris, LGDJ, 1996.

[43] The ALI draft does give that law the power to define the initial title for works of authorship (Section 313 (1) (a)), but proposes thereafter a number of exceptions which do not appear to be absolutely necessary (Section 313 (1) (b) to (d), (2) to (4). The reporters are still hesitant to give that same law the power to also define the transferability of those rights (Section 314 contains two alternatives). I clearly favor alternative B (2).

[44] As far as performers/composers are concerned, I would not apply the place of fixation if by "fixation" we understand the place where the record is made. On the contrary, I consider that the place of first publication also applies to musical works in the sense that, notwithstanding the place of recording, the place where the record is released to the public for the first time is very often a decision taken in careful consideration of all interests at stake.

meet all expected results. Indeed, intellectual property law has two main purposes: one is to foster creativity; the second is to allow the public to benefit from the creations according to conditions set forth. Thus, the creator and the public do "meet" at the place where the work is first made available to the public. This place is not unforeseeable even for the producers, for they know where the work will be made available to the public because they participate in that act. All of this is also true for joint works: all participants in the joint work "meet" at the place of first availability to the public in the sense that, whether or not they have participated in the decision of choosing that place, they have at least agreed to go along with the joint work with all the circumstances attached to it, among which is the place of first public disclosure. This consent should not be and is not given lightly. Some argue that this rule does not work when the work is first published over the Internet.[45] It is true that in that case the place of first disclosure to the public does not exist, so to speak.[46] However, as usual with Internet transactions nowadays, we should work with a presumption. That presumption could be that, in case the place of first disclosure to the public cannot be ascertained (and this rule would apply to both Internet and real-life publication), there is a presumption that that place is located at the habitual residence of the right owner. Hence, it would not be too complicated to say that when the place of first publication cannot be asserted, it is deemed to be at the place of the habitual residence/establishment of the person who makes the decision to first publish as a numeric work. In the case of a joint work published over the Internet, that place should be deemed to be the place of habitual residence/establishment of the person who took the initiative in the joint work.

The law of the place where the rights are exercised or the law of the place for which the rights are claimed goes against the universality principle. It is the basis for the territoriality principle being justified, for a great number of interpreters, by the Berne Convention and the traditional thinking in intellectual property.[47] Some states have adopted this rule as a classic bilateral conflict of laws rule either in a statute[48] or by case law.[49] Some justify the application of this conflict of laws rule by saying that it is the law that must be applied for public policy reasons. But, as was mentioned earlier in this paper, this is not a

[45] For example, Lucas (*supra* note 4), at p. 8.

[46] I do consider that publishing over the Internet is a publication. In agreement, see J. Ginsburg, "The private international law of copyright in an era of technological change," *Collection of Courses, Hague Academy of International Law*, Volume 273 (1998-III) pp. 239-406. Contra, Lucas (*supra* note 4), at p.8.

[47] See the long explanations provided by the ALI draft, notably pp. 106 to 112.

[48] This is the case at least for Italy, Greece, and Switzerland, three countries quoted by Lucas (*supra* note 4), at p. 7 footnote 38.

[49] This is the case in France, as shown by the latest decision of the Cour de cassation (Civ 1) of December 9, 2003, Universal Music et al. vs. SNAM et al. (C01-10.264, decision #1653 F-P). This seems to be contrary to a case decided in 1959 which, although fairly ambiguous, seemed to favor the law of origin: Civ 1 December 22, 1959, D. 1960 p. 93 note G. Holleaux.

pertinent rationale for a conflict of laws rule since the public policy exception (whether *a priori* or *a posteriori*) is always available. Another justification could be that this would also be the law applicable to infringement.[50] It is true that infringement claims are very often faced with a counterclaim to the effect that there is no valid right in the first place, thus there is no infringement; or that the person who claims to be the victim of the infringement is not the right owner. It is perhaps easier for a judge to apply one single law for all these issues. But, then, there is a territorial *morcellement*, and the judge would have to apply as many laws as there are countries in which the right has been exercised. This does not seem practical.

All things considered, it seems that the law of the first making available to the public is that which represents the fewest inconveniences and the most advantages.

4. *Infringement*

First, I should clarify that I consider unfair competition or passing off as being of the same nature as infringement, and thus the same conflict analysis is applied in both cases. It remains that whatever law is applicable to the issues identified above in section IV.3., the question of infringement may have to be dealt with separately. The traditional private international law of tort can apply to intellectual property torts (whether infringement or unfair competition). We should first address one new issue of dépeçage, namely whether two different laws should be applied to liability on the one hand and compensation on the other.[51] It is true that tort law has two main purposes: (1) to compensate the victim for the damages suffered and (2) deter similar activities by potential tort feasors. This dépeçage actually avoids the lengthy and almost impossible-to-solve discussion between supporters of the law of tort feasor[52] and supporters of the law of destination, namely the law of the victim or, for others, that of each place of the damage;[53] in other words, the place where the effects are felt or the law of the market. Indeed, it allows application of the law of the tort feasor on liability and that of the victim on compensation. This solution has the advantage of furthering both policies behind tort law. We could refine the rule for cases when the tort feasor cannot be identified, or is located in a

[50] See AIPPI's Resolution Q 174 on Cross-Border Infringement, adopted October 26, 2003. Article 2 of that Resolution reserves "special circumstances" but without explaining what they may be.

[51] For the demonstration that this division is pertinent, see Olivera Boskovic, *La réparation du préjudice en droit international privé,* Paris, LGDJ, 2003.

[52] By the law of the tort feasor, I mean the law of the country in which the alleged infringer is situated, i.e., habitual residence for an individual and principle place of business or "siège" for a legal entity.

[53] For such an exposition, see Lucas (*supra* note 4), at p. 11-13.

legal/numeric heaven. In those cases, a default rule would lead to the law of the domicile of the injured party or that of the place of damage.

If the division between liability and compensation is not acceptable, the person who claims to be the victim of a tort could be given the choice to claim protection under those laws where the tort is alleged to have taken place and damage is suffered (cumulative condition), or under the laws of the place of habitual residence/establishment. The latter would apply as the sole conflict of laws rule when the infringement is alleged to have taken place over the Internet. Should that also be the only conflict of laws rule for torts committed in the analogue world? It certainly carries strong arguments with it. It seems quite clear that the tort feasor knows or ought to know the place of habitual residence of the right owner(s). An exception could probably be carved out for cases where that law would be entirely unpredictable for the tort feasor. Is this workable when the intellectual property right is held collectively by several right owners? In such a case, could we expect the tort feasor to know all these laws? Should we find a single law for that particular case? All things considered, I would argue for a single exception when the result is clearly unpredictable for the tort feasor, whether it is because the work is a joint one or for other reasons. However, the subsidiary rule is not an easy one to agree upon. This is why I favor the division between liability and compensation as a better solution.

V. Conclusion

A few general remarks on the ALI project may be necessary in the guise of a conclusion.

It is unfortunate that the reporters did not free their rules on applicable law from the old conundrum of private international law, which makes it impossible to think about applicable law without having first ascertained the court seized of the matter. It is true that it is sometimes impossible to escape that web, but sometimes it is possible. This is unfortunate for at least two reasons. First, individuals and entities very often need to know the extent of their rights independent of any dispute and long before they even consider bringing a case before a court. Second, it is not uncommon now that some of the issues covered by Part III of the ALI project will be adjudicated by arbitration or will be submitted to mediation/conciliation. This is why I think it would be most appropriate to free Part III of the project from the other parts, so that whoever has to resort to applicable law rules, in whatever context, would be able to rely on those proposed by the ALI. And although I agree with the previous move by the reporters to refrain from speaking extensively about arbitration because it is a different world by itself, it is still unfortunate that, at least in the introduction of Chapter III, they do not suggest that arbitrators, *mutatis mutandis*, could avail themselves of the ALI applicable law rules if they find them useful.

A second general remark refers to Section 321 of the draft.[54] For a reason unclear to me, the reporters thought it important to import a rule on "proof of applicable law," when in three lines they actually cover three very difficult issues of private international law, namely: 1) to what extent a court may/must apply *sua sponte* a foreign law; 2) whether a foreign law must be "proven;"[55] and 3) if so, how that proof is given. In their comment and notes, the reporters do not do justice to the extensive literature and case law which has occupied many scholars and courts, at least in Europe, for many decades. In some countries, it is now settled law that a court – apart from contractual relations, perhaps – must apply *sua sponte* the foreign law applicable to the case at stake. Importing the second rule in Section 321 may be considered a step backward without exercising any positive influence on the courts, which are still reluctant to apply foreign law. The reporters' note[56] rightly quotes the still relatively unknown London Convention of the Council of Europe of 1968. However, in all fairness, we should not forget that the mechanism put into place by that Convention is complicated and, in consequence, is seldom used. Another good opportunity to favor direct cooperation between courts has been lost here. Finally, the reporters have forgotten an important coda to this matter, which is to provide for a rule explaining what happens if the foreign law cannot be established.[57] It is true that they provide for that rule in Section 302, second rule in that sentence. However, I believe that it should be a general rule and not reserved to some instances only.[58]

A third general remark is directed at Section 322. This rule which, on its face, is devoted to excluding the use of "*renvoi*," in fact pretends to solve all at once another complex issue of private international law. Whether a conflict of laws rule designates the law of a country – i.e., the state law – or the rules of law admitted in that country – i.e., any rule including those rules made by operators, usages, general principles, and the like – is a very controversial issue. This is a controversy that has arisen from the very Article 15 of the Rome Convention which the reporters quote as a justification for their own rule, without going into further discussion on this issue.[59] There is extensive literature on

---

[54] If the reporters accept the remarks in this paragraph, they should also consider amending the last few lines of their road map on page 105.

[55] The law of the forum is never "proven" so to speak. Thus, in its generality, the title of Section 321 is erroneous.

[56] See p. 133.

[57] Compare Article 16 of the Swiss Statute on Private International Law.

[58] As far as the first rule in Section 302 ("if these norms do not supply a rule") is concerned, the reporters may wish to consider the literature which argues that any system of law always contains general rules which may very well give a solution to the problem, even if a specific rule has not been developed yet. This line of reasoning is certainly more in line with the minimum respect due to foreign systems of law.

[59] I am not convinced either by the call to logic as a justification for the exclusion of *renvoi* (see Reporters' Comment on p. 134).

this issue and it is not feasible to cover it here. I only wish to call the attention of the reporters to a matter which needs further analysis.

A fourth comment goes to Section 323 (2), which deals with the question of statute of limitations only linked with party autonomy, hence applying *lex causae* to the statute of limitation. However, it would be interesting to know whether countries for which the statute of limitation is procedural would actually agree to depart from that conception only in cases where party autonomy has been exercised. Is there less need for uniformity and predictability[60] when the parties have not exercised the freedom to choose the applicable law, or when their choice has been displaced for some reason (mandatory rule, public policy, or otherwise invalidity of the choice)? I am not entirely convinced.

A fifth comment is directed at Sections 324 and 325. There are two ways in which public policy may displace the initial conflict of laws analysis: either a mandatory rule exists which prevents the conflict of laws analysis to function properly and impose a solution *a priori*, or it is used *a posteriori* as a limited exception to the law otherwise held applicable after the conflict of laws analysis has been conducted. States are not often very clear when using one or the other method, but it does function in concrete terms in the sequence I just indicated. Consequently, I think Sections 324 and 325 should be inverted. On the substance of the two provisions, I think that some modifications may be necessary. We should first consider that the world of international law-making is changing, notably under the pressure of globalization. As mentioned above, the extension of party autonomy leaves states with little power other than their public policy or mandatory rules to safeguard the values of their societies. Hence, it has become common to say that we have replaced conflict of laws by conflict of public policies. Having said that, however, it is probably not a good idea to signal to states that they can disguise any kind of rules under a public policy mask or a characterization as mandatory rules. This is why I think it would be appropriate to accept the public policy exception only if foreign law is "manifestly" contrary to public policy in order to avoid an abusive use of the exception.[61] As far as mandatory rules are concerned, it is important to separate two hypotheses. The first concerns mandatory rules of the forum. It is clear that they must be applied. There is a large international consensus on this solution. To the contrary, whether foreign mandatory rules must be applied has not reached the same consensus. If the foreign law applicable according to the

---

[60] These are the justifications given in the comment at p. 135.

[61] It is important to recall that, at least in the United States, the interest analysis theory was a response to what was considered at the time as an application of the public policy exception that was too broad, too systematic, and without nuance. Of course, the public policy exception is probably not needed any more, or to a much lesser extent, if one proceeds with an interest analysis since the policies behind the rules are already built in the conflict of laws analysis. However, such a conflict rule renders much more complex the search for the applicable law and much less foreseeable its outcome.

conflict of laws rule contains mandatory rules, it is quite clear that they must be applied as any other rules. However, if the foreign mandatory rules are that of a third country with which the case has a link, it is accepted by some that these rules may be given effect, but seldom that they may be applied, and even less so that they must be applied. This is the very reason why the Rome Convention treats both hypotheses separately, and that states party to that Convention have been authorized not to apply the second rule if they so declare.[62]

My final comment is directed at the structure of Chapter III as a whole. I have always found it awkward to draft legislation-like norms from a theoretical point of view and not from a practical point of view, be they Convention, model laws, or sets of rules such as the ALI draft. If the latter is adopted, then the rules should probably be structured around the following: (1) mandatory rules, with a clear signal to states that they should keep these to the absolute essentials; (2) law applicable to the definition of the right owner – which, in my view, should also define the nature and amount of rights and their transferability – principle and conditions; (3) party autonomy for contracts; (4) default rule for contracts if the latter is silent; (5) law applicable to tort (infringement and unfair competition); (6) public policy exception left to the absolute minimum; and (7) general provisions. In my view, such a structure could also help non-specialists in private international law get their reasoning straight.

I will close with another excerpt from the discourse by Victor Hugo quoted as a preface to this paper: "La propriété littéraire est d'utilité générale. Toutes les vieilles législations monarchiques ont nié et nient encore la propriété littéraire. Dans quel but ? Dans un but d'asservissement. L'écrivain propriétaire, c'est l'écrivain libre. Lui ôter la propriété, c'est lui ôter l'indépendance." And later: "Le principe est double, ne l'oublions pas. Le livre, comme livre, appartient à l'auteur ; mais comme pensée, il appartient … au genre humain. Toutes les intelligences y ont droit. Si l'un des deux droits … devait être sacrifié, ce serait certes le droit de l'écrivain, car l'intérêt public est notre préoccupation unique, et tous, je le déclare, doivent passer avant nous. Mais … ce sacrifice n'est pas nécessaire." I wish that the same wit and *sagesse* would be applied to private international law issues for intellectual property.

---

[62] This is very unusual since reservations are normally never accepted under European Law. It could be done in the Rome Convention because it was not strictly adopted as a matter of European law since it was not mentioned in the former Article 220 of the Treaty of Rome (now Article 293). It may not be maintained if and when the Rome Convention is transformed into a Community Act.

The Hague Project of a Global Judgments Convention and IP Rights: Recent Developments

ANDREA SCHULZ

I. The History of the Hague Conference Project of a Global Convention on Jurisdiction, Recognition, and Enforcement in Civil and Commercial Matters (the Hague Judgments Project)

Following a U.S. proposal put forward in 1992,[1] the 17th Session of the Hague Conference on Private International Law decided – first tentatively at the Centenary of Hague Conference meetings in 1993, then definitely at the conclusion of the 18th Session in 1996, "... to include in the Agenda of the Nineteenth Session the question of jurisdiction, and recognition and enforcement of foreign judgments in civil and commercial matters."[2]

Some preparatory work was carried out between 1992 and 1996 until, in accordance with the decision taken in 1996, the Secretary General of the Hague Conference convened a Special Commission, which held five meetings of one or more weeks between June 1997 and October 1999.[3] At the meeting in

[1] By letter from the Legal Adviser of the Department of State to the Secretary General of the Hague Conference; see *Pfund*, Contributing to Progressive Development of Private International Law: The International Process and the United States Approach, Recueil des Cours 249 (1994-V), p. 13 (83).

[2] Final Act of the Eighteenth Session, Part B, No 1, Hague Conference on private international law, Proceedings of the Eighteenth Session, Tome I, 1999, p. 47.

[3] For further details, see *Nygh & Pocar*; Report on the Preliminary Draft Convention on Jurisdiction and Foreign Judgments in Civil and Commercial Matters adopted by the Special Commission, Hague Conference, Prel. Doc. No 11, p. 25 *et seqq.* (also available at <www.

October 1999, which was supposed to be the last meeting of the Special Commission,[4] a "Preliminary Draft Convention[5] on Jurisdiction and Foreign Judgments in Civil and Commercial Matters"[6] was adopted by vote. In its structure and content, the text very much resembled the Brussels Convention of September 27, 1968,[7] and the Lugano Convention of September 16, 1988,[8] both on Jurisdiction and the Enforcement of Judgments in Civil and Commercial Matters. The text contained rules on jurisdiction as well as on the recognition and enforcement of judgments rendered in a Contracting State by a court having Convention-based jurisdiction. The chapter on jurisdiction provided for a general defendant's forum (in the defendant's state of habitual residence; Article 3) where all actions against a particular defendant could be brought, as long as they fell within the scope of the Convention (Article 1) and were not subject to exclusive jurisdiction under the Convention. Equally open to all actions independent of the subject matter were fora based on a choice of court

---

hcch.net> under "Work in Progress." Whenever reference is made to the website of the Hague Conference in this paper, only the top-level address will be indicated; during the course of 2004, the Hague Conference will be moving to a new website format which will affect the path indicating the location of individual documents.).

[4] According to the working methods so far largely followed by the Hague Conference, each session lasts roughly four years and is concluded by a Diplomatic Conference which normally adopts (1) the main elements of the work program for the four years to follow, in particular the next convention project, and (2) the text of a "Draft Convention" elaborated by a Special Commission during the four years since the last Diplomatic Conference.

[5] The Special Commission constituted for each project will normally end its work about one to one and a half years before the envisaged date of the Diplomatic Conference with the adoption of a "Preliminary Draft Convention," thereby leaving time for consultations on the text in the Member States of the Conference and other states participating in the negotiations. The final text then adopted during the Diplomatic Conference, as mentioned above, is called "Draft Convention" as long as it has not been signed by any state or other entity entitled to do so. Normally, the Draft Convention is opened for signature on the closing day of the Diplomatic Conference, when the Final Act is signed by all delegations and the text thereby approved as being the result of their negotiations. The first signature promotes the "Draft Convention" to a "Convention," which will subsequently be referred to as bearing the date of the first signature.

[6] The text of the Preliminary Draft Convention 1999 and its Explanatory Report by *Nygh* (Australia) *& Pocar* (Italy) have been published in Prel. Doc. No 11 (*supra* note 3). On the website of the Hague Conference at <www.hcch.net>, the two documents are available under separate covers.

[7] OJ EC C 27/1998, p. 1. On March 1, 2002, the Brussels Convention was replaced by Regulation (EC) No. 44/2001 on Jurisdiction and the Recognition and Enforcement of Judgments in Civil and Commercial Matters of December 22, 2000 (OJ EC L 12/2001, p. 1) (the Brussels I Regulation) for 14 of the then 15 EU Member States. Since May 1, 2004, the Regulation also binds the ten new Member States. The Convention is, however, still in force between Denmark, on the one hand, and the 14 EU Member States party to it. It is envisaged to be replaced by an agreement between the Community and Denmark along the lines of the Brussels I Regulation.

In this paper, the Conventions of Brussels and Lugano, together with the Brussels I Regulation, will be referred to as "the European instruments."

[8] OJ EC L 319/1988, p. 9.

agreement (Article 4), on appearance and submission by the defendant (Article 5), on a joinder of actions against multiple defendants (Article 14), counter-claims (Article 15), and third-party claims (Article 16). In addition, there were rules on specific jurisdiction for certain subject matters – some exclusive (Article 12), but most of them not (Articles 6 – 11).

The validity of intellectual property rights required to be registered or deposited was subject to exclusive jurisdiction of the state of deposit or registration where a finding on the validity or invalidity of the IP right was the subject of the action (Article 12(4) of the 1999 text). This meant that the Convention's bases of jurisdiction provided for contracts (e.g., license litigation), tort (e.g., infringement of IP rights), or choice of court agreements would not apply in those cases. The delegates present in October 1999, however, were not able to agree on whether exclusive jurisdiction should also extend to proceedings where validity could arise as an incidental question, in particular infringement proceedings (Article 12(5) and (6)). At that time, the IP community largely ignored the negotiations in The Hague and provided very little input.

During the consultations carried out in the Member States of the Hague Conference on the Preliminary Draft Convention adopted in October 1999, it turned out that the text was mainly interesting for those states party to the Conventions of Brussels and Lugano and, perhaps, a few others with similar or at least compatible legal – and in particular procedural – systems. This was partly attributed to the fact that the text had been adopted by vote, and on many occasions there had been a very narrow majority, thus leaving a large minority of more than one-third of the delegations unsatisfied.

Moreover, in the late 1990s, the Internet and electronic commerce were becoming ever more important, and legislators were struggling to deal with them. In the United States, the Digital Millennium Copyright Act (DMCA) was being discussed; in the European Union there was a debate on the Directives on Electronic Commerce and on Copyright in the Information Society (all of them involving, e.g., the problem of liability of Internet Service Providers [ISPs] for content posted by one of their clients, and the questions of jurisdiction and applicable law for such liability); and the Conventions of Brussels and Lugano were revised and stirred up the waters with regard to the Internet and electronic commerce in the area of consumer contracts.[9] In addition, some specialized international organizations started to look across the neatly drawn boundaries between IP and PIL. The World Intellectual Property Organization (WIPO), for example, was faced with conflict of laws issues concerning trademarks on the Internet and copyright (during the negotiations on a Treaty on Audiovisual

[9] What had been seen by the delegates revising the Conventions of Brussels and Lugano (to whom the author belonged) as a mere clarification of Article 13(1) No 3 of the Brussels Convention (the issue of targeting of electronic advertisements) was seen by e-commerce businesses as a major change to their detriment in the jurisdiction rules.

Performances in December 2000, which as of now has still not been finalized), and the IP community was finally alerted[10] that the Hague Judgments Project could affect IP rights.

For all these reasons, it was felt that more time and study was needed in order to appropriately deal with the factual changes brought about by the new digital media, in particular in the difficult borderline area between PIL and IP. The negotiating parties in The Hague therefore decided in April 2000 to suspend formal negotiations on the Judgments Project and conduct informal discussions on how to reach consensus on specific issues, including IP and e-commerce. Informal meetings hosted by individual states were held in Noordwijk (The Netherlands), Washington, D.C. (U.S.A.), Ottawa (Canada), Basel and Geneva (Switzerland), and Edinburgh (Scotland/United Kingdom) in 2000 and 2001.[11] The Geneva meeting in January 2001 was the first meeting on the Judgments Project ever to focus exclusively on IP issues. Following a two-day conference organized by WIPO on "Private International Law of Intellectual Property," which also touched on the Hague Judgments Project, the Hague Conference organized a one-day meeting on the IP aspects of the Judgments Project, taking advantage of the presence of numerous IP experts as well as many "habitual" Hague delegates. The major aim was to examine whether different IP rights might require different treatment under the Hague draft. As in 1999, there was a strong preference to reserve issues of validity of registered industrial property rights exclusively to the state of registration where this was the principal issue of the claim, but there was still no clear tendency as to whether exclusive jurisdiction should be extended to infringement proceedings, bearing in mind that in many infringement proceedings, invalidity is the standard defense.[12]

Discussions on infringement proceedings continued at a meeting in Ottawa in March 2001 where the tort jurisdiction under Article 10 of the 1999 draft was examined, in particular in light of the Internet. Discussions focused on cases where an act occurring in one single state produced effects in a number of different states, as can be the case for defamation, environmental damage, or IP infringement, and the tort working group found the draft of Article 10 partly unsatisfactory.[13]

---

[10] See, i.a., *Dreyfuss*, An Alert to the Intellectual Property Bar: The Hague Judgments Convention, University of Illinois Law Review 2001, No 1, p. 421.

[11] For a summary description of the informal meetings, see the report produced by the Permanent Bureau of the Hague Conference (Prel. Doc. No 15) at <www.hcch.net> under "Work in Progress."

[12] The meeting was chaired by the author. A report (Prel. Doc. No 13) is available at <www.hcch.net> under "Work in Progress."

[13] For further details, see *Schulz*, The Hague Conference Project of a Global Convention on Jurisdiction, Recognition and Enforcement in Civil and Commercial Matters – an update, in: *Drexl/Kur (ed.)*, IP and Private International Law: Heading for the Future (publication pending in 2004).

After this series of informal meetings, delegations felt sufficiently confident that they could now come to agreement when going back to formal negotiations. Moreover, it was agreed that the next step should not be based on voting but be consensus-based. Because it was felt that the latter might require more time, it was decided to split the Diplomatic Conference (which was the only remaining "formal" step because the Special Commission had terminated its work in October 1999) in two parts. The first part took place in June 2001 and produced a draft entitled "Interim Text."[14] Wherever it was impossible to reach unanimity – even in the case of a single delegation opposing a proposal – square brackets were placed. The number of square brackets, options, variants, and alternatives makes the text very difficult to read, to say the least. For those who did not participate in the meeting, it is almost incomprehensible. Moreover, it does not reflect how weak or strong the support or opposition to a particular provision was, because strict unanimity was required.

In April 2002, the Special Commission on General Affairs and Policy of the Hague Conference[15] convened to decide how to proceed further. While some delegations still had a strong interest in a global instrument covering all kinds of civil and commercial cases, and containing specific bases of jurisdiction for all of them, others stressed that the meeting in 2001 had demonstrated that it would be impossible to reach unanimity on all these issues within a reasonable time. In light of the time and effort already spent on the project and in an attempt to reconcile both positions, it was therefore decided to change first of all the working method: The Permanent Bureau of the Hague Conference was requested to establish an informal working group, reflecting the legal traditions of the Member States of the Hague Conference, which should try to draft a text that could then serve as a basis for future work. The group was supposed to use a "bottom-up approach," starting from the basis of jurisdiction in previous drafts that seemed least controversial, namely choice of court clauses in Business to Business (B2B) cases. The group was supposed to subsequently examine other bases of jurisdiction on which consensus seemed possible. As possible "candidates," the Commission on General Affairs listed general defendant's forum, submission, counter-claims, branches, trusts, and physical torts.[16]

The informal working group was chaired by Professor Allan Philip from Denmark and encompassed participants from Argentina, Brazil, China, Egypt, the European Commission, Germany, Italy, Japan, Mexico, New Zealand, the Russian Federation, South Africa, Spain, Switzerland, the United Kingdom, and the United States. The Permanent Bureau prepared a paper to facilitate the

---

[14] Available at <www.hcch.net> under "Work in Progress."

[15] This is a plenary meeting of Member State representatives which now meets annually and decides on the work program of the Conference, within the four-year framework set up by the Diplomatic Session (*supra* note 4).

[16] This last expression was used in order to exclude mere financial damages and damages to intangible rights (intellectual property, reputation). For the Conclusions of the Commission, see <www.hcch.net> under "General Affairs and Policy."

discussions of the group. It dealt with choice of court clauses in B2B cases as well as with submission, counter-claims, and the general defendant's forum.[17] During the three meetings held by the group between October 2002 and March 2003,[18] a text on choice of court clauses in B2B cases was drafted.[19] However, it was not possible to reach consensus on other bases of jurisdiction.

The text elaborated by the group was submitted to the Commission on General Affairs and Policy of the Conference at its meeting in April 2003. This meeting as well as further consultation subsequently carried out by the Secretary General of the Hague Conference in 2003 demonstrated that there was sufficient support for a Special Commission to be convened on the basis of the draft produced by the informal working group. It met in The Hague from December 1–9, 2003,[20] and, because it had not been able to complete its work at the December 2003 meeting due to a lack of time, again from April 21–27, 2004.[21] The latter meeting was preceded by an informal meeting hosted by the U.S. Department of State and the U.S. Patent and Trademark Office (USPTO) in Alexandria (Virginia, U.S.A.) from March 28–30, 2004 which focused exclusively on IP issues.

II. The Draft Text on Exclusive Choice of Court Agreements in B2B Cases

1. *The Aims of the 2004 Hague Draft*

The Convention draft is currently limited to exclusive choice of court clauses in B2B cases. It has three aims, namely to ensure that

(1) the chosen court *must* hear the case when seized by one of the parties, thereby excluding any discretion, e.g., under the doctrine of *forum non conveniens* (Article 5);
(2) any other court has to decline jurisdiction, unless one of the exceptions applies (Article 7); and

---

[17] Prel. Doc. No 19, available at <www.hcch.net> under "Work in Progress."

[18] See the reports of the three meetings (Prel. Docs No 20, 21 and 22) at <www.hcch.net> under "Work in Progress."

[19] Prel. Doc. No 8 (General Affairs), available at <www.hcch.net> under "Work in Progress." The same draft text, accompanied by a report with comments on the provisions, subsequently drawn up by the Permanent Bureau of the Hague Conference and reflecting the discussions in the informal working group (Prel. Doc. No 22), is available *ibid.*

[20] The text produced at the December 2003 Special Commission, together with a draft Explanatory Report drawn up by *Hartley* (United Kingdom) and *Dogauchi* (Japan) (Prel. Doc. No 25), is available at <www.hcch.net> under "Work in Progress."

[21] The text produced at the April 2004 Special Commission (Work. Doc. No 110 E Revised – Proposal by the Drafting Committee) is available at <www.hcch.net> under "Work in Progress." The draft Explanatory Report on the December 2003 text (see previous note) is currently being amended in order to reflect the latest draft. This work is expected to be completed in Summer 2004.

(3) a judgment rendered by the chosen court is recognized and enforced under the Convention, unless one of the exceptions applies (Article 9).

The Convention deals only with *exclusive* choice of court clauses. That is, the obligation of the chosen court to take the case and not to exercise any discretion to decline jurisdiction does not exist where the choice of court agreement was non-exclusive, thereby allowing one or all parties to seize a court other than the chosen court. If they have another option, there is no need to limit any discretion not to take the case which might exist under the national law of the court chosen and seized. The same is true for the obligation of any court other than the chosen court to decline jurisdiction: Where the parties themselves retained the freedom to seize a court other than the chosen court by making their clause non-exclusive, the Convention does not impose any obligation on the court seized but not chosen to decline jurisdiction. This means that in case of a non-exclusive clause, parallel proceedings may lawfully be brought if one party seizes the court (not exclusively) chosen, and the other party seizes a different court. In light of the complexity of the "package solution" achieved in 1999[22] on a combination of *lis alibi pendens* and *forum non conveniens*, it was considered disproportionate to include such a complex solution for parallel proceedings in a convention dealing only with choice of court agreements. A limitation to exclusive choice of court agreements therefore decreases the need to include a rule on parallel proceedings: Where the agreement is exclusive, no parallel proceedings are expected to occur, and if they do, it would be for the court seized but not chosen to dismiss proceedings under Article 7.[23] It was therefore decided to limit the Convention to *exclusive* choice of court agreements.

Nevertheless, this limitation is less far-reaching than it may seem, for several reasons: A very important change brought about by the new instrument is the presumption of exclusivity of the choice of court agreement in Article 3(b). Unless expressly provided otherwise by the parties, the agreement is deemed to be exclusive. This reverses the current law and practice in many, if not all, common law states. Moreover, "exclusive" in the sense of the Convention are (1) agreements designating the courts of one state, (2) agreements designating one specific court, and (3) agreements designating several courts in the same Contracting State. This means that, in fact, a large number of choice of court agreements will be covered by the Convention.

The limitation, which allowed a clearer focus on how best to strengthen party autonomy with regard to choice of court clauses in B2B cases, has led to a complete departure from the structure of the 1999 and 2001 Hague drafts. This concerns in particular the previous division of grounds of jurisdiction into

---

[22] See Articles 21 and 22 of the 1999 text (*supra* note 6).

[23] It may be necessary to include a rule covering situations where the court seized but not chosen may apply one of the exceptions mentioned in Article 7, and take the case, while the other party has seized the chosen court.

"good grounds" (the so-called white list of Conventional bases of jurisdiction, the use of which entitled the judgment rendered to recognition and enforcement under the Convention), "bad grounds" (the so-called black list of jurisdictional bases available under some national laws which would even prevent a court from rendering a judgment on such a basis, and not only exclude trans-frontier recognition and enforcement), and "tolerated grounds" (the remaining "gray area" of bases of jurisdiction available under national law: their use was permitted as long as the jurisdictional basis in question was not black-listed, although the resulting judgment would not be entitled to recognition and enforcement under the Convention regime).

The 2004 draft, while focusing on just one basis of jurisdiction – namely exclusive choice of court agreements – aims at a minimum degree of harmonization while leaving everything going beyond choice of court clauses in B2B cases to national law. With regard to the formal validity of a choice of court agreement, Article 3(c) harmonizes the requirements necessary and sufficient under the Convention. The agreement must be entered into or evidenced (i) in writing or (ii) by any other means of communication which renders information accessible so as to be usable for subsequent reference. The latter formulation was taken from Article 6 of the 1996 UNCITRAL Model Law on Electronic Commerce. A choice of court agreement is not covered by the Convention if it does not comply with these requirements, but if it does, no further requirements of a formal nature may be imposed under national law.[24]

As to substantive validity, the text does not establish direct Convention standards. However, a common denominator in numerous legal systems is the restriction or even exclusion of party autonomy concerning the choice of a court for litigation regarding certain subject matters. Many of these subject matters may therefore be found in Article 2 of the Convention, which lists the matters excluded from its substantive scope. This is true for consumer and employment contracts, rights *in rem* in immovable property, entries in public registers, etc. Another indirect definition of a Convention standard on substantive validity may be found in Article 7(a)–(e) and Article 9(1)(a)–(f). These Articles contain exhaustive lists of reasons that allow a court other than the chosen court which is seized on the merits (Article 7) or requested to recognize and enforce a judgment rendered by the chosen court (Article 9) to disregard the choice of court agreement and either take the case itself (under Article 7) or refuse recognition and enforcement of the chosen court's judgment (under Article 9). The harmonization achieved here is the choice of law rule in *lit.* a) of both Article 7 and Article 9(1): When examining whether the choice of court agreement is valid, the court seized has to apply the law of the state of the chosen court, including its choice of law rules. This is to ensure that there is no "double standard," and that all courts which are seized during the various

[24] See *Hartley & Dogauchi* Report (*supra* note 20), paras. 55 – 60.

stages of the proceedings apply the same law to the substantive validity of the choice of court agreement.

Given its focus on exclusive choice of court agreements, the text no longer contains grounds of jurisdiction for specific subject matters such as contracts, torts, or the validity of certain IP rights. However, the jurisdiction based on a choice of court clause is "content-neutral," as long as the matter at issue is not excluded from the scope of the Convention (Articles 1 and 2) and "arises in connection with a particular legal relationship," as agreed by the parties (Article 3(a)).

It is hoped that a Convention along those lines could provide a valuable alternative to arbitration, in particular in cases where the costs of an arbitration might seem out of proportion as compared to the value of the case, or in cases where, for some reason, e.g., effects on third parties or the possibility to join them to the proceedings even against their will, it seems desirable to obtain a court judgment instead of an arbitral award. The Convention therefore does not aim at entering into competition with the – most successful – 1958 New York Convention on the Recognition and Enforcement of Foreign Arbitral Awards, but wants to complement it. This complementarity is also reflected to some extent in some wording of the draft which echoes the New York Convention.

2. *The 2004 Hague Draft and IP Rights*

Party autonomy is the value most cherished by the draft. What does this mean for IP rights? As stated above, they are not excluded from the (limited) scope of the envisaged new Convention,[25] with the exception of

- agreements to which a natural person acting primarily for personal, family, or household purposes (a consumer) is a party (Article 2(1)(a));
- and proceedings relating to "[intellectual property rights other than copyright or related rights, except in proceedings pursuant to a contract which licenses or assigns such intellectual property rights [including proceedings for infringement of the right to which the contract relates]]" (Article 2(2)(k)).

The first exclusion mentioned means that, e.g., a license agreement between a consumer and a business would not be covered by the Convention. The meaning of the second exclusion is less obvious because, on its face, Article 2(3)(k) seems to exclude *all* IP litigation – even in B2B cases – from the scope of the Convention, with some exceptions from this general exclusion. But, as will be shown below, this is not the case.

[25] Article 2 defines the exclusions from the scope of the Convention.

a) Validity as the Subject of the Claim

There was consensus at the Special Commission that claims directly aiming at a determination of the validity of a patent or registered trademark with effect *erga omnes* (and therefore also affecting the entry in the register concerned) should be excluded from the scope of the Convention. This consensus also extends to unregistered trademarks and other registered industrial property rights.

The question, however, was which other intellectual property rights should be covered by this exclusion from the scope of the Convention, and in which words to express this – by listing individual IP rights, by referring to certain *categories* of rights (e.g., "registered intellectual [or industrial] property rights"), or in some other way. The problem with the latter solution, however, is that some rights may be – or even have to be – registered in some countries, while in other states they are unregistered. In addition, some rights exist in a registered and an unregistered form within the same state. The latter applies, e.g., to designs, copyrights, and trademarks. Furthermore, new registration duties are sometimes created for some rights. Therefore, making the exclusion from the scope of the Convention dependent on registration could lead to somewhat arbitrary results, depending on whether the national legislators choose to require registration or not. It could sometimes also be difficult for a court chosen and seized with proceedings concerning the validity of a foreign IP right to know whether there is a registration requirement in the state whose law protects the right. Moreover, one would have to find a solution for those rights for which registration is possible but not mandatory. The solution of mentioning specific IP rights, on the other hand, bears the risk of casting in stone solutions which might need to be adapted over time, e.g., with the creation of new IP rights.

Therefore, some favored a general catch-all phrase excluding proceedings that have the validity of *any* intellectual property right as their principal issue.[26] Others preferred an exclusion limited to the obvious and undisputed area of proceedings having the validity of patents and (registered or unregistered) trademarks as their principal issue. A third option, suggested at the March 2004 IP meeting in the U.S., was a declaration system providing utmost flexibility and transparency.

While the drafting policy of these solutions seems to be fundamentally different, the results would probably not differ very much in practice for the following reasons.

The Convention as it is drafted now is limited to exclusive choice of court agreements in B2B cases. This means that it will cover litigation concerning IP

[26] One suggestion in this context was to exclude "proceedings relating to the registration and validity of intellectual property rights, but not to licensing." Others felt that the last part should be better covered by a general "incidental question" rule which may also be necessary for the other exclusions mentioned in Article 2(2).

rights only where the parties to the proceedings have entered into some kind of contract beforehand, which contains *inter alia* a choice of court clause. Such a contract could either be a licensing agreement, an agreement that one party should not make use of a certain IP right, or another alternative. Where a dispute then arises between the parties, a decision must be made as to whether it arose "in connection with a particular legal relationship" (see Article 3(a)) in order for the Convention to apply. So far, reports from practitioners seem to suggest that validity as a principal issue arises in particular with regard to patents, to a lesser extent with regard to trademarks and other (registered) industrial property rights, and almost never with regard to copyright and (other) unregistered rights. Therefore, even if one chose to exclude "proceedings relating to the validity of intellectual property rights" while at the same time making clear that this applies only to claims where this is the principal issue, the exclusion would in practice not cover very many cases beyond patents and trademarks, if any at all. And where it does, those cases would be subject to exclusive jurisdiction in most states concerned anyway, which means that *not* excluding them would involve difficult disconnection issues with regard to other existing and future international instruments.

Article 2(2)(k), by excluding proceedings relating to *any* IP right except copyright and related rights from the scope of the Convention, therefore ensures that proceedings having as their principal subject the validity of an IP right would not be covered by the Convention. If parties agree on a court in a state other than the state whose law protects the right, the court chosen and seized may well be able to take the case under its internal law if the latter so permits, but the resulting judgment would not benefit from recognition and enforcement under the Convention.

However, unlike previous versions of this provision, the wording of Article 2(2)(k) is no longer limited to excluding proceedings "on the validity" of an IP right. On the contrary, it excludes in principle *all* IP litigation except for "proceedings pursuant to a contract which licenses or assigns such intellectual property rights."[27] Again, the underlying reason is the reach of exclusive jurisdiction on validity under national law, and the corresponding restriction on party autonomy.

b) Contractual Litigation (Licenses, Assignment of IP Rights)

There was a common wish among delegations to include license litigation and litigation concerning the assignment of IP rights within the scope of the Convention. For example, two parties bound by a license contract which contains a choice of court agreement should be held to that agreement, and the judgment should benefit from recognition and enforcement under the Con-

[27] The further addition in square brackets will be discussed below under c).

vention. This was felt appropriate even in cases where the licensee – who may be being sued for the payment of royalties, for injunctive relief putting an end to his exploitation of the IP right which allegedly exceeds the license granted, or for other grounds – raises invalidity of the right as a defense. Article 2(2)(k) in conjunction with Article 2(3)[28] makes sure that such litigation – where (in)validity arises only as an incidental question[29] – is indeed covered by the Convention.[30]

c) Infringement

Concerning infringement litigation, the picture was less clear. Some[31] felt that these cases were more closely connected to validity, which is often subject to exclusive jurisdiction, does not permit party autonomy, and should therefore be excluded from the scope of the Convention. In patent and (to a lesser extent) trademark cases, the defendant often objects to a claim by alleging the invalidity of the IP right. This is most often the case in situations of "sheer piracy," i.e., where there is no contractual relationship between the rightholder and the alleged infringer – which would also mean that there is no choice of court agreement – and the Convention would therefore not apply. It also happens, however, in cases that would be covered by a Convention along the lines of the 2004 Hague Draft, i.e., where there is an agreement between the parties that contains a choice of court clause for disputes arising between them in connection with a particular legal relationship. Examples could be the same

---

[28] Article 2(3) provides that "Notwithstanding paragraph 2, proceedings are not excluded from the scope of the Convention where a matter referred to in that paragraph arises merely as an incidental question and not as an object of the proceedings."

[29] In some countries invalidity is raised as a defense, while in other legal systems a counter-claim is required. These cases would, in many jurisdictions, not be considered as "incidental question cases" because the subject of the counter-claim is validity, and consequently the general IP exclusion in Article 2(2)(k) applies to the counter-claim. Jurisdiction for the counter-claim on validity is then governed by national law, and so are the effects of the judgment.

[30] Many license agreements, e.g., for trademarks, contain a "no challenge clause." The licensee undertakes a contractual obligation not to challenge the validity of the right. However, if (s)he does so in spite of the clause, e.g., when being sued for non-payment of the license fee, it depends on national procedural law which influence the clause will have on the proceedings. In many cases, it will not make them inadmissible or ill-founded, but will only give the licensor a right to damages for breach of contract. The fact that such clauses are widely used does not therefore make an "incidental question rule" in the Convention superfluous.

[31] UK courts have interpreted the rule on exclusive jurisdiction concerning the validity of patents, trademarks, and designs in Article 16 No 4 of the Brussels Convention (now Article 22 No 4 of the Brussels I Regulation) as also covering infringement where invalidity is raised as a defense. The traditional position of the German courts used to be different, but currently a case referred to the ECJ by the Düsseldorf Court of Appeal (OLG) for a preliminary ruling on this question is pending in Luxembourg. A decision is expected for September 2004.

as above: cases where the licensor sues for royalties which have not been paid, or for damages arising from an alleged exploitation of the IP right beyond what was permitted by the license either in quality, quantity, or time. The latter example, in some jurisdictions, would be considered a contract case, while in others it would be a tort case, or it could be brought as either. This shows that it would be wise to move away from the opposition of "infringement" versus "contract." The wish of delegations was – to put it simply – to have proceedings aimed at the enforcement of a license or other contractual agreement concerning an IP right within the scope of the Convention, even if the rightholder chooses to bring proceedings in tort rather than in contract (provided, however, that there *is* a contract), e.g., in order to benefit from the application different rules of procedure.[32] This result is ensured by the last addition in square brackets to Article 2(2)(k): "[including proceedings for infringement of the right to which the contract relates]." Moreover, a mere invalidity defense will not make the Convention inapplicable.

d) Stay of Proceedings

Article 6 states that nothing in the Convention prevents the chosen court from suspending the proceedings before it, in particular to allow the courts of the state under whose law an intellectual property right arose, to give judgment on its validity. It also permits the proceedings to be dismissed, provided that such dismissal does not prevent the proceedings from being recommenced – for instance, once the decision on validity has been rendered by the other court. This applies to both contractual litigation and infringement proceedings, as far as they fall within the scope of the Convention. Where invalidity is raised as a defense, the court chosen and seized can either decide this incidental question as described *supra* under b) and c)[33] or it can suspend or dismiss under Article 6. Article 6 does not create the right to do this under the Convention; it is a mere reference to national law. Legal systems such as the German patent litigation system, which provide for the possibility or even obligation to stay proceedings and have the validity issue decided by "the proper court," may therefore continue to use it, while others are not obliged by the Convention to introduce such a possibility for their courts.

---

[32] In other countries such as Germany, the plaintiff only has to plead the facts, and it is for the court to find the legal basis. There are countries where the court would apply tort and contract rules cumulatively or alternatively, and the application of this Convention should not depend on such differences of national procedural law.

[33] On the effects of such a ruling on the incidental question under the Convention, see *infra* under 3.

3. *IP-Specific Rules on Recognition and Enforcement*

As a general rule, a judgment given by a court of a Contracting State designated in an exclusive choice of court agreement has to be recognized and enforced under the Convention in other Contracting States (Article 9), unless one of the grounds for refusal applies. It is not required that the court of origin actually base its jurisdiction on the choice of court agreement, e.g., where another basis of jurisdiction is more readily available (general defendant's forum; location of property, etc.). Moreover, it is worth mentioning that the chapter on recognition and enforcement also applies to judgments given in a case that was purely internal to the state of origin[34] if the judgment is then taken to another Contracting State for recognition or enforcement. However, as at the jurisdiction stage, IP rights will receive some special treatment at the stage of recognition and enforcement as well.

a) Effects of an Incidental Finding on Validity in Other Contracting States

Validity proceedings leading to a judgment which creates effect *erga omnes* are normally excluded from party autonomy under national law[35] because the state that grants the protection of the IP right concerned also wants to reserve the decision on the existence of the right to the authorities it deems fit. As stated above, such a judgment would be outside the scope of the Convention by way of Article 2(2)(k).

However, the same reasoning does not necessarily apply if the principal issue is contractual litigation between private parties, and the court has to decide on an invalidity defense before rendering judgment on royalties or other issues. However, the effect of an implicit or incidental finding on validity is different in different legal systems. Sometimes the implicit finding does not create any binding effect for subsequent proceedings, even between the same parties; in other legal systems the finding acquires the effect of *res judicata*, but only *inter partes*; and in a third group of states, there may be broader (and even non-mutual) collateral estoppel effects. The theory of "*Wirkungserstreckung*" defines recognition of a foreign judgment as extending the effect it has in the state of origin to the recognizing state. Thus, for example, a German court in a case concerning the validity of a German trademark might be obliged to apply

---

[34] See Article 1(3).

[35] National law, as a coherent and conclusive system, can exclude certain matters from party autonomy by simply establishing a rule of exclusive jurisdiction for it. The same mechanism can be used in a double convention like the Conventions of Brussels and Lugano. There, the provision on choice of court clauses is always "subject to" the provisions on exclusive jurisdiction. In a convention limited to choice of court clauses only, however, the limits set by any rules on exclusive jurisdiction are not contained in the same instrument, because it does not establish any such rules. Therefore, the respective subject matter as such would have to be excluded from the scope of the convention.

issue estoppel to a judgment (even, as the case may be, with regard to third parties that were not involved in the original proceedings) – such as dismissing a claim for royalties on the basis of a defense of invalidity of the trademark – provided that the judgment has such collateral effect in its state of origin. This was considered not only impractical but highly undesirable. Therefore, Article 10(2) provides that, where a matter referred to in Article 2(2) (e.g., the validity of an IP right) arose as an incidental question, the ruling on that (incidental) question shall not be recognized and enforced under the Convention.[36] The judgment as such (the "order," "*Tenor,*" "*dispositif*"), however, will normally be covered by the chapter on recognition and enforcement. There are some exceptions to this rule, though.

b) Limits on Recognition and Enforcement of a Judgment Containing an Incidental Finding on Validity

During the IP discussions at the USPTO as well as during the Special Commission meeting in April 2004, another question was raised which is illustrated by the following example: Two parties resident in Canada enter into a licensing agreement concerning a French patent. They agree that the Canadian courts shall have jurisdiction for any litigation arising out of this licensing agreement. One party then sues the other in Canada for unpaid royalties and gets a payment order. Assuming that this order needs to be enforced in France because that is where the assets of the judgment debtor are, what would a French court requested to declare the Canadian money judgment enforceable do if, in the meantime, the French patent were declared invalid in proceedings before the

---

[36] However, this does not exclude giving effect to the ruling on the incidental question under the internal law of the requested state. The matter is simply not governed by the Convention. The previous version of the text as suggested by the informal working group in 2003 had tried to draft an autonomous Convention rule stating that the incidental finding on validity, which was reached in litigation between private parties linked by a contract, would create subsequent effects only between the parties to these proceedings. This was supposed to make clear that neither third persons nor, in particular, the registering institution would be bound by the finding on the incidental validity issue under this Convention. Important parts of the IP community, however, preferred a rule excluding *any* – even *inter partes* – effect of the incidental validity finding in subsequent proceedings. Therefore, a suggestion was made to go back to Article 12(6) of the 2001 Interim Text – an approach also taken by paragraph (2) of the draft produced by a working group of the Max Planck Institute for Intellectual Property, Competition, and Tax Law <http://www.ip.mpg.de/Enhanced/Deutsch/Arbeitsgruppen/int_zustaen_haag-Projekt/dhcalternativedraft5amended.htm>.

Article 12(6) of the 2001 Interim Text reads:

[6. Paragraphs 4 and 5 shall not apply where one of the above matters arises as an incidental question in proceedings before a court not having exclusive jurisdiction under those paragraphs. However, the ruling in that matter shall have no binding effect in subsequent proceedings, even if they are between the same parties. A matter arises as an incidental question if the court is not requested to give a judgment on that matter, even if a ruling on it is necessary in arriving at a decision.].

Patent Office? It was mentioned that many license agreements contain a clause which states that royalties are due on the basis of the licensing agreement, even if the right is declared invalid *ex nunc* or *ex tunc*. Article 10(2) provides:

> "Where an incidental ruling on the validity of an intellectual property right other than copyright or related rights was necessary for the judgment of the court of origin, recognition or enforcement of the judgment may be refused to the extent that it is inconsistent with a judgment on the validity of the intellectual property right rendered in the State under the law of which the intellectual property right arose."

The draft contains a general rule allowing the refusal of recognition and enforcement where there is an irreconcilable judgment on validity rendered or capable of being recognized in the requested state (Article 9(1)(f)) which may be sufficient to deal with the case described above. In Germany, for instance, "irreconcilable" is understood as also covering incidental rulings that are incompatible with the "main" order of another judgment.[37] However, this may not be the case in all legal systems. In some systems, the rule on irreconcilable judgments will only apply to cases where the "order," "*dispositif*," or "*Tenor*" would be irreconcilable – in particular where states are involved that do not attribute any or much effect to the other parts of the judgment. Article 10(2) goes further in that it would cover the case described above. In the example, the French court would not be obliged to recognize the Canadian money judgment awarding royalties for a French patent that French authorities had found invalid. However, the rule is discretionary, so it leaves room for the requested state to recognize the foreign (money or other) judgment anyway, e.g., if it considers the effect of *res iudicata* to be decisive, if it regards the contractual payment obligation as unaffected by the invalidity of the right, or if it simply does not investigate the grounds on which the money judgment was rendered because in its own legal system, the only part of the judgment that matters is the payment order.

Article 10(3) adds a parallel rule covering situations where there has not yet been rendered an irreconcilable judgment on validity in the "proper forum," i.e., in the state under the law of which the IP right arose, but (in)validity proceedings are pending. It allows the court addressed to suspend recognition and enforcement of the foreign judgment or dismiss the proceedings without prejudice until the validity case is decided. Again, this is a discretionary rule.

4. *Interim Relief (Provisional and Protective Measures)*

Under the 1958 New York Convention on Foreign Arbitral Awards, the courts of some states parties are hesitant to grant interim relief where the parties have

---

[37] See, e.g., *Thomas/Putzo-Hüßtege*, ZPO, 25th ed. 2003, § 328 ZPO No 13; *Kropholler*, Europäisches Zivilprozessrecht, 7th ed. 2002, Article 34 (of Regulation 44/2001 – Brussels I), No 49 – 51.

opted for arbitration. In other states, such an arbitration agreement is interpreted as applying only to the merits of the case. In order to avoid any doubt, Article 8 of the draft makes clear that the Convention does not prevent any court from granting interim relief, even if another court was exclusively chosen by the parties. Moreover, the Convention makes clear that a request to this effect from either party would not normally be considered a breach of contract, giving rise to liability. It is, of course, conceivable that the parties have entered into a choice of court agreement expressly covering not only the merits of the case but also interim relief. Such a clause should then be honored. But even in such a case, Article 4(1), second sentence, makes clear that such an interim measure would not be entitled to recognition and enforcement under the Convention.

While the draft produced by the informal working group in March 2003 led to the same results, it was felt by a number of stakeholders (in particular by Internet Service Providers) that, psychologically speaking, the new draft went far beyond just remedying the ambiguities of the New York Convention and unduly encouraged parties to seek interim relief. Therefore, the text is now phrased in a somewhat cumbersome but strictly neutral language.

III. Conclusion

The completed version of the Explanatory Report, an indispensable tool for consultation within Member States, is expected to be ready in summer 2004. Consultations within Member States and at a regional level, e.g., within the European Community, normally take between six months and a year. If there is sufficient political support, the next step would then be a Diplomatic Conference in 2005, based on the Draft Text on Exclusive Choice of Court Clauses in B2B Cases. Time will show whether agreement on such a limited – but nevertheless novel – Convention can be achieved. It would be the first global instrument on jurisdiction, recognition, and enforcement in civil and commercial matters. Even with a limited scope, this would be a major achievement. And according to a survey[38] carried out by the International Chamber of Commerce among businesses about business practices with regard to choice of court agreements, both as to quantity and content, 74% responded that more than half of their international contracts drafted have IP implications; as a result, the Convention would clearly have an impact on IP-related litigation in the future and provide a valuable alternative to arbitration. Consultations carried out so far demonstrate that both the business community and the arbitration community seem to share this perception and endorse the project. It

[38] Available at the ICC's website at <http://www.iccwbo.org/law/jurisdiction/>, together with a further breakdown of the data according to business sectors and/or geographical regions.

has to be admitted that particularly the IP-specific provisions described in this article, which were added in April 2004, do complicate the Convention and take away a lot of its initial resemblance to the New York Convention. However, the additions will certainly facilitate consultation because now it is clear what a possible solution for the IP-related problems such as "the incidental question issue" could look like. This will facilitate the political decision to be taken by the negotiating governments on whether to insert these rules or whether to hope that these cases would probably not be so numerous as to require specific provisions – as was the case in other existing instruments.

Discussion: Current Political Agenda

FRIEDRICH WENZEL BULST and CHRISTIAN A. HEINZE

Dessemontet, one of the reporters of the American Law Institute project on intellectual property, complemented what had been said about the ALI project: He characterized it as being less an American draft than an endeavor to reconcile different sensitivities in the EU and the U.S. The main aim of the project was the consolidation of the law relating to multi-state patent litigation. By focusing on principles rather than binding rules, the project served primarily an educative purpose comparable to the UNIDROIT principles. The ALI draft built upon the TRIPS rules and took into consideration that modern intellectual property law was concerned primarily with "big businesses" and no longer solely with individual authors. Nonetheless, the ALI drafters accepted the European notion of "weaker party protection."

Dessemontet commented on the individual provisions as follows: Section 301 embodies the concept of territoriality, with its paragraph 1 laying out the principle of "legal territoriality," paragraph 2 the principle of "economic territoriality," and paragraph 3 dealing with the difficult case of personal rights. Section 302 paragraph 2 lit. a was described as less exceptional than its wording might suggest. Section 311 paragraph 2 was regarded as solving the problem of "multi-author situations," given that there usually was a contract in cases of multiple authorship. Section 311 paragraph 1 preserves the principle of territoriality for initial title to registered rights. Section 313 paragraph 2 lit. a partially answers the question of who is the creator in the American style by way of definitions. The explanatory comments of the ALI on section 321 ("proof of applicable law") advocate an alleviation of the burden of proof of applicable law to the benefit of the weaker party. Section 323 paragraph 2 establishes that the forum should treat statutes of limitations as questions of substantive law, and thereby tries to reach over to the legal traditions of many countries outside the U.S. Section 315 stipulates that there is no longer *dépeçage* within a contract with the exception of transferability of rights. Section 315 paragraph 2 establishes the criterion of the assignor's main business establishment as the connecting factor in the absence of a contractual choice of law.

In the ensuing discussion, the attempt embodied in the ALI draft to provide for legal certainty in international transactions was welcomed. Nonetheless, sections 313 paragraph 1 lit. c and 315 paragraph 2 of the draft were regarded as furthering American commercial interests. The ALI draft was also seen as overly differentiated and as insufficiently integrating intellectual property rights into general conflict of laws thinking.

The discussion then turned to *Tell's* presentation. It was proposed to allow for an *ex post* choice of law for the consequences of a multi-state infringement of an intellectual property right in article 8 of the Rome II Proposal. This would foster party autonomy and avoid a mosaic application of different tort laws, while the question of infringement would still be governed by the law of the protecting country. There was also a concern as to whether the wording of Article 8 of the Rome II Proposal allowed the plaintiff to determine the applicable law by designating the country for which he or she seeks protection. It was proposed to replace "country for which protection is sought" by "country where the infringement took place." In response, it was argued that Article 8 aimed at establishing the *lex loci protectionis* principle and did not leave the determination of the applicable law to the plaintiff. The rule of Article 8 was included in the proposal because the general provision of Article 3 and its section 2 in particular was considered inappropriate for infringements of intellectual property rights.

Part 2: Contractual Obligations

Transfer of Rights, License Agreements, and Conflict of Laws: Remarks on the Rome Convention of 1980 and the Current ALI Draft

AXEL METZGER

I. Introduction

If one observes the current international activities on private international law and intellectual property rights, the challenge for scholars should be clear. It consists in comparing the two law reform projects of the European Commission ("Rome I" and "Rome II")[1] and the American Law Institute[2] and being inspired by the drafts from the other side of the Atlantic. The following contribution will take this challenge and analyze the law applicable on transfer of IP rights, license agreements, and conflict of laws. The focus will be that of a European scholar. First, the European situation will be analyzed (I),[3] which is unfortunately not very transparent, especially for copyright issues, although we have about 15 years of practical experience with the Rome Convention. Second, some remarks will be made on the current ALI Draft (II).

---

[1] See the contribution of *Olivier Tell* p. 7 et seq. in this volume.
[2] See the contribution of *Catherine Kessedjian* p. 19 et seq. in this volume.
[3] Only English, French, and German law will be analyzed.

II. Transfer of Rights and License Agreements under the Rome Convention

1. Sources of Choice of Law Rules

The conflict of laws rules governing the transfer of intellectual property rights and license agreements are not very clear under the Rome Convention of 1980.[4] The Convention neither contains an explicit provision about these contracts, nor are they excluded from the scope of the Convention in Article 1. The Convention is tacit on this type of contracts.

In contrast, the *Guiliano/Lagarde* Report[5] addresses the applicable conflict rules:

> "Since the Convention is concerned only with the law applicable to contractual obligations, property rights and intellectual property are not covered by these provisions. An Article in the original preliminary draft had expressly so provided. However, the Group considered that such a provision would be superfluous in the present text, especially as this would have involved the need to recapitulate the differences existing as between the various legal systems of the Member States of the Community."

One can conclude from these remarks that non-contractual questions are not governed by the *lex contractus* but by the law governing the IP right itself.

However, there can be no doubt that license agreements and contractual transfer of intellectual property rights fall within the scope of the Convention as far as contractual matters are concerned. Most of the typical contracts on IP rights predominantly concern purely contractual issues. Let us take as an example a distributor agreement on products with a grant to the distributor to use a trademark.[6] Here, the duty of the distributor to buy and sell the products, exclusivity for a certain territory, after-sales activities, information requirements, and termination clauses give the contract its character. The license grant is only one provision among others. Therefore, the question of which law is applicable to the contract cannot be answered with an exclusive focus on the trademark license provision.

If the *lex contractus* is determined independently from the IP right, the question arises of whether the so-determined *lex contractus* also governs the transfer or license provision. Here the main problem is whether questions such as the transferability of the IP right, interpretation of the license grant, and formal requirements are to be characterized as contractual and therefore within the scope of the *lex contractus*, or whether they are non-contractual. The following remarks will elucidate these difficulties of characterization.

---

[4] Rome Convention of 1980 on the law applicable to contractual obligations (consolidated version), OJ EC, C 27, 26.01.1998, 34.

[5] *Giuliano/Lagarde*, Report on the Convention on the law applicable to contractual obligations, OJ EC, C 282, 31.10.1980, 1.

[6] See as an example the "Distributor Agreement" at Münchener Vertragshandbuch[5]*(-Graf von Westphalen)* (2002), 86 et seq.

Moreover, the application of the Rome Convention to the "contractual issues" is not always obvious. Problems may arise regarding the applicable law in the absence of choice (Article 4), the scope of the *lex contractus* (Article 10), formal validity (Article 9), and internationally mandatory provisions (Article 7).

2. *Industrial Property Rights*

Starting with industrial property rights, especially patents and trademarks, means starting with the less complicated issue.

a) Lex loci protectionis

It seems that for patents and trademarks, the principle of territoriality is undisputed. The *lex loci protectionis* governs not only the protection of the immaterial good and the initial ownership of the IP right, but also the answer to the question of whether an industrial property right can be transferred or whether a license agreement may be concluded.[7] The *lex loci protectionis* is also to be applied if the law of the protecting country does not allow partial assignments or territorially restricted license agreements. All other questions are governed by the *lex contractus*. The same principles apply to the international registered trademark under the Madrid Agreement Concerning the International Registration of Marks[8] and the European Bundle Patent.[9]

b) Contractual Issues

For all contractual questions, the parties may choose the applicable law as long as the conditions of Article 3 of the Convention are respected. The freedom of choice does not raise particular questions with regard to IP rights. A more complicated issue is to determine the applicable law in case of absence of choice (Article 4 Rome Convention). The *Landgericht Düsseldorf*[10] and the majority of scholars – at least in Germany – seem to prefer the application of the *lex loci protectionis* and – in case of a license for more than one state –

---

[7] For Germany: *Busse(-Keukenschrijver)*, Patentgesetz[6] (2003), § 15, note 15; *Staudinger (-Fezer)*, Kommentar zum BGB: Internationales Wirtschaftsrecht[13] (2000), note 773; *Beier* GRUR Int. 1981, 299, 306. For UK: *Fawcett/Torremans*, Intellectual Property and Private International Law (1998), 546; *Dicey/Morris*, The Conflict of Laws[13] II (2000), note 24-062. For France: *Mayer/Heuzé*, Droit international privé[7] (2001), 449.

[8] See Münchener Kommentar zum BGB[3] *(-Kreuzer)* (1998), Nach Art. 38 Anh. II, note 63.

[9] See Art. 72 – 74 European Patent Convention of 05.10.1973.

[10] Landgericht Düsseldorf, 04.08.1962, GRUR Ausland- und Internationaler Teil 1962, 256, 257 – *Tubenverschluss*.

subsidiarily the law of the licensor.[11] Other scholars provide different solutions for different situations. If the licensee has no duty but to pay a lump sum, the law of the licensor is to be applied.[12] In more complicated cases – for example, the distributor agreement mentioned above – the law of the licensee[13] or the *lex loci protectionis* are promoted if the license is only granted for one state.[14] For contracts that include mutual rights and duties, a simple rule covering all cases does not exist.

A question of particular interest is the determination of the scope of the *lex contractus* (Article 10 Rome Convention). Here again, contractual and non-contractual issues have to be clearly separated. It is apparently not disputed that all questions concerning the formation of contract, the consequences of non-performance, royalties, and all other questions concerning rights and duties of the parties that are not directly linked to the transfer of rights or grant of license are governed by the *lex contractus*. The same is true for all issues mentioned in Article 10 Rome Convention. However, particular issues may raise difficult questions of characterization. The interpretation of the contract is one example. Under Article 10 para. 1 lit. a), the interpretation of the contract is governed by the *lex contractus*. Whether a license grant is territorially restricted has to be analyzed by interpretation of the contract. This interpretation has to respect the rules of interpretation of the *lex contractus*, comprising all special rules of interpretation that may exist in this legal order regarding IP rights. By contrast, the question of whether a territorial restriction is possible or not is governed by the *lex loci protectionis*.[15]

The issue of formal validity of the contract is sometimes confused with the formalities required for the transfer or license of a registered right.[16] Here, two questions must be distinguished.

The law governing the formal validity of the contract, especially the requirement that a transfer or license must be in writing, is to be determined pursuant to the rule of Article 9 Rome Convention.[17] Article 9 refers to the proper law of the contract or, alternatively, to the *lex loci contractus* and – with regard to

---

[11] *Beier* GRUR Int. 1981, 299, 304 et seq; *Staudinger(-Fezer)*, Kommentar zum BGB: Internationales Wirtschaftsrecht[13] (2000), note 758 and 766; *Benkard(-Ullmann)*, Patentgesetz[9] (1993), § 15, note 135.

[12] *Busse(-Keukenschrijver)*, Patentgesetz[6] (2003), § 15, note 137; *Fawcett/Torremans* (*supra* note 7), 558 et seq.

[13] *Ulmer*, Die Immaterialgüterrechte im internationalen Privatrecht (1975), 103.

[14] *Fawcett/Torremans* (*supra* note 7), 566 et seq.

[15] See, e.g., the French Art. L. 714-1 al. 1 Code de la Propriété Intellectuelle ("La cession, même partielle, ne peut comporter de limitation territoriale"). See *Chavanne/Burst*, Droit de la propriété industrielle[5] (1998), 653.

[16] See, e.g., *Ulmer* (*supra* note 13), 98.

[17] For Germany: *Staudinger(-Fezer)*, Kommentar zum BGB: Internationales Wirtschaftsrecht[13] (2000), note 774 (trademark). For UK: *Fawcett/Torremans* (*supra* note 7), 547 (general). For France: Cour de Cassation, 07.04.1992, Bull. civ. 1992, Quatrième partie N° 151 (trademark).

contracts made *inter absentes* – the respective laws of the countries in which either party is present at the time of formation. The rationale of this provision is to increase the chances of validating the contract.

Notwithstanding the formal validity of the contract, the formalities required by the *lex loci protectionis* for a transfer of the IP right or a license have to be respected.[18] If an IP right is licensed for more than one country, then the requirements of each country have to be respected. However, these requirements concern the performance of the contract. They do not concern its validity.

As far as a contracting party is working as an employee of the other party, the special provision of Article 6 Rome Convention for individual employment contracts has to be applied. A case of practical relevance concerns the employee's inventions provisions in some European legal orders.[19] As long as the employee habitually carries out his work in one country,[20] a choice of law made by the parties may not deprive him of the protection that he enjoys under the mandatory employee invention provisions of that country.[21]

Difficult questions may appear with regard to internationally mandatory provisions. First, national and European rules of competition law, especially rules on technology transfer agreements, have to be taken into account as mandatory provisions irrespective of the law otherwise applicable to the contract (see Article 7 para. 2 Rome Convention).[22] Second, a remarkable number of mandatory technology transfer rules exist, especially for developing countries.[23] These rules can be ignored by the courts of those Member States which used their right to make a reservation regarding Article 7 para. 1 of the Rome Convention. This is the case for Germany, the United Kingdom, and Luxem-

---

[18] For Germany: *Staudinger(-Fezer)*, Kommentar zum BGB: Internationales Wirtschaftsrecht[13] (2000), note 773; *Beier* GRUR Int. 1981, 299, 306. For UK: *Fawcett/Torremans* (*supra* note 7), 547.

[19] For the German "Arbeitnehmererfindungsgesetz" of 25.07.1957 (BGBl. 1957 I, 756). For UK, see para. 40 et seq. esp. 43 (4) UK Patents Act 1977. For France, see Art. L. 611-7 CPI.

[20] For the case of an employee who does not habitually carry out his work in any one country, see Art. 6 para. 2 lit. b.

[21] For the German "Arbeitnehmererfindungsgesetz," see *Busse(-Keukenschrijver)*, Patentgesetz[6] (2003), § 1 ArbEG, note 16. For the provisions of the UK Patents Act 1977, see *Fawcett/Torremans* (*supra* note 7), 586 et seq.

[22] This is particularly the case for the provisions of the Commission Regulation (EC) No 240/96 of 31.01.1996 on the application of Article 85 (3) of the Treaty to certain categories of technology transfer agreements, OJ L 31, 09.02.1996, 2 et seq. See *Reithmann/Martiny (-Hiestand)*, Internationales Vertragsrecht[5] (1996), 1047. See also the contribution of *Josef Drexl* p. 79 et seq. in this volume.

[23] See *Stoll*, Technologietransfer: Internationalisierungs- und Nationalisierungstendenzen (1994), 54 and 199 et sequel; *Fawcett/Torremans* (*supra* note 7), 547.

bourg.[24] In the other Member States of the Rome Convention, courts have a discretionary power to apply foreign mandatory rules.

c) Tentative Conclusion

Generally speaking, one can say that the instruments of the Rome Convention seem to be suitable for contracts in the field of industrial property rights. Although some particular questions are disputed in practice, the interpretation is more or less uniform. With regard to industrial property rights, there is no need for a reform of the Convention.

3. *Copyright*

Agreements in the field of copyright raise a lot of complicated questions. Here, the Rome Convention has as of now failed to unify the private international law of the Member States.

a) Author as the Weaker Party (1): Overview of the Different Approaches

The reason for this diversity seems to be the particular situation of the author as the weaker party in typical contractual situations.[25] Agreements on copyrights are mostly characterized by the non-equality of parties. The publishing house, music industry, or film producer can choose from a myriad of "young talents" who are willing to sign any contract to get their chance in the cultural industries. It is obviously true that there are also counterexamples of successful artists who can freely negotiate. But they do not represent the typical case. Therefore, some Member States, especially in the so-called *droit d'auteur* states, introduced author-protective provisions in their substantive copyright legislation.[26]

The Rome Convention does not provide for a special conflicts of law rule, such as Article 5 or 6, that protects self-employed persons in general and authors in particular from a non-favorable choice of law. Nevertheless, the Member States developed two techniques to protect the author in international contracts. Some countries characterize the protective provisions as non-contractual issues; by consequence, freedom of choice is denied. This is the German and English solution ("Anglo-German approach"). Other countries declare the protective provisions as internationally mandatory. By consequence, the forum

---

[24] *Audit*, Droit internationale privé[3] (2000), 700.

[25] All questions arising with regard to performing artists will not be treated in this contribution.

[26] E.g., France and Germany.

can apply the author-protective rules irrespective of the law otherwise applicable to the contract. This is the solution provided by French courts ("French approach"). The following remarks will compare both solutions.

b) Law Governing the Right

For English[27] and German[28] courts, the question of whether the copyright in whole or in part or particular copyright claims can be transferred, waived, or licensed is governed by the law that governs the right, i.e., the *lex loci protectionis*. This approach can only be evaluated if the corresponding provisions of substantive law are brought into view. One technique used by the *droit d'auteur* states to protect the author is to prohibit the transferability or licensability of the copyright or of particular claims.[29] It is beyond the scope of this paper to go into the details of substantive copyright law. However, some remarks may be useful to illustrate how author protection is achieved in Germany and France.

For the German "monistic" approach, the copyright is one unitary right protecting both the economic and moral interests of the author. German copyright law states that the copyright cannot be transferred in whole or in part. The transferability of moral and exploitation rights is excluded; only the grant of a license is possible (see § 29 Urheberrechtsgesetz (UrhG)). Moreover, special provisions deny the licensability of future forms of exploitation (see § 31 para. 4 UrhG) or the transfer of claims out of the so-called resale right (see § 26 UrhG). Two new examples for non-transferable claims were introduced by the 2002 Amendment[30] of the UrhG.[31] These claims have the character of internationally mandatory provisions (see § 32b UrhG).[32]

Although the French copyright law adopts a different basic approach to copyright law, the consequences are similar. French copyright law is based on the idea of a dualistic copyright, whereby the author's right is considered to consist of two different elements, the economic right and the moral rights. Moral rights are neither transferable nor waivable (see Article L. 121-1 al. 3

[27] See High Court of Justice, Chancery Division, 13.11.1962, [1963] 1 All ER 237 – *Campbell Connelly & Co. Ltd./Noble*. Cf. *Fawcett/Torremans* (*supra* note 7), 548.

[28] See Bundesgerichtshof, 02.10.1997, GRUR 1999, 152 – *Spielbankaffaire*. This is also the view of the majority of academic opinions in Germany; see *Schricker(-Katzenberger)*, Urheberrecht: Kommentar^2 (1999), Vor §§ 120 ff, note 150; *Ulmer* (*supra* note 13), 50; *Drobnig* RabelsZ 40 (1976), 195, 204. Contrary to that point of view, *Schack*, Urheber- und Urhebervertragsrecht^2 (2001), 409 (*lex originis*).

[29] Other techniques are interpretation rules, non-mandatory reservations of the consent of the author, and requirements on the formal validity.

[30] "Law on Strengthening the Contractual Position of Authors and Performers," BGBl. 2002 I, 1155. For a consolidated English translation of the provisions of the new law, see IIC 2002, 842.

[31] See *Dietz* IIC 2002, 828 et seq.

[32] See the contribution of *Haimo Schack* p. 107 et seq. in this volume.

Code de la Propriété Intellectuelle (CPI)). Exploitation rights can be transferred, but here too certain restrictions have to be respected. First, Article L. 131-1 states that a total transfer of future works is null and void. Second, Article L. 131-3 al. 1 CPI provides that the contract must enumerate every form of exploitation and that every form of exploitation must be defined to its scope and purpose as well as to place and duration. If the parties fail to fulfill these requirements, the author can claim the invalidity of the contract (*nullité relative*).[33] One could thus conclude that a general transfer of exploitation rights is not possible. Third, under Article L. 131-6, a transfer of the right to exploit future forms of exploitation is only possible under the condition that the transfer is explicit and provides participation correlated to the profits from exploitation. It seems that French courts tend to use these provisions for a restrictive interpretation of the contract.[34] Nevertheless, the provision could also be interpreted as denying the validity of a license grant without a special remuneration for future forms of exploitation.

As demonstrated above, German and English courts characterize the question of transferability of the copyright as a whole or the transferability of a particular claim as governed by the law that governs the right itself. As a result, the substantive provisions of non-transferability can be enforced in international contracts. It is clear that one should not overstress the parallels between intellectual property and other rights. However, with regard to Article 12 para. 2 Rome Convention, this solution seems to be suitable. As a consequence, every rule that can be qualified as denying the transfer of the right or other claims can automatically supersede the *lex contractus*. The German *Bundesgerichtshof* applied this approach with regard to § 31 para. 4 UrhG.[35] The majority of German scholars agree with this approach in the case of moral rights[36] or the author's claim out of the resale right under § 26 UrhG.[37] The English High Court follows the same approach.[38] English scholars are also favorable to this solution.[39]

In French courts, the transferability is rarely characterized as a non-contractual issue. One reason might be that French law accepts the *lex loci protectionis*

---

[33] See *Lucas/Lucas*, Traité de la Propriété Littéraire et artistique[2] (2001), N° 494.

[34] See, e.g., TGI Strasbourg, 03.02.1998, Légipresse 149-III (1998), 22; TGI Paris, 14.04. 1999, Légipresse 162-III, 81.

[35] See Bundesgerichtshof, 15.10.1987, GRUR 1988, 296, 298 – *Gema-Vermutung IV*; *Ulmer* (*supra* note 13), 50. Contrary *Schricker(-Katzenberger)* (*supra* note 28), Vor §§ 120 ff, note 150.

[36] *Ulmer* (*supra* note 13), 51.

[37] *Ulmer* (*supra* note 13), 51; *Schricker(-Katzenberger)* (*supra* note 28), Vor §§ 120 ff, note 150;

[38] See High Court of Justice, Chancery Division, 13.11.1962, [1963] 1 All ER 237 – *Campbell Connelly & Co. Ltd./Noble*.

[39] *Fawcett/Torremans* (*supra* note 7), 548; *Dicey/Morris* (*supra* note 7), note 24-062.

rule only for infringement cases,[40] while initial ownership is governed by the *lex originis*, i.e., the country where the work was first published.[41] By consequence, protective provisions of the French copyright law can only be applied as non-contractual issues if the work was first published in France. Against this background, one can understand why only one decision of a French court applied the French provision that denies a waiver of moral rights as part of the *lex originis*. In this case, the work was first published in France.[42] By contrast, pursuant to the *lex originis* rule, it is not possible for French courts to apply French protective provisions as rules of the law that governs the right if the work is not first published in France.[43] Therefore, French law has developed another technique to protect the author in international contracts, which is an extensive application of the concept of internationally mandatory provisions.[44]

c) Contractual Issues

For all contractual issues, freedom of choice is given to the party (see Article 3 Rome Convention). The determination of the *lex contractus* in the absence of an explicit choice of law raises the same difficulties as industrial property rights. Article 4 seems to be interpreted in a uniform way in Germany, France, and England for simple cases. If the licensee has no duty but to pay a certain amount of money, the law of the licensor is to be applied.[45] For more complicated cases, different approaches exist. Some suggest the application of the *lex loci protectionis* if the license is granted for only one country.[46] Other scholars advocate the application of the law of the licensee if he has a duty to publish the work.[47] In the case of a contract for a work that has not yet been created by the author, the law of the author shall apply.[48] It is therefore also

[40] See Cour de Cassation, 05.03.2002, JCP 2002 II, N° 1008 – *Sté informatique service réalisation organisation (Sisro)/ Sté de droit néerlandais en liquidation Ampersand Software BV.*

[41] Cour de Cassation, 22.12.1959, Rev. crit. DIP 1960, 361 – *Sté Fox Europa/Sté Le Chant du monde*. See *Josselin-Gall*, Les contrats d'exploitation du droit de propriété littéraire et artistique (1995), 283 et seq.

[42] Only exception: Tribunal de Grande Instance Paris, 30.05.1984, RIDA N° 122 (1984), 220 – *Marius Constant/Warner Bros Transatlantic et Sté Warner Columbia Film.*

[43] This was the situation in the following cases: Cour d'Appel Paris, 06.07.1989, D. 1990, Jur. 152 – *Sté la Cinq/Angelica Huston et autres* (film published first in the U.S.).

[44] See *infra* II.3.c) (p. 71).

[45] For Germany: *Ulmer* (*supra* note 13), 54; *Schricker(-Katzenberger)* (*supra* note 28), Vor §§ 120 ff., note 56 et seq. For UK: *Fawcett/Torremans* (*supra* note 7), 573. Contrary for France: *Josselin-Gall* (*supra* note 41), 366 et seq.

[46] For UK: *Fawcett/Torremans* (*supra* note 7), 575.

[47] For Germany: *Ulmer* (*supra* note 13), 54; *Schricker(-Katzenberger)* (*supra* note 28), Vor §§ 120 ff, note 56 et seq. For France: *Josselin-Gall* (*supra* note 41), 379.

[48] *Josselin-Gall* (*supra* note 41), 398.

true for copyright contracts that a simple rule covering all cases does not seem to exist.

The scope of the *lex contractus* is determined by Article 10 Rome Convention. The *lex contractus* governs formation of the contract, performance of the contractual obligations, remedies for breach of contract including the assessment of damages, prescription and limitation of actions, and consequences of nullity of the contract.

An issue of particular interest here, too, is the interpretation of copyright contracts. The legislations of the *droit d'auteur* states include special rules of interpretation intended to protect the author. The most important rule of this type is the German "*Zweckübertragungslehre*" (see § 31 para. 5 UrhG). According to this rule, if the contract does not enumerate the forms of exploitation for which the rights are transferred, the author will not be deemed to have granted more extensive rights than would be required by the purpose envisaged in making the grant. French copyright law provides in Article L. 122-7 CPI a set of similar but more detailed rules of interpretation. Under Article 10 para. 1 lit. 1), these rules can be applied only if the respective law governs the contract as *lex contractus*.[49]

Formal validity has to be determined by the provisions of Article 9 Rome Convention.[50] Requirements of form can be found in French[51] and English[52] copyright law. Therefore, Article 9 is of some importance in the field of copyright contracts.

Article 6 is to be applied if the author works as an employee. A choice of law may not deprive the employee of the mandatory provisions of the country in which he habitually carries out his work.[53] In the absence of a choice of law, the provisions of this country are to be applied. Article 6 refers not only to special provisions that are intended to protect the employee, but to all mandatory provisions that are more favorable to the employee in general. If the author habitually carries out his work as an employee in a *droit d'auteur* state, he is given the benefit of that country's internally mandatory copyright provisions that are more favorable to him.[54]

---

[49] For UK: High Court of Justice, Chancery Division, 13.11.1962, [1963] 1 All ER 237 – *Campbell Connelly & Co. Ltd./Noble*; *Fawcett/Torremans* (*supra* note 7), 548 et seq. For France: *Josselin-Gall* (*supra* note 41), 449. For Germany: *Schricker(-Katzenberger)* (*supra* note 28), Vor §§ 120 ff, note 160.

[50] For France: *Josselin-Gall* (*supra* note 41), 446. For an application of the rule *locus regit actum* see Cour d'Apell Paris, 06.02.1986, JCP I 3376 Annexe 7 – *Rowe/Société Walt Disney Production*. For Germany: *Schricker(-Katzenberger)* (*supra* note 28), Vor §§ 120 ff, note 169. For UK: *Fawcett/Torremans* (*supra* note 7), 588 et seq.

[51] See Art. L. 131-2, 131-3 al. 3, 132-7 al. 1 CPI.

[52] See Art. 90 para. 3 Copyright, Designs and Patents Act 1988 (CDPA).

[53] For the case of employees that do not habitually carry out their work in any one country, see Art. 6 para. 2 lit. b) Rome Convention.

[54] See *Hilty/Peukert* GRUR Int. 2002, 643, 648.

The issues of internationally mandatory provisions under Article 7 Rome Convention and *ordre public* under Article 16 are, as mentioned above, of particular interest in French copyright law. French courts characterize the rule that moral rights cannot be transferred or waived either as an internationally mandatory provision[55] or as *ordre public*.[56] By contrast, provisions restricting the transfer of exploitation rights are not characterized as internationally mandatory. French courts refrained from characterizing the protective provisions of Article L. 131-6[57] and L. 131-2 CPI[58] as internationally mandatory. French scholarship is in favor of this approach.[59]

French copyright law is not alone in using the instrument of internationally mandatory provisions. The 2002 Amendment of the UrhG[60] introduced a provision in § 32b stating that the non-waivable claims of the author for an equitable remuneration (see § 32) and additional participation, the so-called "bestseller provision," § 32a, are internationally mandatory.[61]

d) Author as the Weaker Party (2): Evaluation of the Different Approaches

As seen above, two approaches of author protection under the Rome Convention exist. The following remarks attempt to compare the two approaches by an example based on the *John Huston* case.[62]

The film director Hudson, domiciled in the U.S., made a black-and-white movie called "Deep Jungle" for the producer MGM, transferring by written contract all economic and moral rights to the film for all countries. The contract declared U.S. law applicable. The movie was first published in the U.S. MGM later colorized the film. MGM Europe, domiciled in the UK, sold the colorized version as DVDs in France and the United Kingdom. Hudson objected that this distribution violated his moral rights and asked an English court for a prohibitive injunction for France and the UK.

Does the British court have jurisdiction for both countries? Under Article 2 of the Brussels I Regulation,[63] the question has to be answered in the

[55] Cour d'Appel Paris, 06.07.1989, D. 1990, Jur. 152 – *Sté la Cinq/Angelica Huston et autres*.

[56] Cour d'Appel Paris, 01.02.1989, RIDA N° 142 (1989), 301, 305 – *Bragance/Éditions Olivier Orban et autres*.

[57] Cour d'Appel Paris, 01.02.1989, RIDA N° 142 (1989), 301, 305 – *Bragance/Éditions Olivier Orban et autres*.

[58] Cour d'Appel Paris, 29.04.1959, D. 1959, Jur. 402 – *Soc. Roy Export Company Establishment et Charlie Chaplin/Soc. Les films Roger Richebé (The Kid)*.

[59] *Josselin-Gall* (*supra* note 41), 438 et seq.

[60] See *supra* II.3.b) (p. 67).

[61] See *Schack* GRUR 2002, 853, 856; *Hilty/Peukert* GRUR Int. 2002, 643 et seq.

[62] Cour d'Appel Paris, 06.07.1989, D. 1990, Jur. 152 – *Sté la Cinq/Angelica Huston et autres*.

[63] Council Regulation (EC) No 44/2001 of 22.12.2000 on jurisdiction and the recognition and enforcement of judgments in civil and commercial matters, OJ EC L 12, 16.01.2001, 1.

affirmative. The defendant is domiciled in the United Kingdom, and subject matter limitations on jurisdiction for infringement cases do not exist under the Brussels I Regulation. Article 22 (4) does not preclude a British court from affirming jurisdiction regarding a foreign copyright.[64]

For the territory of the United Kingdom, both approaches obtain the same result. If one follows the Anglo-German approach, British copyright law as *lex loci protectionis* applies to the question of whether moral rights can be waived in a contract or not. The transferability of the copyright as a whole or of special claims is governed by the law that governs the right, i.e., the *lex loci protectionis*. Moral rights can be waived under British copyright law.[65] By consequence, the judge will deny the injunction for the United Kingdom. The French approach leads to the same result: the law of the forum, i.e., British law, does not provide a mandatory provision that denies the transfer of moral rights.

By contrast, different results will be obtained for French territory. If the court adopts the Anglo-German approach, it has to give the injunction. Under this approach, the *lex locis protectionis*, i.e., French law, governs the question of whether moral rights are waivable or not. Because French law denies the waiver of moral rights, the infringement of MGM cannot be justified by the contractual consent. If the court adopts the French approach and characterizes the principle of "non-transferability" of moral rights as a mandatory provision, it cannot grant the injunction. The United Kingdom made a reservation regarding Article 7 para. 1 Rome Convention. In consequence, British courts do not take into account mandatory rules of a foreign country.[66] The result is that no injunction can be given for France. Moreover, Hudson cannot request a French court for a second proceeding because of Article 33 Brussels I Regulation.[67]

If one compares the two approaches, the French seems to be inferior – although it is true that the Rome Convention does not express a preference for either one of the two approaches. There are three arguments for the Anglo-German point of view. First, the most effective way to protect the author in international contracts is to characterize all questions of transferability as governed by the *lex loci protectionis*. This solution guarantees the author that no contract can deprive him of the protection given by the *droit d'auteur* states.

---

[64] See *Rauscher(-Mankowski)*, Europäisches Zivilprozessrecht (2004), Art 22 Brüssel-I-VO, note 44.

[65] See Copyright, Designs and Patents Act 1988, para. 87. See also *Cornish*, Intellectual Property^{3} (1996), 395.

[66] With regard to Article 16 Rome Convention, strong arguments can be found that UK courts will follow the characterization of the French courts. The question of whether a provision of substantive law has to be qualified as internationally mandatory or not has to be interpreted in a uniform manner.

[67] See European Court of Justice, 30.11.1976, Case 42/76, ECR 1976, 1759 – *Jozef de Wolf/Harry Cox B.V.* See also *Kropholler*, Europäisches Zivilprozessrecht^{7} (2002), Vor Art. 33, note 12

Second, the French approach supports forum-shopping.[68] If Hudson had brought his claim before a French court, the result would have been different. Internationally mandatory provisions disturb the harmony of laws. The third argument relies on a more general observation. The principle of territoriality is justified by the specific nature of intellectual property rights.[69] An intellectual property right is a grant of monopoly by a state for certain acts in the territory of that state. This is not only true for registered rights, but also for non-registered rights.[70] Here, the scope of protection is defined by national legislation. Intellectual property rights are part of the national trade policy of each state (or federation of states, such as the European Community).[71] The principle of territoriality reflects the natural barriers of national policies. Not only the scope of protection and actions for infringements, but also the transferability of the granted rights is part of this policy. Whether the copyright can be transferred without any restrictions or not is relevant for the stimulation of the relevant players of the cultural industries. This is especially true for those who finance creative efforts. Therefore, the transferability of IP rights is part of the market rules set by the granting state. States that follow a utilitarian philosophy of copyright emphasize freedom of contract. The *droit d'auteur* countries provide a more restrictive set of market rules. Both policies should end at the frontiers of the granting state. British and German courts already apply this approach. Therefore, one can hardly say that the Rome Convention ought to be changed with regard to license agreements.

III. Transfer of Rights and License Agreements under the ALI Draft

1. Introduction

To refresh our old European minds, let's see how the American Law Institute's draft "Principles Governing the Jurisdiction, Choice of Law and Judgments in Transnational Disputes" regulate the transfer of rights and license agreements.[72] The draft is of particular interest for contracts, including a transfer of copyright or a license grant, because its § 315 section para. 3 provides for another model

---

[68] For a critical stand against the concept of mandatory provisions in general, see *Siehr*, Festschrift Ulrich Drobnig (1998), 443, 447.

[69] Another argument for the principle of territoriality in the field of copyright can be found in Art. 5 para. 2 phrase 2 and 14bis para. 2 of the Berne Convention, see *Schricker (-Katzenberger)* (*supra* note 28), Vor §§ 120 ff., note 120; *Cornish* (*supra* note 65), note 9-25 ff.; *Fawcett/Torremans* (*supra* note 7), 466 f.; *Gebrandy*, Kort commentaar op de Auteurswet 1912, Arnheim 1988, 412. For a contrasting viewpoint, see *Schack*, Zur Anknüpfung des Urheberrechts im IPR (1979), 28 et seq.

[70] For a contrary viewpoint, see *Schack*, Zur Anknüpfung des Urheberrechts im IPR (1979), 50 et seq.

[71] See, e.g., *Ullrich* GRUR Int. 1995, 623, 625; *Cornish* (*supra* note 65), note 9-41 et seq.

[72] These remarks refer to the Preliminary Draft N° 2 of 20.01.2004.

to protect the weaker party, i.e., especially the author. François Dessemontet, one of the three reporters of the draft, calls this approach a "European test of the weaker party" comparable to Artt. 5 and 6 Rome Convention.[73] The question here will be whether we should introduce a comparable provision in the future Rome I Regulation. The desirability of the ALI Draft for the U.S. private international law will not be analyzed. The question will only be whether an introduction of the proposed rules into a future Rome I Regulation should be promoted. This will be done in two steps. It is clear that the ALI rules were not drafted for the future Rome I Regulation. They are made for another legal context and would need a "conversion" into the Rome I system. This will be the first step. The second step consists of analyzing the underlying policy. Do we want a special conflict rule for authors?

2. *Some Remarks on the ALI Draft*

These remarks concern the wording of the draft. Although it is clear that this is not the right place to evaluate every detail of the draft, some remarks should be admitted. As already mentioned above, these remarks are not meant to criticize the suitability of the draft for the U.S. system. The aim is to show the parallels and differences between the draft and the Rome Convention.

a) § 314, § 315 para. 1 and 2

The "Draft No. 2" of January 20, 2004, provides two alternatives for the law governing transferability (§ 314). For registered rights, the *lex loci protectionis* seems to be undisputed, while two alternatives are given for the transfer of unregistered rights. Following alternative A, the *lex loci protectionis* would also govern the transferability of non-registered rights; alternative B promotes the application of the *lex originis* for copyright cases.[74] It seems that the Philadelphia meeting of the ALI project[75] has shown that a broad majority of the participants prefers alternative A. If one follows the territorial approach of copyright law advocated in this paper, then this result is to be welcomed.

The first para. of § 315 also deserves approval. The principle of freedom of choice is undisputed and would fit perfectly in the Rome I system. From a European point of view, one must also welcome the reservation in paragraph 1 for the question of transferability. As demonstrated above, British and German courts have successfully relied on this approach in the past.

[73] *Dessemontet*, Festschrift Wilhelm Nordemann (2004), 415, 422.

[74] The initial title referred to in § 314 Alternative B para. 2 is to be determined under § 312 and § 313.

[75] The last meeting of the ALI Project was held in Philadelphia in February 2004.

By contrast, the presumption in § 315 para. 2 phrase 2 would not really fit within the European choice of law system. Most European scholars think that this presumption is only correct in simple cases, where the licensee has only the duty to pay a certain amount of money. In more complicated cases, the presumption seems to be misleading.[76]

b) § 315 para. 3

§ 315 para. 3 allows the judge to control the designated law, especially with regard to the interests of the weaker party. Prima facie, the ALI draft seems to propose a protective rule analogue to those for consumers and employees under Articles 5 and 6 Rome Convention.[77] However, the legislative technique used is typical of U.S. private international law. The concept of controlling the "reasonability" of the designated law is well known from the Restatement Conflict of Laws Second, Rule 187.[78] The same observation can be made for the "substantial connection" test of lit. a). This concept differs apparently from the Rome Convention, which does not allow for a general control of the choice made by the parties.[79] Under the Rome Convention, the parties are free to choose any law. Only in a limited number of special situations, namely consumer and employment agreements, are reservations for the internally mandatory rules made. European conflicts of law thinking works with rules and exceptions. If a result is not acceptable for the forum's substantive law, the *ordre public* reservation has to serve as a backdoor. As a result, less discretionary power is given to the judge. This is clearly not the right forum to discuss the pros and cons of these basic approaches to private international law. Nevertheless, we should accept that a European special conflict rule for author protection would have to follow the model of Articles 5 and 6 Rome Convention more closely to fit within the system.

Another interesting point of the ALI Draft seems to be the restrictive scope with regard to non-negotiated contracts. In the Rome Convention, protection of weaker parties is not restricted to standard contracts. I'm not convinced that contracts which are disadvantageous for the author are always non-negotiated. It seems that two different needs for protection have been cumulated. As a consequence, the available protection is narrowed down.

The elements related to the location and sophistication of the "weaker party" are in the center of interest. The wording of this element provokes questions. It

---

[76] See *supra* at II.2.b) (p. 63) and II.3.c) (p. 69).

[77] *Katzenberger* pleaded as early as 1988 for an analogues application of the general principle laid down in Art. 5 and 6 Rome Convention to copyright contracts; see IIC 1988, 731, 739.

[78] *American Law Institute*, Restatement of the Law, Conflict of Laws^2 (1971), 561.

[79] See *Lorenz* RIW 1987, 569 et sequel.; *Junker* IPrax 1993, 1 et seq. *Heiss* RabelsZ 65 (2001), 634, 637.

will not always be easy to determine the "weaker party." Which evidence can be given to prove "weakness" in a particular contractual relation? A more specific term would be preferable. One should ask if there is a remarkable number of cases in the fields of industrial property rights. In trademark and patent cases, businesses are on both sides of the contractual relationship. Therefore, the rule should be restricted to the relevant copyright cases. Instead of "weaker party," the term "author" should be introduced in the rule.

With regard to the consequences of an "unreasonable" choice, the protection mechanism of the Draft seems to be rather radical. If the chosen law is "unreasonable" in light of the listed elements, the law of the weaker party shall apply (lit. f). First, one could ask whether the law of the weaker party is also to apply if it is less desirable for the weaker party. Articles 5 and 6 of the Rome Convention adopt another approach. Under the Rome Convention, the law of the consumer or employee is only to be applied if it is more favorable for him.[80] Although it is intended to be an advantage, the Draft could turn out to be disadvantageous for the weaker party. Second, it will be hard to convince a European PIL lawyer that not only the mandatory provisions of the law of the weaker party are to be applied, but all legal provisions. This issue is of particular interest in the field of copyright law because some of the most effective protective provisions are not mandatory: as an example, take the German "*Zweckübertragungslehre*" (§ 31 para. 5 UrhG) mentioned above. It would not be logically coherent to prohibit a contractual choice of law if the parties are free to resolve a question with an explicit provision in a purely national contract.

3. *Protective Provision Desirable in the Future Rome I Regulation?*

A special provision analogue to those of Articles 5 and 6 Rome Convention is not needed if one follows the Anglo-German approach in characterizing the question of transferability as non-contractual and governed by the *lex loci protectionis*. Under this solution, the protective provisions of the *droit d'auteur* states that deny the transferability of the copyright or special claims are to be applied irrespective of whether another law is chosen and whether the author is domiciled in another country.

For the French approach (*lex originis*), a provision analogue to Articles 5 and 6 Rome Convention would also not be very helpful to the author. Protection would only be available to authors domiciled in a *droit d'auteur* state. In cases such as the *"Hudson"* case, this provision would not protect any author from an unfavorable choice of law. The disadvantages of the French approach cannot be outweighed by the introduction of a special provision for copyright contracts.

---

[80] See *Kropholler*, Internationales Privatrecht[4] (2001), 463 and 465.

IV. Conclusion

The results can be summarized as follows:

(1) The transferability of IP rights should be governed by the law that governs the right, i.e., the *lex loci protectionis*. This is true for industrial property rights and copyrights. The principle also applies to the question of whether a license grant is possible and which restrictions have to be respected.

(2) For all contractual questions, the provisions of the Rome Convention are to be applied.

(3) A special provision for the protection of the author similar to Articles 5 and 6 Rome Convention is not needed, as long as the *lex loci protectionis* governs the transferability of the copyright.

Which Law Protects Consumers and Competition in Conflict with Intellectual Property Rights?

Josef Drexl

I. Introduction

Private international law in the field of licensing agreements is governed by the general principle of free choice of law. The legal basis for this very principle in the EU is to be found in Article 3(1) of the Rome Convention on the law applicable to contractual relationships of 1980.[1] This provision applies to licensing contracts, since Article 1(2) does not exclude intellectual property law matters from the scope of application of the Convention.[2]

The free-choice-of-law principle covers both the obligation of the parties to a licensing agreement and the assignment of the right as such.[3] However, the

[1] OJ EC of 26 January 1998 No. C 27, p. 34.

[2] *James J. Fawcett & Paul Torremans*, Intellectual Property and Private International Law, Oxford (Oxford University Press) 1998, p. 551.

[3] This is also true in countries where the law distinguishes between the obligatory part of the transaction and the agreement on the assignment of the right. On the situation in Germany, where application of Art. 3(1) of the Rome Convention to the transfer of the property right is the dominant opinion in legal doctrine, see *Eugen Ulmer*, Die Immaterialgüterrechte im internationalen Privatrecht, Cologne etc. (Carl Heymans) 1975, p. 47-50; *Paul Katzenberger*, in: Gerhard Schricker (ed.), Urheberrecht, Kommentar, Munich (C.H. Beck), Vor §§ 120 ff.

issue of whether and to what extent a specific right can be assigned is governed by the law of the country of protection (*lex loci protectionis*).[4]

In this contribution on licensing agreements, we will not consider the details of the free-choice-of-law principle and of the default rule of Article 4 of the Rome Convention, the latter applying to cases in which the parties have not made a choice as to the applicable law.[5] We will rather look at the exceptions from free choice of law to be made under the Rome Convention and a future Rome I Regulation in the sense of mandatory choice-of-law rules. The Convention provides for exceptions in situations in which certain interests deserve special protection and, therefore, may not be set aside by the consent of the parties to the contract. Two interests seem most relevant in the context of licensing agreements, namely the interest in protecting consumers and that in protecting competition.

As to the contractual protection of consumers, Article 5(2) of the Convention, based on certain connecting factors, provides for the application of the mandatory rules of the law of the country in which the consumer has his habitual residence.

Competition law, which may invalidate a licensing agreement, is not explicitly mentioned in the Convention. However, domestic competition law rules have to be considered mandatory rules in the sense of Article 7(1) of the Convention. According to Article 7(1), courts may apply such mandatory rules of the law of another country with which the situation has a close connection.

This article aims at highlighting the choice-of-law issues at the interface of the law applicable to licensing agreements on the one hand and consumer law and competition law on the other hand.[6] The protection of both consumers and competition is a strong concern of European Community law, resulting in

---

note 148 et seq.; *Gerhard Schricker*, Verlagsrecht, Kommentar, Munich (C.H. Beck) 2001, Einl. note 38; dissenting, e.g., *Dieter Martiny*, in: Münchner Kommentar, Bürgerliches Gesetzbuch, Band 10, Internationales Privatrecht, Munich (C.H. Beck) 1998, Art. 28 EGBGB note 262; the practice of the courts follows the dominant opinion: see *Bundesgerichtshof* (Federal Supreme Court), [1959] Gewerblicher Rechtsschutz und Urheberrecht [GRUR] 331, at 333 – "Dreigroschenroman". The view of the dominant opinion in Germany promotes the likelihood that different national courts in the EU will apply the same domestic law to assignment on the basis of the Rome Convention.

[4] See *Fawcett & Torremans* (*supra* note 2), p. 546; *Katzenberger* (*supra* note 3), Vor §§ 128 ff. note 150; *Schricker* (*supra* note 3), Einl. note 38.

[5] As to the application of default rule of Art. 28(1) German Einführungsgesetz zum Bürgerlichen Gesetzbuch (EGBGB) implementing Art. 4 of the Rome Convention to software licenses, see *Mathias Lejeune*, Anwendbares Recht, Rechtswahl- und Schiedsgerichtsklauseln in internationalen Software-Lizenzverträgen (Teil 1), [2003] IT-Rechtsberater (ITRB) 247, 248.

[6] Therefore, the article will not discuss the application of the Rome II Regulation to infringement of IPRs; see, however, *Josef Drexl*, Rome II – European Choice of Law in the Field of Intellectual Property, in: Josef Drexl & Annette Kur, Intellectual Property and Private International Law – Heading for the Future, Oxford/Munich (Hart & C.H. Beck) 2004 (forthcoming).

extensive European legislation. Correspondingly, the article investigates the need of taking the two issues into account for the future design of the Rome I[7] and Rome II[8] Regulations on the law applicable to contractual and non-contractual obligations, respectively. In the following, we will first look at existing European rules in the context of electronic commerce, which constitutes a special technical and legal environment for our investigation (*infra* II.). Then, we will continue with the law applicable to consumer contracts (*infra* III.) and the private international law analysis of the interface of licensing and competition law (*infra* IV.). On both issues, some proposals will be made for future legislation.

II. Electronic Commerce and Licensing

The Internet has become a most useful instrument for cross-border marketing of products involving intellectual property rights (IPRs), for instance of copyrighted music, copyrighted or even patent-protected software, of information stored in databases as well as of goods and services carrying a trademark. Cross-border marketing on the Internet, of course, raises the issue of the applicable law.[9]

In 2000, the European legislature adopted the so-called Electronic Commerce Directive.[10] As a means of facilitating business and transactions on the Internet the Directive opts for the principle of mutual recognition (principle of the country of origin). According to this principle each Member State has to ensure that service providers established on its territory comply with the national provisions applicable in that Member State,[11] and no Member State may restrict the freedom to provide services from another Member State.[12] Consequently, service providers can rely on the law in the country of their estab-

---

[7] See Green Paper of 14 January 2003 on the conversion of the Rome Convention of 1980 on the law applicable to contractual obligations into a Community instrument and its modernisation; COM(2002) 654 final <http://europa.eu.int/eur-lex/en/com/gpr/2002/com2002_0654en01.pdf>.

[8] See Proposal of 22 July 2003 for a Regulation of the European Parliament and the Council on the law applicable to non-contractual obligations ("Rome II); COM(2003) 427 final <http://europa.eu.int/eur-lex/en/com/pdf/2003/com2003_0427en01.pdf>.

[9] Until now, only legal commentators focused very much on admittedly more important choice-of-law issues relating to infringement of IPRs on the Internet; see, e.g., *Ansgar Ohly*, Choice of Law in the Digital Environment – Problems and Possible Solutions, in: Josef Drexl & Annette Kur, Intellectual Property and Private International Law – Heading for the Future, Oxford/Munich (Hart & C.H. Beck) 2004 (forthcoming).

[10] Directive 2000/31/EC of the European Parliament and of the Council of 8 June 2000 on certain legal aspects of information society services, in particular electronic commerce, in the Internal Market (Directive on electronic commerce); [2000] OJ EC No. L, p. 1.

[11] Art. 3(1) of the Directive.

[12] Art. 3(2) of the Directive.

lishment and do not face additional legal requirement in the country of the recipient of the service.

This is not the place to decide on the issue of whether rules of Article 3(1) and (2) of the Electronic Commerce Directive should be understood as choice-of-law rules.[13] In any instance, the principle of mutual recognition of these provisions does not apply in the field of competition law and the law concerning the applicable law relating to consumer contracts. According to Article 1(5)(c) no provision of the Directive applies to questions relating to agreements or practices governed by cartel law. In addition, an annex to the Directive makes clear that, *inter alia*, the freedom of the parties to choose the law applicable to their contract and contractual obligations concerning consumer contracts do not fall within the scope of application of the mutual-recognition principle. By these limited exemptions expressed in the annex, the European legislature means to guarantee application of the Rome Convention on the Internet. This approach is underlined by Article 1(4), stating that the Directive does not establish additional rules on private international law.[14]

Consequently, for the following analysis, there is no need to take into account any Internet-specific rules that would influence the general application of choice-of-law rules regarding licensing agreements, consumer contracts and competition law.

III. Licensing and the Law Applicable to Consumer Contracts

The choice-of-law rule on consumer contracts contained in Article 5 of the Rome Convention also applies to licensing agreements to which consumers are party. (*infra* III.1.). In addition, European consumer contract directives provide for choice-of-law rules aiming at safeguarding the protection of such directives against the choice of the law of a third country (*infra* III.2.). In the context of converting the Rome Convention to a Rome I Regulation, Article 5 of the Rome Convention needs to be amended (*infra* III.3.). Thereby, the particular situation of electronic commerce requires specific consideration (*infra* III.4.). The question remains whether and to what extent specific intellectual property concerns need to be considered for such new rules (*infra* III.5.).

---

[13] This issue is much debated in German legal writing. Private international law experts in particular argue that these rules provide for the application of the law of the country of origin; see, e.g., *Peter Mankowski*, Das Herkunftslandprinzip des E-Commerce-Rechts als Internationales Privatrecht, [2002] Europäisches Wirtschafts- und Steuerrecht (EWS) 401, at 402 et seq; *Brigitta Lurger & Sonja Maria Vallant*, Grenzüberschreitender Wettbewerb im Internet, [2002] Recht der internationalen Wirtschaft (RIW) 188, at 198.

[14] See also Recital No. 23 of the Directive, pointing out that the provisions of the applicable law "designated by rules of private international law" may not restrict the freedom to provide services.

1. Present Situation under Article 5 of the Rome Convention

According to Article 5(2) of the Rome Convention free choice of law may not deprive the consumer of the protection afforded to him by the mandatory rules of the country of his or her habitual residence if certain connecting factors are met.

This exception to the free-choice-of-law principle also applies to a licensing agreement that meets the criteria of Article 5(1) of the Rome Convention for consumer contracts.[15] According to this provision, a licensing agreement is to be considered a consumer contract if the agreement has as its object the supply of a good or service to a person ("the consumer") for a purpose that can be regarded as being outside his or her trade or profession. This definition of the consumer can be met either for the licensee or for the licensor.

Cases in which the licensee has to be considered "a consumer" can easily be identified. In the field of licensing of copyright-protected computer programs, for example, even the private user needs to get a licence – regarding the reproduction right – in order to use the program[16] for private purposes (outside his or her trade or profession).[17] Cross-border situations may specifically arise when computer programs are provided to consumers over the Internet.

At first glance, reverse situations, in which the licensor has to be considered a consumer, are difficult to imagine. The wording of Article 5(1) specifies that a good or service is provided to a consumer, whereas it is the licensor who provides the protected subject matter to the licensee. Still, such situations exist. In many instances the original right holder grants a licence based on a contract obliging the licensee to reproduce and market the protected subject matter. Such service provided to the licensor may be covered by Article 5(1) of the Rome Convention. Imagine a former Ph.D. student in law who wants to publish his thesis. This Ph.D. student may well be required to pay for the printing. Of course the student has to license his reproduction and distribution right to the publisher. Nevertheless the act of publishing has to be considered the characteristic performance of the contract in the sense of the default rule under Article 4(2) of the Rome Convention, resulting in the application of the law of the country of the publisher's residence.[18] This default rule and the free-choice-

---

[15] The issue of applying Art. 5 of the Rome Convention is rarely discussed in detail; see, e.g., *Lejeune* (*supra* note 5), at 248 and 249 (only indicating that the German implementation provision may apply to software licensing agreements).

[16] According to Art. 4 a) Computer Program Directive (Council Directive 91/250/EEC of 14 May 1991 on the legal protection of computer programs, OJ EC 1991 No. L 122, p. 42), any loading, displaying, transmission or storage of the computer program that necessitates a reproduction shall be subject to authorisation by the right holder.

[17] See also *Fawcett & Torremans* (*supra* note 2), p. 579.

[18] In this sense *Katzenberger* (*supra* note 3), Vor §§ 120 ff. note 156; *Martiny* (*supra* note 3), Art. 28 note 263a (for contracts obliging the exclusive licensee to use the license); cf. also *Fawcett & Torremans* (*supra* note 2), p. 564-570 and 572-575 (discussing different options for the application of Art. 5(2) and (5) of the Rome Convention and rejecting the

of-law rule of Article 3 are set aside, however, by Article 5(2) of the Convention if the licensor does not license in the course of his or her trade and profession. In situations in which it is the licensor who has to pay for the exploitation of the right, the requirements of Article 5(1) will often be fulfilled. Let us imagine that our former Ph.D. student, after having acquired his degree, decided to go into practice while still trying to get the thesis published; at this point, he will have to be considered a consumer in the sense of Article 5(1) of the Convention. In addition, Article 5(1) would also apply in situations in which the heir of the original owner of a right markets the acquired rights while the licensee is obliged under the contract to use the license. The administration of the acquired right does not belong to the sphere of the trade or profession of the heir in the sense of the definition of consumer under Article 5(1) of the Rome Convention.

What are the connecting factors for the application of the mandatory rules of the country of the consumer's habitual residence under Article 5(2) of the Convention? In the Internet environment, to be considered in particular for the adoption of the Rome I Regulation, the first of the three indents of Article 5(2) is most problematic. This indent requires the conclusion of the contract to be preceded by a specific invitation to the consumer or an act of advertising in the consumer's country of habitual residence and, in addition, requires that the consumer has taken all necessary steps for the conclusion of the contract in this country. Of course, the Internet may nowadays be used as a very effective means of addressing consumers. But how can we possibly localise such action in individual countries? It is obvious that the Internet argues for a reformulation of this provision.[19] For the moment it suffices to note that Article 5(1), 1st indent of the Convention only protects the so-called passive consumer who is addressed by the business operator and whose actions for the conclusion of the contract take place in his home country.

In applying Article 5(2) of the Convention to licensing agreements we also have to decide what rules of the country of the consumer's habitual residence have to be considered "mandatory rules" in the sense of the provision. Of course, provisions specifically protecting consumers fall within the scope of protection of this provision, covering those situations in which the licensee has to be considered a consumer. However, in situations in which the licensor is a consumer in the sense of Article 5(1), the issue arises of whether specific mandatory rules of national law protecting the author against overwhelming bargaining power of the licensee fall within the scope of application of that provision. The scope of application of the choice-of-law rules of the Convention are

general application of the exploiter's law, especially in a situation in which the right holder is paid by the exploiter).

[19] See, e.g., *Wulf-Henning Roth*, Grundfragen im künftigen internationalen Verbrauchervertragsrecht der Gemeinschaft, in: Michael Coester, Dieter Martiny & Karl August Prinz von Sachsen Gessaphe (eds.), Privatrecht in Europa, Festschrift für Hans Jürgen Sonnenberger, Munich (C.H. Beck) 2004, p. 591, at 602 et seq., and the discussion on this reform *infra* III.3.

defined in Article 10 of the Convention. This provision, however, does not specifically deal with intellectual property matters. The Convention certainly applies to "performance".[20] But does Article 5(2) of the Convention also cover national rules restricting the assignment of intellectual rights? Consequently, there are two arguments that might be brought forward against applying Article 5(2) of the Convention to the licensor. Firstly, rules protecting the licensor do not belong to the group of rules to be considered consumer contract rules. Secondly, rules protecting the right holder against economically unreasonable assignment do not fall within the scope of the Convention. Still, both arguments are not clear-cut and therefore may incite clarification by the European legislature in adopting a Rome I Regulation.

Additional problems arise from the relationship between Article 5(2) and Article 7 of the Rome Convention. According to Article 7(1) the courts of the Member States may even apply mandatory rules of another country with which the situation has a close connection, if and in so far as, under the law of that country, those rules must be applied regardless of which law is applicable to the contract. In the licensing context, the issue arises, for instance, of whether other EU Member States have to apply the German law granting authors a right to fair remuneration, which, under certain circumstances defined in Sec. 32b of the German Copyright Act, also apply internationally.[21] In addition, Article 7 might be applied to the situation of the passive consumer. However, it is very much in dispute whether Article 7 is not excluded by Article 5 regarding consumer contracts.[22]

2. *European Consumer Law Directives and Licensing*

European consumer law directives provide for mandatory protection of the consumer in contractual relationships. National implementation of such directives gives rise to domestic consumer law rules in the sense of Article 5(2) of

---

[20] Art. 10(1)(b) of the Convention.

[21] On Sec. 32b Copyright Act see *Reto Hilty & Alexander Peukert*, Das neue deutsche Urhebervertragsrecht im internationalen Kontext, [2002] Gewerblicher Rechtsschutz und Urheberrecht Internationaler Teil (GRUR Int.) 643 (discussing application of Art. 34 of the German Einführungsgesetz zum Bürgerlichen Gesetzbuch (EGBGB)); *Eva Inés Obergfell*, Deutscher Urheberschutz auf internationalem Kollisionskurs, [2003] Kommunikation und Recht (K&R) 118; *Haimo Schack*, Internationally Mandatory Rules in Copyright Licensing Agreements (p. 107 et seq. in this volume). Germany, on the occasion of the ratification of the Rome Convention, made a reservation as to the application of Art. 7 of the Convention. Art. 34 EGBGB implements this rule in the sense of only applying mandatory rules of German law. Similar reservations were made by Ireland, Luxembourg and the United Kingdom.

[22] The *German Federal Supreme Court (Bundesgerichtshof)* of 26 October 1993, 123 BGHZ 380, at 391, opts for a principle of exclusivity regarding the application of Arts. 29 and 34 EGBGB, implementing Arts. 5 and 7 of the Rome Convention, thereby excluding the application of Art. 34 EGBGB to consumer contracts in a situation in which the connecting factors of Art. 29 EGBGB are not met.

the Rome Convention.[23] In the light of this legal framework, the European consumer law approach, building on harmonisation of the domestic law, does not create any problem for the functioning of the Internal Market as long as consumer protection is essentially the same in all EU Member States. However, apart from the most recent Directive on Distance Marketing of Financial Services,[24] European consumer law directives only pursue minimum harmonisation, allowing the Member States to go beyond the European level of protection. Consequently, even within the scope of application of such directives, business operators have to be aware of the mandatory application of diverging domestic consumer contract law when marketing their products across borders within the EU. Without questioning the validity of the consumer law policy of the European legislature as such, the combination of mandating the Member States to adopt mandatory consumer law rules in the framework of minimum harmonisation and continued application of Article 5(2) of the Rome Convention negatively affects the exercise of the fundamental freedoms of the EC Treaty for traders of goods and service providers although European consumer law directives are deemed to be internal market directives based on Article 95 EC Treaty, ex-Article 100a EC Treaty and ex-Article 100 EEC Treaty (Article 94 EC).[25]

Whereas European consumer law directives do not seem to take into account the choice-of-law consequences of Article 5(2) of the Rome Convention within the EU, more recent directives provide for specific choice-of-law rules safeguarding the respect of European consumer law standards against the choice of the law of a third state. For instance, according to Article 6(2) of the Unfair Contract Term Directive,[26] Member States "shall take the necessary measures to ensure that the consumer does not lose the protection granted by this Directive by virtue of the choice of the law of a non-Member country as the law applicable to the contract if the latter has a close connection with the territory of the Member State." Compared to the connecting factors of Article 5(2) of the

---

[23] This is very obvious in the case of the Consumer Sales Directive (Directive 1999/44/EC of the European Parliament and the Council of 25 May 1999 on certain aspects of the sale of consumer goods and associated guarantees, [1999] OJ EC No. L 171, p. 12. The Directive provides for mandatory rules on the protection of consumers, whereas only some EU Member States had such mandatory rules for consumer sales at the time of the adoption of the Directive.

[24] Directive 2002/65/EC of the European Parliament and of the Council of 23 September 2002 concerning the distance marketing of consumer financial services and amending Council Directive 90/619/EEC and Directives 97/7/EC and 98/27/EC, [2002] O.J. EC No. L 271, p. 16.

[25] In more detail, see *Josef Drexl*, Continuing Contract Law Harmonisation under the White Paper of 1985? – Between Minimum Harmonisation, Mutual Recognition, Conflict of Laws, and Uniform Law, in: Stefan Grundmann & Jules Stuyck (eds.), An Academic Green Paper on European Contract Law, The Hague etc. (Kluwer International) 2002, p. 103, at 116-120.

[26] Council Directive 93/13/EEC of 5 April 1993 on unfair terms in consumer contracts, OJ EC 1993 No. L 95, p. 29.

Rome Convention, this formula, repeated in later directives, is not limited to the "passive" consumer. It may also be applied to the "active" consumer with a habitual residence in one Member State who, for instance as a tourist, may be confronted by the marketing of a product or service in another Member State and concludes the contract in application of the law of a non-Member State.[27]

In the field of licensing, we have to take into account in particular the application of the law based on the Directive on Unfair Contract Terms[28] and the Distance Selling Directive.[29] Their provisions also protect the consumer acquiring protected subject matter, like a computer program, under a licensing agreement.

3. *Reforming Article 5(2) of the Rome Convention*

In the Green Paper on a Rome I Regulation of 14 January 2003,[30] the Commission asks two questions relating to consumer protection rules. Question 12 deals with Article 5 of the Rome Convention, whereas Question 12A more specifically asks whether the provision is appropriate in the light of the development of electronic commerce. Question 13 asks whether the Rome I Regulation should specify the meaning of the "mandatory provisions" in Articles 3, 5, 6 and 9 and in Article 7.

A remarkable number of comments has been submitted so far in reaction to the Green Paper.[31] Two academic comments by institutions, namely the Nordic Group of Private International Law[32] and the Hamburg Max Planck Institute for Foreign Private and Private International Law,[33] will be referred to in this analysis, since both comments submit drafts for a future Rome I Regulation.

All comments, including the two to be considered in more detail, confirm the need to reformulate Article 5(2), 1st indent, for Internet purposes. Many com-

---

[27] Cf. the German implementation rule of Art. 29a of the Einführungsgesetz zum Bürgerlichen Gesetzbuche (EGBGB) that specifically covers such situations.

[28] *Supra* note 26.

[29] Directive 97/7/EC of the European Parliament and of the Council of 20 May 1997 on the protection of consumers in respect of distance contracts, OJ EC 1997 No. L 144, p. 19.

[30] *Supra* note 7.

[31] The 80 or so replies are assembled on the website of the European Commission: <http://europa.eu.int/comm/justice_home/news/consulting_public/rome_i/news_summary_rome1_en.htm>.

[32] *Nordic Group of Private International Law*, Proposal for Amendments to the Convention on the Law Applicable to Contractual Obligations, <http://europa.eu.int/comm/justice_home/news/consulting_public/rome_i/doc/nordic_group_private_international_law_en.pdf>.

[33] *Max Planck Institute for Foreign Private and Private International Law*, Comments on the European's Commission's Green Paper on the conversion of the Rome Convention of 1980 on the law applicable to contractual obligations into a Community instrument and its modernisation, <http://europa.eu.int/comm/justice_home/news/consulting_public/rome_i/doc/max_planck_institute_foreign_private_international_law_en.pdf>.

ments propose to synchronise Article 5(2) with Article 15 of the Brussels I Regulation[34] defining the competent court in consumer law litigation. Actually, in the context of Article 15 of the Brussels I Regulation, the European legislature had to solve the same problem of adapting the former rule of the Brussels I Regulation, formulated in similar terms as Article 5(2) of the Rome Convention, to the needs of the Internet. Adopting this model of the Brussels I Regulation would considerably extend the scope of application of Article 5(2) of the Rome Convention by covering the "mobile" or "active" consumer in addition to the "passive" consumer.[35]

The Nordic Group on Private International Law is most progressive in protecting consumers. According to its proposal the free-choice-of-law principle should be excluded for consumer contracts altogether by extending the mandatory application of the law of the country of the consumer's habitual residence beyond the sphere of mandatory rules.[36] In situations in which the proposed connecting factors, to be synchronised with Article 15 Brussels I Regulation, are not met, the Nordic Group would not allow free-choice-of-law rule but would apply the general default rule of Article 4 as a general mandatory choice-of-law rule to consumer contracts.[37] This proposal is based on the two arguments that, firstly, party autonomy is considerably limited for consumers in contractual relationships and, secondly, that a simplification of Article 5(2) is needed insofar as it currently requires a distinction between the mandatory rules of the law of the consumer's habitual residence and other rules of the law chosen by the parties.[38] As we were able to see, such distinction is difficult, in particular when it comes to the application of mandatory rules protecting the copyright owner against the overwhelming bargaining power of the licensee.[39] However, the Nordic Group ignores a number of counter-arguments. Firstly, the law applied under Article 4 is not necessarily the law of the country of the consumer's residence. On the contrary, the characteristic performance is typically effectuated by the other party. Free choice of law would give the consumer at least a chance to agree with the other party on the application of the law of the country of the consumer's habitual residence in situations in which application of that law would not be mandatory. Secondly, the proposal would aggravate already existing problems for the Internal Market. The possibility of

---

[34] Council Regulation (EC) No 44/2001 of 22 December 2000 on jurisdiction and the recognition and enforcement of judgments in civil and commercial matters, OJ EC 2001 No. L 12, p. 1.

[35] See, in more detail, *infra* III.4.

[36] Proposed Art. 5(2) of the Rome I Regulation would simply read as follows: "Consumer contracts shall be subject to the law of the State in which the consumer has his habitual residence if (...)".

[37] Proposed Art. 5(4) Rome I Regulation.

[38] *Nordic Group for Private International Law* (*supra* note 32), p. 35-37.

[39] See *supra* III.1. The Nordic Proposal highlights the issue of whether Art. 5(2) of the Rome Convention also applies to mandatory rules that are not intended to protect consumers (*supra* note 32), p. 36.

implementing Europe-wide marketing strategies following the rules of a single jurisdiction would be made impossible, though such strategies would be needed by small and medium-sized enterprises (SMEs) in particular that cannot easily adapt to the different laws of the growing number of Member States.[40] The Nordic Group relies on a comparative approach and cites Article 120 of the Swiss Federal Act on Private International Law as the model of the proposal.[41] However, Swiss law does not have to take into consideration the special needs of the Internal Market.

The Hamburg Max Planck Institute also opts for a synchronisation of Article 5(2) with Article 15 of the Brussels I Regulation but does not go beyond the application to mandatory rules. By extending the scope of Article 5(2) to protect the active consumer as well, the Hamburg Max Planck Institute argues that the scope of the general public-order rule of Article 7 may be reduced considerably without harming the consumer.[42] For Article 7 the Max Planck Institute generally advocates a reduction to "international" mandatory rules.

4. Problems of Electronic Commerce

There are two problems that need to be solved in order to identify the applicable law to consumer contracts concluded on the Internet. Firstly, European law has to localise business activity on the Internet. Secondly, the legislature has to decide whether to protect the passive consumer only or to extend protection to the active consumer. The latter option seems to impose itself given the fact that in the Internet environment it is the "active" consumer who often takes the first step and uploads the website of a provider situated abroad.

Actually, the European legislature has already made its decision on both problems in the framework of converting the Brussels Convention into the Brussels I Regulation.[43] According to Article 15 and 16(1) of the Brussels I Regulation the consumer may sue in his country of domicile if the defendant "pursues commercial or professional activities in the Member State of the con-

---

[40] Also supporting an approach similar to the Nordic Proposal, *Stefan Leible*, Verbesserungen des kollisionsrechtlichen Verbraucherschutzes, in: Jenaer Expertentagung, Das Grünbuch zum internationalen Vertragsrecht, Stellungsnahmen zum Grünbuch über die Umwandlung des Übereinkommens von Rom aus dem Jahre 1980 über das auf vertragliche Schuldverhältnisse anzuwendende Recht in ein Gemeinschaftsinstrument sowie über seine Aktualisierung <http://europa.eu.int/comm/justice_home/news/consulting_public/rome_i/doc/jenaer_expertentagung_27_28_06_2003_de.pdf>, p. 96, at 106 et seq. *Leible* argues against a violation of the fundamental freedoms since the general application of the law of the consumer's habitual residence may be justified by mandatory requirements of consumer protection. Thereby, the author takes impediments to the exercise of the fundamental freedoms for granted. Then, however, the author would have to accept that the European legislature would have to live up to its duty to combat such impediments by total harmonisation of consumer laws.

[41] *Nordic Group for Private International Law* (*supra* note 32), p. 37.

[42] *Max Planck Institute* (*supra* note 33), p. 61.

[43] *Supra* note 34.

sumer's domicile or, by any means, directs such activities to that Member State or to several States including that Member State, and the contract falls within the scope of such activities."

Commentators on the Green Book tend to adapt this rule in their proposals for a Rome I Regulation. For instance, the Hamburg Max Planck Institute proposes the following formula for a new Article 5(2):

> Notwithstanding the provisions of Article 3, a choice of law made by the parties shall not have the result of depriving the consumer of the protection afforded to him by the internally mandatory rules of the law of the country in which he has his habitual residence at the time of conclusion of the contract, if the contract has been concluded with a supplier who pursues commercial or professional activities in that state or, by any means, directs such activities to that state or to several states including that state and the contract falls into the scope of such activity.

The electronic commerce scenario would be covered by the formula of an activity directed at a State "by any means". Despite the interactive nature of the Internet, the European legislature in the Brussels I Regulation did not give up the idea of taking the supplier's activity as the connecting factor for the localisation of the contract. This approach is not without doubt. Still, it is the only possible one. Otherwise a limitation of the number of laws applicable to Internet commerce would not be possible. However, the formula might go too far in some other respects. It does not only apply to the Internet, but gives broad protection to the active consumers who may conclude a contract even on the business premises of a supplier abroad. In such a situation the law of the country of the consumer's habitual residence would still apply if the provider also uses the Internet to reach consumers based in this country. Article 15 of the Brussels I Regulation does not require a causal link between the defendant's activity in the country of the consumer and the contract concluded by the consumer.

In addition, the problem remains that a business operator has to face the application of a considerable number of domestic consumer laws; this problem would even be aggravated. This multiplicity of laws would especially hamper the marketing of IP protected intangible subject matter involving licensing agreements. Three principles may be thought of that would limit this multiplicity of laws.

(1.) A broadening of the free-choice-of-law principle may be acceptable to the extent that the consumer is adequately informed about the rules of the applicable law. It may be true that many consumers will not readily conclude contracts under a foreign law. But this could be left to the competitive process; the supplier may find customers abroad willing to accept the law of the provider. Still, the counter-argument is obvious. Workable competition, including workable competition of legal orders depends on many factors. For many Internet users the content of the applicable law will be overlooked, being part of standard contract terms. In addition, the quality of the law cannot be judged easily by the consumer.

(2.) Another problem with the formula chosen for the Brussels I Regulation arises from the fact that it applies irrespective of whether the business operator is aware of the customer's domicile. In particular, in a situation in which products are distributed online, like software, databases and music, knowledge of the customer's domicile is not acquired by the provider. This would argue for a strict awareness test according to which the law of the country of the consumer's habitual residence does not apply if the consumer lies about his or her residence.[44] Under such a rule, even the provider on the Internet would be able to control which national laws apply. Evidence of deceitful conduct on the part of the consumer could easily be produced by the specific technical design of the provider's website that only allows the provision of digital goods if the consumer confirms a country of habitual residence listed on the website.

(3.) A last option for limiting the number of applicable laws could consist in a broadening of the free-choice-of-law principle within the EU. This idea leads to more detailed choice-of-law rules on consumer contracts for a Rome I Regulation.

5. *Principles for the Law Applicable to Consumer Contracts in a Rome I Regulation*

In order to promote the exercise of the fundamental freedoms in the Internal Market, secondary Community law increasingly prefers the application of the principle of mutual recognition to harmonisation of substantive standards. This is also true in areas in which the fundamental freedoms conflict with the interest of protecting consumers. Within the scope of application of the Electronic Commerce Directive,[45] the principle of mutual recognition, relying on the application of the legal standards in the country of origin, applies in particular in the field of advertising. Of course, the principle of mutual recognition runs the risk of lowering legal standards within the Community. How-

---

[44] Such a rule is also argued by the business community; see *EuroCommerce (The Retail, Wholesale and International Trade Representation to the EU)*, Comments on the Green Paper on the Rome Convention of 1980 on the Law Applicable to Contractual Obligations into a Community Instrument and its Implementation, September 2003, p. 8; <http://europa.eu.int/comm/justice_home/news/consulting_public/rome_i/doc/eurocommerce_en.pdf>. Even the European Consumers' Organisation BEUC, Rome I – BEUC Position Paper concerning the Commission's Green Paper, p. 13, <http://europa.eu.int/comm/justice_home/news/consulting_public/rome_i/doc/beuc_en.pdf>, is of the opinion that Art. 5(2) should not apply in cases in which the business operator is not aware of the consumer's residence as a result of the consumer's conduct. In many cases this rule will not be needed. If the consumer lies about his or her habitual residence, most frequently the provider of the online services will not have directed the commercial activity to the real habitual residence. However, the situation is different if the provider also covers the country of the real habitual residence, be it over the Internet or, e.g., by a subsidiary stationed in that country. In any case the provider should be sure about the consumer law to be applied to the contract.

[45] *Supra* note 10.

ever, the Community legal order is in possession of the means to balance such threats by raising, in a second step, the level of protection through substantive harmonisation.

Mutual recognition, however, does not work in the field of contract law for a very simple reason. It is for the rules of private international law to define the applicable law. According to private international law, based on the idea of freedom of contract, the parties to a contract can generally decide which law governs the formation of the contract and the rights and obligations flowing from the contractual relationship. Consequently, there was no alternative to the exclusion of the application of the principle of the country of origin in the Electronic Commerce Directive with regard to the free-choice-of-law principle and consumer contract law.[46]

Actually, in the field of contract law, the free-choice-of-law principle achieves the same goals of promoting the fundamental freedoms and the Internal Market as does the principle of mutual recognition in other fields of the law. Therefore, there is a need for clarifying to what extent the free-choice-of-law principle might nowadays be applied instead of the mandatory application of the law of the consumer's habitual residence. This question quite rightly has to face strong concerns of weakening the attained level of consumer protection. However, Article 5(2) of the Rome Convention was adopted in 1980, at a time when no European consumer law legislation existed and harmonisation was extremely difficult to achieve under the former Article 100 EEC Treaty (Article 94 EC), requiring unanimity on the Council.[47]

Any reform of Article 5(2) of the Rome Convention resulting in a limitation of the scope of application of the law of the country of the consumer's habitual residence has to balance appropriately the interests of the free movement principles and consumer protection. Therefore, the scope of application of the free-choice-of-law principle has to be implemented in an extremely cautious approach. A number of principles should limit free choice of law in order to guarantee due respect of the needs of consumer protection.

(1.) Broader application of the free-choice-of-law rule is only possible within the geographic area of application of European consumer law, including not only the EU, but also the EEA and other associated states in which respect of European standards is guaranteed.

(2.) Free choice of law should not be extended to the whole area of consumer contract law. It should rather be limited to legal instruments to be identi-

---

[46] See *supra* II.

[47] Relying on this argument and in light of European consumer law harmonisation, the *European Internet Services Providers Association (EuroISPA)*, Position Paper of September 2003, p. 3, <http://europa.eu.int/comm/justice_home/news/consulting_public/rome_i/doc/euroispa_en.pdf>, argues that application of the country-of-reception principle of Art. 5(2) is unnecessary. See, however, *Roth* (*supra* note 19), at 611-614 (still defending Art. 5(2) against a free-choice-of-law rule with very valid arguments).

fied by the European legislature.[48] Such a decision is necessary in particular for directives following the minimum harmonisation approach. Member States may be able to agree on a minimum standard, but such standards might still be too low, allowing the parties to opt against a law providing higher standards of protection for consumers. With regard to directives that now follow an approach of total harmonisation,[49] like the recent Directive on Distance Marketing of Financial Services,[50] a decision as to the applicable choice of law rule is not superfluous since the directive may give limited options to national legislatures. Still, the Directive on Distance Marketing of Financial Services clearly marks a policy change, limiting the Member States' ability to provide for ever higher levels of consumer protection without giving consideration to the functioning of the Internal Market. Similar concerns were also expressed by the ECJ in its decision on the Tobacco Advertising Directive, when it held that the European legislature has no power to allow Member States to go beyond the European level of consumer protection without simultaneously implementing a rule that guarantees the free movement of goods that are in conformity with the standards of the minimum directive.[51] This decision obviously questions the legality of minimum harmonisation in the field of consumer contract law as well. Minimum harmonisation needs to be balanced with a second, Internal Market principle. In the Tobacco Advertising case, this would be the principle of mutual recognition; in the field of consumer contract law the legislature would have to apply a principle of free choice of law. Still, minimum harmonisation in the field of consumer contract law can reduce discrepancies between national laws and thereby improve the situation for the Internal Market without implementing a principle of free choice of law. Therefore, it should be acceptable to leave it to the European legislature to decide for which legal instruments on consumer contract law the free-choice-of-law principle would apply. This decision would best be made in the framework of an additional paragraph in Article 5 of a Rome I Regulation, listing the legal instruments for which the free-choice-of-law principle applies.

---

[48] Cf. European Mail Order and Distance Selling Trade Association (EMOTA), Comments on the Green Paper on the conversion of the Rome Convention of 1980 on the law applicable to contractual obligations into a Community instrument and its modernisation, p. 4, <http://europa.eu.int/comm/justice_home/news/consulting_public/rome_i/doc/emota_en.pdf>, going one step further in claiming that Art. 5(2) should not apply in the field of European harmonisation, which is deemed to provide adequate consumer protection in general.

[49] This approach of total or maximum harmonisation is opposed by some consumer lawyers; see *Geraint Howells*, European Consumer Law – The Minimal and Maximal Harmonisation Debate and Pro Independent Consumer Law Competence, in: Stefan Grundmann & Jules Stuyck (ed.), An Academic Green Paper on European Contract Law, The Hague etc. (Kluwer International) 2003, p. 73, at 75 et seq.

[50] *Supra* note 24.

[51] Case C-376/98, *Federal Republic of Germany v. European Parliament and Council*, [2000] ECR I-8599, para. 104.

(3.) General application of the free-choice-of-law principle beyond the scope of current harmonisation in all Internet-related intra-European situations would correspond to the general application of the mutual-recognition principle to other fields of law under Article 3 of the Electronic Commerce Directive. Such application – and exception from the mandatory choice-of-law rule of Article 5(2) of the Rome Convention[52] – can only be justified by the goal of specifically promoting the development of electronic commerce; it would help SMEs in particular, who cannot as easily as larger competitors provide individual websites complying with the requirements of different European countries.[53] In order to keep the risks for consumers low, special legal disciplines might be come up with to inform the consumer appropriately of the fact that it is not the law of the country of his or her habitual residence that will apply. Such information could reduce the chances of attracting consumers abroad. Nevertheless, it is necessary for guaranteeing workable competition of different national laws in the field.

The situation with regard to the law of third states, i.e. not covered by European consumer law legislation, is completely different. Here, alignment of Article 5(2), 1st indent, of the Rome Convention with the wording of Article 15 of the Brussels I Regulation seems to be the appropriate rule that nevertheless should be complemented with a stringent awareness test according to which a consumer who has lied about his residence may not rely on the application of the law of country of his or her habitual residence. If such alignment with the Brussels I Regulation were implemented, special choice-of-law rules safeguarding the standards of given directives against the choice of the law of a third state would become superfluous. Active consumers would also be protected, but should sustain the application of the law of a third country if the other party to the contract is not active in the country of the consumer's habitual residence.

As to the specific intersection of licensing agreements and consumer contracts, the rules proposed here would specifically promote cross-border

---

52 Such an exception for Internet cases is actually argued by Internet providers; see *Yahoo! Europe*, Comments on the Green Paper on a "Rome I Regulation" of 15 September 2003, p. 5 (answering Question 12 of the Green Paper); <http://europa.eu.int/comm/justice_home/news/consulting_public/rome_i/doc/yahoo_europe_en.pdf>; *Amazon Europe*, Response to the European Commission Green Paper on the Conversion of the Rome Convention of 1980 ("Rome I") on the Law applicable to Contractual Obligations into a Community Instrument and its Modernisation, p. 8, <http://europa.eu.int/comm/justice_home/news/consulting_public/rome_i/doc/amazon_europe_en.pdf> (arguing that Art. 5(2) puts an undue compliance burden on Internet providers in Europe regarding the number and respect of a high number of different domestic rules).

53 Cf. *EuroCommerce (The Retail, Wholesale and International Trade Representation to the EU)* (*supra* note 44), p. 8, <http://europa.eu.int/comm/justice_home/news/consulting_public/rome_i/doc/eurocommerce_en.pdf>, criticising minimum harmonisation in general and the Distance Selling Directive that led to 15 different laws in the Member States, harming the interests of SMEs in particular.

marketing to consumers of protected subject matter that requires licences without unduly reducing the level of consumer protection. In addition, the European legislature should bring more precision to the Rome I choice-of-law rules in two regards: firstly, in Article 10(1) it should be clarified that the applicable law also governs the transfer of intellectual property rights. Secondly, the European legislature would be well advised to specify whether Article 5(2) only provides for rules specifically formulated for the contractual protection of consumers. Since consumer contract law reacts to situations of an imbalance of bargaining power in contractual relationships, and since such situations may arise in very different relationships, it would probably be best to adopt a wider scope of application. Accordingly, Article 5(2) should cover all mandatory rules intended by the national legislature to protect against such market failures of unequal distribution of bargaining power as long as the protected person meets the definition of a consumer. Thereby, the Article 5(2) of a future Rome I Regulation would also protect copyright owners in particular who, outside their own trade or profession, license their rights to an exploiter. This provision provides much greater legal certainty than the ill-defined general rule of Article 7(1) of the present Rome Convention applicable to right holders granting licenses within their trade or profession.

IV. Licensing and Competition Law

As pointed out before, another area in which the general principle of free choice of law may be restricted relates to the application of competition law to licensing agreements. For further analysis we first have to identify the choice-of-law rules regarding competition law (*infra* IV.1.). The interface with competition law needs to be considered both for the adopting of a Rome I Regulation on contractual obligations (*infra* IV.2.) and for a Rome II Regulation on non-contractual obligations (*infra* IV.3.). The true significance of the private international law issue is underscored by the recent evolution of Community competition law (*infra* IV.4.). From this, certain consequences need to be drawn for a future Rome I and Rome II Regulation (*infra* IV.5.).

1. Choice-of-Law Rules Regarding Competition Law

The application of domestic competition laws is based on the idea of territoriality. Domestic competition law only pursues protection of competition in the home market.[54] As a guiding principle for choice of law, territoriality is very convincing in the field of administrative and criminal enforcement of domestic competition law. Public international law does not allow extension of such

---

[54] For an extensive discussion of the applicable law relating to competition law, see, e.g., *Jürgen Basedow*, Weltkartellrecht, Tübingen (Mohr-Siebeck) 1998, p. 11-30.

enforcement across borders. However, territoriality does not suffice to decide on the applicability of domestic competition law in cross-border situations. Quite often restraints of competition are initiated from abroad but restrain competition in the domestic market.

With the objective of avoiding gaps in the effective protection of enforcement, many jurisdictions opt for the application of the so-called effects doctrine. According to this doctrine, even if the respective action is taken abroad, a restraint of competition is covered by domestic competition law insofar as this restraint affects competition in the domestic market. The application of the effects doctrine is nowadays considered to be in conformity with public international law, at least as long as authorities appropriately respect essential interests of other states according to the general principle of international comity.[55] The effects doctrine is applied in most EU Member States for the application of their domestic competition law.[56] In contrast, the European Court of Justice (ECJ) sticks to a concept of territoriality but does not require that the alleged infringer of competition law actually acts in the territory of a Member State. It suffices that the restraint is only "implemented" within the European Union.[57] Otherwise, the Court argues, the infringer could easily evade Community competition rules, if the application of such rules depended on the place where the agreement, decision or concerted practice was formed.[58] This "implementation" doctrine comes very close to the effects doctrine, although it may not be identical with it in all regards.[59]

When it comes to the question of which competition law applies to a licensing agreement, consideration has to be given to the co-existence of the supranational competition law of the European Community and domestic competition laws. Article 81(1) EC on restrictive agreements and other collusive behaviour applies whenever the restraint affects trade between Member States. Actually, this requirement would regularly be met in the case of licensing agreements covering the whole territory of a given Member State.[60] The new

---

[55] In this sense also the European Court of First Instance: Case T-102/96, *Gencor*, [1999] ECR II-753, para. 90. See also *David Gerber*, The European Commission's GE/Honeywell Decision: US responses and their implications, [2003] Zeitschrift für Wettbewerbsrecht (ZWeR) 87, at 91.

[56] See, e.g., Sec. 130(2) German Act against Restraints of Competition: "This Act shall apply to all restraints of competition having an effect within the area of application of this Act, also if they were caused outside the area of application of this Act."

[57] Joint Cases 89, 104, 114, 116, 117, and 125 to 129/85, *Ahlström Osakeyhtiö and others v. Commission*, Slg. 1988, 5193, para. 16-18.

[58] Id., at para. 16.

[59] Cf. *Basedow* (*supra* note 54), at 19, citing the example of sales below cost just across the external borders of EU attracting customers from within the EU. In such a case, the practice should not be deemed capable of implementation in the territory of the EU though it affects the EU market.

[60] According to settled case law Art. 81 EC applies on restrictive agreements extending over the whole territory of a Member State; see Case 8/72, *Vereniging van Cementhandelaren*

Implementation Regulation 1/2003[61] allows parallel application of domestic competition law along with Article 81 EC;[62] but it also states that domestic law may not prohibit any agreement that is to be considered legal under Article 81(1) and (3) EC.[63] Hence, Community law conclusively defines the standard of illegality of licensing agreements under competition law within the EU. However, choice-of-law rules have to define the scope of application of Community competition law with regard to the application of the domestic competition law of a third state. The domestic courts of the Member States may also have to deal with such situations, as highlighted by the following example:

A French company named F holds a pharmaceutical patent in Switzerland. F grants a licence on production and distribution to the Swiss company named S. The licensing agreement fixes the prices S will take from Swiss customers. In addition, the agreement provides for the application of French contract law and for jurisdiction of French courts. Later, S argues that the contract is void according to Swiss competition law. F sues S for royalties before the competent French court. Here, the issue arises of whether the French court should apply Swiss competition law under Article 7(1) of the Rome Convention. The court may be hesitant to do so. Actually, there is a concern that such application would enforce the public policy of Switzerland. However, as to the legal consequences in the field of private law, competition law also balances the interests of private parties. Therefore, application of foreign competition law under Article 7(1) of the Rome Convention should not be excluded per se.[64]

Identifying the applicable competition law is further complicated by different approaches of domestic laws regarding the enforcement of competition laws. Legislatures may choose between criminal, administrative and private enforcement or combine some or, as the U.S. legislature does, all of them. Whereas criminal and administrative enforcement are clearly covered by the territoriality principle, private enforcement of competition law, seen from a private international law perspective, belongs to the area of contract law, as far as the validity of an agreement is concerned, and to torts and delicts when it comes to damages. Contract law is covered by the existing Rome Convention; torts and delicts would fall within the scope of application of a future Rome II Regulation. Therefore, in formulating a Rome I and Rome II Regulation, the

---

v. Commission, [1972] ECR 977, para. 29. See also *Bellamy & Child*, European Community Law of Competition, 5th ed., London (Sweet & Maxwell) 2001, note 2-138 (on the applicability of EC competition law to patent licenses).

[61] Council Regulation (EC) No 1/2003 of 16 December 2002 on the implementation of the rules on competition laid down in Arts. 81 and 82 of the Treaty, [2003] OJ EC No. L 1, p. 1.

[62] Art. 3(1) Regulation 1/2003.

[63] Art. 3(2) Regulation 1/2003.

[64] See *Andreas Heinemann*, Die Anwendbarkeit ausländischen Kartellrechts – Probleme der Qualifikation und der Anknüpfung im internationalen Kartellprivatrecht, in: Mélanges en l'honneur de Bernard Dutoit, Geneva (Librerie Droz) 2002, p. 115 (on the application of foreign competition law by domestic courts).

European legislature should take into account the applicability of said Regulations to competition law that may affect licenses.

2. *Situation under the Existing Rome Convention*

Competition law rules, under the existing Rome Convention, may have to be taken into account in the framework of Article 7 of the Convention.[65] The two paragraphs of the provision highlight different scenarios of controlling licensing agreements by competition law.

Under Article 7(2) of the Convention, rules of the forum may be applied in a situation where these rules are mandatory irrespective of the law otherwise applicable to a contract. According to this formula a competent domestic court within the EU may apply EC competition law in order to confirm the invalidity of a licensing agreement concluded under the law of a third state. Application of Article 81(1) and (2) EC by courts in the EU is already mandated by the primacy of Community law, regardless of which national law applies to the contract. Therefore, the legal effect of Article 7(2) of the Rome Convention as to the mandatory character of EC competition law is close to zero; at best, the provision confirms the legal situation under existing and directly applicable EC competition law.

Under Article 7(1) of the Convention, domestic courts of the Member States would also be authorised to apply the competition law of a third country as the "mandatory rules of the law of another country". Such application is possible if and insofar as, under the law of that country, those rules must be applied even if the law applicable to the contract is that of a different country. This provision would apply to the case formulated above,[66] in which a French court, applying French contract law, has to consider whether the licensing agreement is void according to Swiss competition law. Actually, Swiss competition law follows the effects doctrine[67] and, therefore, has to be considered of a mandatory nature as a matter of Swiss rules on choice of law.[68] Although application of Swiss competition law in the case may meet with opposition by French judges, applying Swiss competition law under Article 7(1) of the Rome Convention has to be preferred to the other choice-of-law approach of entrusting control of

---

[65] See *Fawcett & Torremans* (*supra* note 2), p. 580, mentioning competition law rules as possible mandatory rules in the sense of Art. 7(2). Application of Art. 7(1) to competition rules is not discussed by the authors because of the reservation filed by the British guaranteeing the non-application of this provision.

[66] *Supra* IV.1.

[67] See Sec. 2(2) of the Swiss Competition Act (*Kartellgesetz*) of 6 October 1995, as amended by the Act of 20 June 2003. The Amendment became effective on 1 April 2004 without changing Sec. 2(2) of the Competition Act; on the reform see *Patrick Krauskopf & Sabrina Carron*, Die Schweizer Kartellrechtsnovelle, [2004] Wirtschaft und Wettbewerb (WuW) 495.

[68] Cf. also *Heinemann* (*supra* note 64), p. 118 et seq. (indicating the possibility of applying Art. 7(1) to competition law).

restrictive agreements exclusively to competition law of the *lex causae* (the law applicable to the contract). Applicability of the *lex causae* would allow the parties to the restrictive agreement to choose the weakest competition law, thereby evading the stricter law of the market. In our case cited above, EC competition law would not help at all, since the agreement was only implemented outside the territory of the EU. Accordingly, domestic competition law needs to be applied irrespective of the law applicable to the contract.[69]

3. *Situation under the Proposed Rome II Regulation*

Whereas the effects doctrine of domestic competition law certainly applies to administrative and criminal sanctions, the choice-of-law situation is not as clear with regard to non-contractual obligations arising from a restraint of competition.[70] In Germany, for example, the effects doctrine of Sec. 130(2) of the Act against Restraints of Competition also captures the private law effects of a restraint, but, according to its wording, only works unilaterally. It does not provide for the application of the law of the affected market of another country.[71] To the extent that there are no special choice-of-law rules for the non-contractual obligations arising from a restraint of competition, domestic courts have to identify the applicable law on damages according to the domestic choice-of-law rules relating to torts and delicts.[72] This is also the case in Germany, where Sec. 130(2) of the Act against Restraints of Competition only prevails as the *lex specialis* regarding protection of competition in the German market.[73]

Within the scope of application of EC competition law the situation is even more complex. EC competition law covers the legal consequences of the illegality of a restraint only to a very limited extent. In Article 81(2) EC, it provides for the nullity of a contract that violates the cartel prohibition of Article 81(1) EC, but remains silent on the issue of damages. However, this does not mean that there is no right to recover damages. On the contrary! According to the general principle of full effectiveness of Community law, as derived from Article 10(1) EC, the Member States are generally responsible for

---

[69] See the very convincing arguments made by *Heinemann* (*supra* note 64), p. 120.

[70] Cf. *Heinemann* (*supra* note 64), p. 127 et seq.

[71] See *Ullrich Immenga*, in: Münchner Kommentar Bürgerliches Gesetzbuch Band 10, Munich (C.H. Beck) 1998, Nach Art. 37 EGBGB note 19 et seq., who opposes a multilateral interpretation of the provision.

[72] In favour of a tort law qualification also *Heinemann* (*supra* note 64), p. 127 et seq., still arguing that in Germany, the choice-of-law rule for torts is to be applied in the light of the effects doctrine of Sec. 130(2) Act against Restraints of Competition. According to this rule, the law of the affected market has to be considered the *lex loci delicti commissi*.

[73] Cf. *Heinemann* (*supra* note 64), p. 127 et seq., suggesting that the *lex loci delicti* rule should always apply to the non-contractual obligations arising from restraints of competition. However, Sec. 130(2) Act against Restraints of Competition would remain relevant insofar as the affected market would define the *lex loci delicti*.

providing for effective means of enforcement. According to the ECJ in its *Courage* decision of 2001, this general principle amounts to an obligation to grant damages under domestic law if the denial of a right to compensation would put at risk the full effect of the prohibition provided for in Article 81(1) EC.[74] As to the substance of such a Community right to damages, the ECJ relies on the two principles of equivalence and effectiveness.[75] According to the principle of equivalence, such national rules granting a right to compensation may not be less favourable than those governing similar domestic actions. The principle of effectiveness requires that such national rules do not render practically impossible or excessively difficult the exercise of the rights conferred by Article 81(1) EC.[76] Summing up, *Courage* makes clear that Member States have to provide for a right to damages under their domestic law, whereas EC competition law applies to the standards of illegality. This raises the private international law question of which domestic law applies to the issue of damages when EC competition law is violated.[77]

Application of the effects doctrine under the law of a Member State seems highly inappropriate for identifying the law of a Member State that governs the non-contractual obligations arising from a violation of EC competition law. For the future, the European legislature has to decide whether the issue should be covered by the Rome II Regulation and, if so, according to which rules.

Article 1(2) of the Proposed Rome II Regulation of 2003[78] does not exclude non-contractual obligations arising from a violation of competition law from its scope of application. Neither does the Proposal provide a specific choice-of-law rule on competition law in the sense of a European effects doctrine. Article 5(1) proposes such a rule for unfair competition only. Therefore, the general choice-of-law rules as contained in Article 3 of the Proposal would apply, superseding any diverging national conflict-of-laws rule.

---

[74] Case C-453/99, *Courage v. Crehan*, [2001] ECR I-6297, para. 25-27; see also *Josef Drexl*, Do We Need "Courage" for International Antitrust Law? Choosing between Supranational and International Law Principles of Enforcement, in: Josef Drexl (ed.), The Future of Transnational Antitrust – From Comparative to Common Competition Law, Berne etc. (Staempli & Kluwer International) 2003, p. 311, at 337 et seq.

[75] Case C-453/99, *Courage v. Crehan*, [2001] ECR I-6297, para. 29.

[76] The ECJ refers to his earlier decision in Case C-261/95, *Palmisani v. Istituto Nazionale della Previdenza Sociale (INPS)*, [1997] ECR I-4025, para. 27, dealing with the right of individuals to seek compensation from a Member State for belated implementation of directives.

[77] In *Courage*, neither the referring national court nor the ECJ had to raise this issue since application of English law was not in dispute. Art. 81(1) EC was applied to a contract of exclusive delivery of beer between an English brewery and an English pub operator.

[78] *Supra* note 8.

4. *Impact of Recent Evolution of EC Competition Law*

The growing significance of choice-of-law rules with regard to non-contractual obligations resulting from a violation of EC competition law in the context of licensing agreements can be illustrated by three recent developments.

(1.) The already mentioned decision of the ECJ in *Courage*[79] highlights the duty of Member States to provide for a right to damages of victims of a restraint of competition. More specifically, the ECJ made it clear that such a right may not be excluded as a matter of principle for a victim who is party to a contract in violation of Article 81(1) EC.[80] According to these principles, the licensee, or more rarely the licensor, may sue the other party for damages if the licence agreement restrains competition. In general, *Courage* increases the incentives for private enforcement of EC competition law.

(2.) Such additional incentives are needed in particular after the entry into force of the Implementation Directive 1/2003[81] on 1 May 2004. The Directive provides for the direct application of Article 81(3) EC, with the effect that domestic courts are now enabled to test the legality of restrictive agreements in the sense of Article 81(1) EC themselves without having to wait, as was required under the previous law, for a decision of the European Commission on the individual exemption. Undertakings now enjoy more economic freedom in drafting their contracts, but, as a considerable drawback, can no longer refer cases to the Commission to get its authoritative opinion on the legality of a given contract. Thereby, undertakings run the risk of nullity of their contracts and also of having to compensate the other party of the contract suffering financial loss as a consequence of the restrictive contract.

(3.) The date of 1 May 2004 also marks the entry into force of the new Block Exemption Regulation on Transfer of Technology (BERTT).[82] This new Regulation adopts a market-oriented approach and implements market-share thresholds as the decisive criterion for the block exemption. In potentially more dynamic technology markets, the parties to a technology transfer (licensing) agreement will have to face considerable problems of identifying whether the exemption exists or not. Although an exemption may still be possible under the directly applicable Article 81(3) EC, the new legal system on transfer of tech-

---

[79] *Supra* IV.3.

[80] Case C-453/99, *Courage v. Crehan*, [2001] ECR I-6297, para. 24.

[81] *Supra* note 61.

[82] Commission Regulation (EC) No 772/2004 of 27 April 2004 on the application of Art. 81(3) of the Treaty to categories of technology transfer agreements, [2004] OJ EC No. L 123, p. 11. See also the Guidelines on the application of Art. 81 of the EC Treaty to technology transfer agreements, [2004] OJ EC No. C 101, p. 2. These Guidelines give indication to the courts for the application both of the BERTT and Art. 81(3) EC outside the scope of the block exemption.

nology lacks the legal certainty the previous law had.[83] Whereas the instrument of block exemption regulations may in general be used in the new system of the directly applicable Article 81(3) EC as an effective means of increasing legal certainty, thereby reducing the risk of non-contractual liability to the other party of the contract, the new BERTT, with its economic approach in particular, does not seem to be very helpful in this regard.

The practical consequences of these developments are considerable. Private enforcement of EC competition law, including compensation for damages, is of growing importance. In the EU, the issue of damages for competition law violations usually arises in disputes concerning contractual obligations. Defendants often question the legality of a contract under EC competition law and counter-claim for damages.[84] Licence agreements appear to be a typical example for which such situations may arise. These developments argue for giving special consideration to choice of law in competition law matters even in the intra-European context.

5. *Conclusions for Rome I and Rome II*

What are the conclusions to be drawn from the foregoing analysis for the future design of a Rome I and a Rome II Regulation?

Considering the Rome II Regulation first, it is necessary to analyse the adequacy and the consequences of the general choice-of-law rule on non-contractual relationships in Article 3 of the Proposed Regulation. Article 3(1) provides for the application of the law of the country of the so-called direct damages. In competition law matters this formula may effectively be interpreted in the sense of the effects doctrine. However, the overriding rule of Article 3(2) of the Proposed Regulation providing for the application of the law of the common country of habitual residence of the two parties is most inappropriate in the field of competition law, as it sets aside the application of the legislature of the country where the restrictive agreement affects the market. Application of the escape clause of Article 3(3) would be even less appropriate. This clause authorises the courts to apply a different law if the non-contractual obligation is manifestly more closely connected with another country. Such a manifestly closer connection is deemed to be present if the non-contractual obligation is closely connected with a contract. In the field of restrictive agreements, the escape clause of Article 3(3) could have to be understood in the sense of assessing the compliance of the licensing agreement with the competition law of the country whose law is applicable to the contract. However, application of

---

[83] See, in general, *Josef Drexl*, Die neue Gruppenfreistellungsverordnung über Technologietransfervereinbarungen im Spannungsfeld von Ökonomisierungen und Rechtssicherheit, [2004] Gewerblicher Rechtsschutz und Urheberrecht Internationaler Teil (GRUR Int.) p. 716.

[84] This was the situation in the *Courage* case.

this law, which may be chosen freely by the parties to the agreement, would manifestly contravene the public policy of the country of the relevant market.

What rules should then be adopted? The following principles and provisions seem appropriate:

(1.) Non-contractual relationships arising from a restraint of competition, such as an illegal licensing agreement, should be governed by the effects doctrine. The European legislature would be well advised to formulate an Article 5(1) covering both unfair competition and restraints of competition.

(2.) In addition, the effects doctrine should explicitly be made applicable to the nullification of a contract. Insofar as this rule refers to Article 81(1) and (2) EC, this would already be the law under Article 23(1) 2nd indent of the proposed Rome II Regulation, giving precedence to Community rules that apply irrespective of the national law governing the non-contractual obligation in question. However, the rule proposed would provide more transparency from the perspective of private international law.

Another issue relates to the question of whether such a rule on nullification should be implemented in the Rome I or the Rome II Regulation. Nullification of a restrictive agreement is not an issue of non-contractual obligation *stricto sensu* but nevertheless arises from tortuous anticompetitive behaviour. This is why it would seem perfectly appropriate to implement such a rule in a specific choice-of-law provision relating to competition in the Rome II Regulation. Still it is rather a matter of taste whether it should better be adopted in the Rome I Regulation, thereby replacing Article 7(1) of the Rome Convention in the field of competition law.

(3.) Opposition to the application of foreign competition laws also with regard to private relationships largely stems from the concern that such laws might collide with the economic policy of the forum. Such concern counts in favour of a cautious approach and a *loi de police* qualification in the sense of the current Article 7(1) of the Rome Convention. However, maintenance of Article 7(1) would not take into account the fact that a clear choice-of-law approach is needed when courts have to decide on the applicable domestic law of a Member State on damages arising as a consequence of a violation of EC competition law. In addition, within the Community legal system, conflicting goals of domestic competition laws may not arise in the first place, because European law would set aside the application of unjustified domestic laws.[85]

---

[85] According to Art. 3(2) Regulation 1/2003 (*supra* note 61), domestic competition law may be applied along with EC competition law but may not prohibit behaviour that would be allowed under Art. 81 EC. The situation is different in the field of unilateral restraints. Here, domestic competition laws may apply stricter standards within the scope of application of Community law. In addition, domestic merger control law may prohibit mergers below the turnover thresholds of the Merger Control Regulation involving undertakings domiciled in different Member States. Although, under these rules, domestic competition law can have a negative impact on cross-border economic activities within the EU, such cross-border application of domestic law is controlled by the Community principles of the fundamental freedoms.

Consequently, more caution is also needed when, under the proposed bilateral choice-of-law rules, courts have to apply the competition law of a third state, like in our example of the Franco-Swiss licensing case.[86] Nevertheless, a limitation of the proposed rule to intra-EU scenarios does not seem appropriate. Reasons for which competition policies may conflict can be of a very different nature and, therefore, cases relating to third states should not all be dealt with alike.

The first scenario, which should not be exempted from regular choice-of-law application, relates to the well-known exemption of export cartels from domestic competition laws. In more general terms, domestic laws and EC competition law, protecting solely the common market, do not address out-bound restraints initiated in the national territory but affecting only foreign markets. This exemption for out-bound restraints promotes exports and the international competitiveness of domestic undertakings. Conversely, the application by domestic courts of foreign competition law to such restraints in the field of private enforcement would undermine the national policy. However, there is a fundamental difference between the refusal to apply one's own laws to out-bound restraints and the refusal to apply the foreign law of the affected market in such cases. Whereas there is no public international law obligation to prohibit out-bound restraints under domestic law,[87] refusal to apply the foreign law undermines the competition policy of the foreign state, although the competition policy of the foreign state may well be in full conformity with substantive competition policy in the forum. Whereas the application of a rule of public order requires that the foreign law interferes with the policy of the forum, in the context of the export cartel exemption, we rather have to face the reverse situation. The law of the forum and the rejection of the application of the law of the country of the affected market would interfere with the competition policy of that other state. Hence, the argument of public order cannot justify the non-application of the foreign law in such a situation. In addition, application of the foreign law, for example to the issue of nullification, would promote harmony between the decisions of courts of different countries. In the example, French and Swiss courts would both reject the effectiveness of the licensing agreement if Swiss law considered the agreement anticompetitive.

In a second scenario, the result would be different. Foreign competition law may provide for much stricter rules than domestic law, thereby restraining economic freedom to act abroad for undertakings settled in the forum state. In the field of licensing, domestic laws of countries that are net-importers of technology may be excessively restrictive under the clout of competition law so as

---

[86] *Supra* IV.1.

[87] See, however, proposals to provide for an international prohibition of such outbound restraints: *Josef Drexl*, International Competition Policy after Cancún: Placing a Singapore Issue on the WTO Development Agenda, [2004] World Competition (forthcoming); *Eleanor M. Fox*, International Antitrust and the Doha Dome, 43 [2003] Virginia J. Int'l L. 911, at 918-921.

to further the access of domestic undertakings to technology. In such instances, corrective regimes are required, which might be formulated in the sense of a specific *ordre public* clause. The same situation arises if the same behaviour would affect not only the foreign market, but simultaneously the common market or the market of a Member State. In such situations courts within the EU should not prohibit application of the foreign law to a behaviour that is considered legal according to EC competition law. The proposal for a specific provision of public order could read as follows:

> The competent court shall refuse to apply the competition laws of a state that is not a member of the European Union or the European Economic Area to a behaviour which would be considered illegal under such laws but legal under the competition law of the European Community
> i) if that behaviour is implemented by an undertaking settled in the European Union or the European Economic Area or
> ii) if that behaviour also affects competition within the European Union or the European Economic Area.

(4.) Still, this proposed rule does not capture the problem highlighted by the decision of the U.S. Court of Appeals for the District of Columbia in the *Empagran* case according to which foreign plaintiffs can sue foreign defendants before U.S. courts in application of US antitrust laws in order to recover damages sustained exclusively abroad.[88] Since there were also victims of the restraint in the U.S., who had settled their case, there was an anticompetitive effect on the U.S. market. Despite possible application of the effects doctrine and illegality of the horizontal price cartel among pharmaceutical companies under European law, the decision appears illegitimate, since it solely covered damage abroad. Application of U.S. law in this particular sense, which would be the consequence of the choice-of-law rules that have been proposed so far, would not be acceptable. The Supreme Court has recently reversed the decision of the Court of Appeals.[89] Nevertheless, the Rome II Convention should protect against such extraterritorial application. The following provision would serve this objective:

> The competent court shall refuse to apply the law of a state insofar as such law grants a right to recover damages incurred outside the territory of that state.

(5.) Finally, non-contractual obligations arising from restraints of competition should be excluded from the principle of ex-post free choice of law as proposed by the Commission in Article 10 of a Rome II Regulation. Such choice of law would allow the parties to undermine the public policy of the law applicable under the effects doctrine.

---

[88] *Empagran S.A. et al. v. F. Hoffmann-La Roche Ltd. et al.*, 315 F.3d 338 (D.C. Cir. 2003).

[89] *F. Hoffmann-La Roche Ltd. et. al. v. Empagran S.A. et al.* (decision of 14 June 2004; not yet officially reported); <http://a257.g.akamaitech.net/7/257/2422/14june20041300/www.supremecourtus.gov/opinions/03pdf/03-724.pdf>.

V. Concluding Remarks

This analysis highlights the interaction between contract law, tort law and competition law. This interaction requires closer scrutiny of the underlying choice-of-law issues in the Rome II Regulation. Adoption of the effects doctrine in competition law matters should be preferred to the application of the general choice-of-law rules on non-contractual obligations.

The Rome Convention in its present form does not sufficiently take into account the needs of the Internal Market. Application of the mandatory rules of the law of the consumer's habitual residence may produce barriers to cross-border distribution of subject matter protected by IPRs. Cautious reform of Article 5(2) of the Rome Convention in favour of extending the scope of free choice of law seems possible for intra-Community relationships to the extent that harmonised European standards of consumer contract law provide an adequate Community-wide level of protection.

When licensing their rights outside their trade or profession, copyright owners in particular have to be considered consumers as defined by Article 5(1) of the Rome Convention. However, it is doubtful whether this provision covers only mandatory rules drafted to protect consumers or whether Article 5(1) covers all mandatory rules as long as the definition of a consumer is fulfilled. Obviously, the drafters of the Convention ignored a potentially uneven distribution of bargaining power in the area of consumer contracts. The foregoing analysis raises the question of whether European Community law should implement a specific choice-of-law rule protecting creators in contractual relationships.[90]

---

[90] Germany, in 2002, adopted mandatory rules guaranteeing authors fair remuneration for their rights, that are now considered as a model for other jurisdictions in the EU; see *F. Willem Grosheide*, A German Revolution that Deserves Support – Some Reflections on the Introduction of the Iustum Pretium in the German Copyright Contract Law 2002, in: Ulrich Loewenheim (ed.), Urheberrecht im Informationszeitalter, Festschrift für Wilhelm Nordemann, Munich (C.H. Beck) 2004, p. 447 (arguing for a differentiation between two different types of contractual relationships, namely personal copyright and entrepreneurial copyright).

Internationally Mandatory Rules in Copyright Licensing Agreements

HAIMO SCHACK

I. Problem

With the statute of March 22, 2002, on the strengthening of the contractual position of authors and performers,[1] § 32b has been added to the German Copyright Act (UrhG). This section determines under specified conditions (*infra* II) the mandatory application of singular provisions of the German Copyright Act that serve to protect the authors and performers and shall also prevail upon a foreign proper law of the licensing contract. These provisions concern the author's claims to an adequate remuneration and to a further participation in unexpected profits according to §§ 32 and 32a UrhG. These two provisions ensure the enforcement of the basic principle of participation in German copyright law: whenever possible, the author should participate in the economic fruits reaped by the licensee.[2] The legislator has emphasized this function of the copyright in the newly added second sentence of § 11, and elaborated on it in §§ 32 and 32a UrhG.

The intention of § 32 UrhG is to make sure that at the time of the conclusion of the licensing contract the stipulated remuneration is fair and reasonable. If it is not, "the author may request the other contracting party to consent to an adaptation of the contract that grants the author the adequate remuneration"

[1] Bundesgesetzblatt [BGBl.] [Federal Gazette] 2002 I, p. 1155, in force since July 1, 2002.

[2] Entscheidungen des Bundesgerichtshofs in Zivilsachen [BGHZ] 17, 266, 282 – Grundig-Reporter; BGHZ 141, 13, 35 with further references = Juristenzeitung [JZ] 1999, 1000 with annotation *Schack* – Kopienversanddienst; *Schack*, Urheber- und Urhebervertragsrecht, 2d ed. Tübingen 2001, marginal nos. 86, 373 [cited as UrhR].

(§ 32[1] third sentence UrhG). To favor the author, this correction claim has been made unilaterally mandatory and circumvention-proof (§ 32[3] UrhG).

Apart from that, § 32a UrhG takes up the bestseller provision of the old law (former § 36 UrhG) and allows the author to request an adaptation of the licensing contract in case it appears *ex post* "that the stipulated remuneration ... is conspicuously out of proportion to the returns and advantages from the use of the work." In this case, the licensee[3] has to grant the author an additional adequate participation (§ 32a [1], first sentence UrhG). This correction claim may not be waived in advance, nor is the author allowed to assign it in advance (§ 32a[3] UrhG).

After the clarification of 2003, both provisions apply not only to authors but also to performers if they don't transfer their exploitation rights outright (§ 79[1] UrhG[4]), but license them instead (§ 79[2], second sentence UrhG).

In the law of obligations, the general rule is that the parties can freely choose the law applicable to their licensing contract (Art. 27 EGBGB).[5] With that, the intended protection of the author is in danger of getting lost if the exploiting party is in a position to impose the "choice" of a foreign law more favorable to itself.[6] In practice, this will usually be the case. With the vast majority of today's licensing contracts being simultaneously connected to several countries, and the exploitation rarely being confined to the licensee's place of business, Art. 27(3) EGBGB is not applicable. Therefore, the parties are not restricted to a simple choice of the substantive law as in Art. 27(3) EGBGB, which would leave the mandatory provisions of the German copyright contracts law unaffected. Instead, the parties may comprehensively choose the law governing their contract, including one that leaves the author rightless after a total buy-out. The legislators realized this danger when they dropped the (ill-conceived) claim by law to an adequate remuneration and replaced it, in accordance with the system, with a contractual claim for an adaptation of the remuneration.[7] In the very last minute the Law Committee of the German Bundestag inserted the

---

[3] Or, instead, his transferee or sub-licensee if the conspicuous disproportion has occurred with the latter, § 32a(2) UrhG. Regardless of its qualification, this quasi-contractual claim is subject to § 32b no. 2 UrhG. For the comparable situation in § 822 Civil Code [BGB], cf. *Kreuzer*, in: Münchener Kommentar zum Bürgerlichen Gesetzbuch, vol. 10, 3d ed. Munich 1998, I vor Art. 38 EGBGB, marginal no. 22 with further references.

[4] In the version of the statute of September 10, 2003, on copyright in the information society, BGBl. 2003 I, p. 1774.

[5] EGBGB = Introductory Code to the German Civil Code, in conformity with Art. 3 of the Rome Convention of June 19, 1980, on the law applicable to contractual obligations, BGBl. 1986 II, p. 809 (in the version of November 29, 1996, BGBl. 1998 II, p. 1421).

[6] Cf. *Wilhelm Nordemann*, Das neue Urhebervertragsrecht, Munich 2002, § 32b UrhG, marginal no. 1.

[7] In retrospect on the copyright contracts law reform of 2002, cf. *Schack*, Urhebervertragsrecht im Meinungsstreit, Gewerblicher Rechtsschutz und Urheberrecht [GRUR] 2002, 853-859, at p. 853; and with the same title *Erdmann* GRUR 2002, 923-931, at p. 924.

special connecting norm of § 32b UrhG.[8] The aim of this provision is clear: to block the exploiter's flight into a foreign contract law and thus contribute to the author actually receiving an adequate contractual remuneration.

II. Prerequisites of Application of § 32b UrhG

Accordingly, the first of the two alternative prerequisites of application in § 32b UrhG is that in the absence of a choice of law, the licensing agreement would be governed by German law. The objective connecting factor under Art. 28(2) EGBGB = Art. 4(2) of the Rome Convention is the habitual residence, or respectively the central administration, of the party who is to effect the performance that is characteristic of the contract. According to the overwhelming opinion, this leads to the law of the country where the licensee – e.g., a publishing house – has its center of administration, because it is from there that the exploiter organizes the performance of its obligations, such as the reproduction and distribution of the work.[9] This conforms to the so-called "principle of the least disturbance"[10] that protects the conflict of laws interest of businesses in having all their mass transactions, if possible, governed by the same substantial law. Therefore, if the licensee's center of administration is in a foreign country, § 32b no. 1 UrhG won't help the German author. Only in the rare cases that the licensee is under no obligation to actually exploit the work but has to pay only the license fee must the characteristic performance be seen in the granting of the license by the author.[11]

---

[8] Report of the Law Committee, Bundestagsdrucksache [BTDr.] 14/8058 of January 23, 2002, p. 20, based on the second formulation assistance of the Federal Ministry of Justice of January 14, 2002. For a collection of the materials on the reform of the copyright contracts law, see *Hucko*, Das neue Urhebervertragsrecht, Halle 2002, pp. 91 et seqq. As to the course of this piece of legislation, cf. *Haas*, Das neue Urhebervertragsrecht, Munich 2002, pp. 1 et seqq., 125 (with a synopsis of the legal texts at pp. 137 et seqq. and materials at pp. 163 et seqq.); and also *Hilty/Peukert*, Das neue deutsche Urhebervertragsrecht im internationalen Kontext, GRUR International [GRUR Int.] 2002, 643-668, at pp. 643 et seq.

[9] Cf. Bundesgerichtshof [BGH] GRUR 1980, 227, 230 – Monumenta Germaniae Historica; BGH GRUR 2001, 1134, 1136 – Lepo Sumera; *Katzenberger*, in: *Schricker*, Urheberrecht Kommentar, 2d ed. Munich 1999, vor § 120 UrhG, marginal no. 157 with further references; *Hausmann*, Möglichkeiten und Grenzen der Rechtswahl in internationalen Urheberrechtsverträgen, in: Festschrift für Wolf Schwarz, Baden-Baden 1988, 47-74, at p. 54; *Nordemann-Schiffel*, Zur internationalen Anwendbarkeit des neuen Urhebervertragsrechts, in: Festschrift für Wilhelm Nordemann, Munich 2004, 479-491, at pp. 480 et seq.; *Schack*, UrhR, marginal no. 1143.

[10] *Kegel/Schurig*, Internationales Privatrecht, 9th ed. Munich 2004, p. 660.

[11] Cf. *Schack*, UrhR, marginal no. 1144 with further references; *Walter*, in: *Loewenheim* (ed.), Handbuch des Urheberrechts, Munich 2003, § 57, marginal no. 167; *Katzenberger*, Urheberrechtsverträge im IPR und Konventionsrecht, in: Urhebervertragsrecht, Festgabe Schricker, Munich 1995, 225-259, at p. 253; *von Welser*, in: *Wandtke/Bullinger*, Praxiskommentar zum Urheberrecht, Munich 2002, vor § 120 UrhG, marginal no. 24; Law Committee (*supra* note 8), p. 20

In practice, § 32b no. 2 UrhG will be much more relevant as far as the object of the contract is substantial exploiting activities in Germany.[12] These may be the reproduction and especially the distribution of the work and its communication to the public. In the meaning of the statute, *substantial* refers to all exploiting activities that are not so trivial as to be disregarded in common licensing contracts,[13] like an unavoidable over-spill. If the licensee causes a use worth mentioning of the work in Germany, the author is due an adequate remuneration. § 32b no. 2 UrhG thus applies regardless of whether the foreign contract law has been chosen by the parties or rendered applicable by the objective connecting factor of the exploiter's center of administration.[14]

The mandate to apply German law in § 32b UrhG, however, becomes operative only if there is a basis of jurisdiction for the author to bring his action in Germany. For disputes under a licensing contract with a foreign exploiter residing in a country to which the Brussels Regulation[15] applies, this will rarely be the case because foreign exploiters will insist on a choice of a non-German forum,[16] not the least in order to avoid an application of §§ 32 et seqq. UrhG. Thus, even the special choice of law rule of Art. 34 EGBGB[17] is no absolute guarantee for enforcement of the author-protecting norms of the German Copyright Act. This is especially true for the § 32a(2) UrhG claim to an additional remuneration against a sub-licensee residing in a foreign country. If the licensing contract is governed by a foreign law, the German legislators can

---

[12] Only in the case of no. 2 ("soweit") is the correction claim limited to the fruits of the exploitation in Germany; *von Welser*, Neue Eingriffsnormen im internationalen Urhebervertragsrecht, Praxis des Internationalen Privat- und Verfahrensrechts [IPRax] 2002, 364-366, at pp. 365 et seq.; *Nordemann-Schiffel* (*supra* note 9), at pp. 483 et seq. Otherwise, i.e., under German law governing the contract or in the case of § 32b no. 1 UrhG, all acts of exploitation, wherever they occur, are to be taken into account; *Nordemann* (*supra* note 6), § 32b UrhG, marginal no. 4; *Nordemann-Schiffel* (*supra* note 9), at pp. 481 et seq.; *Dreier/Gernot Schulze*, Urheberrechtsgesetz Kommentar, Munich 2004, § 32b UrhG, marginal nos. 7 and 9 with further references. In any case, however, in order to determine the adequacy of the remuneration, the complete set of circumstances has to be examined, including the fruits of exploitation in other countries.

[13] *von Welser* IPRax 2002, 365. *Christian Berger*, Das neue Urhebervertragsrecht, Baden-Baden 2003, marginal no. 338, brings the examples of the buffer storage of a work on a German server and (misguidedly) the production of copies if they are not also distributed in Germany; rightly against the latter, *Dreier/Schulze* § 32b UrhG, marginal no. 9.

[14] Report of the Law Committee (*supra* note 8), p. 20; *Haas* (*supra* note 8), marginal no. 476.

[15] Council Regulation no. 44/2001/EC of December 22, 2000, on jurisdiction and enforcement of judgments in civil and commercial matters [EuGVO]; corresponding to Artt. 2 et seqq. of the Brussels and Lugano Conventions.

[16] Art. 23(1) EuGVO; for salaried authors, see the restrictions in Artt. 23(5), 21 EuGVO.

[17] The provision corresponds to Art. 7(2) Rome Convention (*supra* note 5). As to intervention rules of the forum state, cf. *Heldrich*, in: *Palandt*, Bürgerliches Gesetzbuch, 63d ed. Munich 2004, Art. 34 EGBGB, marginal no. 1; *Kropholler*, Internationales Privatrecht, 5th ed. Tübingen 2004, § 52 IX, pp. 490 et seqq.; *Sonnenberger*, Eingriffsrecht – Das trojanische Pferd im IPR oder notwendige Ergänzung?, IPRax 2003, 104-116, at p. 107.

only hope that the judges in other EU Member States follow Art. 7(1) of the Rome Convention in giving effect to the mandatory rules of the German law (here: §§ 32 and 32a UrhG), i.e., that they apply a third country's intervention norms.[18] Besides, Germany would decline to do so, having made the reservation under Art. 22(1)(a) of the Rome Convention.

That was the comparably easy part. With § 32b UrhG, the German legislator has clearly pronounced what he wants. That he can't ensure the practical realization of those norms on the international level is a different matter, and in the end due to the fact that inside the European Union international jurisdiction according to Art. 3(2) EuGVO can no longer be based upon the presence of property belonging to the defendant as, e.g., in § 23 of the German Civil Procedure Code.[19]

III. Other Mandatory Rules Protecting the Author

The question in how far other author-protecting rules of German copyright law are meant to be internationally mandatory is much more complicated. "Dealings with rights in copyright"[20] are (not only in Germany) in many ways restricted in order to protect the intellectual and personal interests of the author. The starting point in § 29(1) UrhG is the principle of non-transferability of the copyright, allowing merely the licensing of exploitation rights under § 31(1) UrhG. In addition, the transfer or sub-licensing of exploitation rights is in principle subject to the author's consent (§§ 34[1], 35 UrhG). Furthermore, the author enjoys several revocation rights (§§ 41, 42 and most recently § 34[3] second sentence UrhG), and the presumption in § 31(5) UrhG that the scope of his contractual license shall be limited to the purpose of the grant. Very important in practice is § 31(4) UrhG, declaring null and void any licenses and contractual obligations for as-yet-unknown types of uses. And finally, contracts for future works may always be terminated after five years (§ 40 UrhG).

Whoever wants to use Art. 34 EGBGB to push through all kinds of author-protecting rules against any applicable foreign copyright (contract) law[21]

---

[18] Cf. *Schack* GRUR 2002, 857; *Hilty/Peukert* GRUR Int. 2002, 657 et seq.

[19] Cf. only *Schack*, Internationales Zivilverfahrensrecht, 3d ed. Munich 2002, marginal nos. 196, 332.

[20] See the caption of the fifth chapter before §§ 28 et seqq. UrhG containing restrictions on the transfer of copyright und some rules on copyright contract law.

[21] E.g., *Schricker/Katzenberger* (*supra* note 9), vor § 120 UrhG, marginal no. 166; *Katzenberger* (*supra* note 11), pp. 255 et seq.; *Hartmann*, in: *Möhring/Nicolini*, Urheberrechtsgesetz Kommentar, 2d ed. Munich 2000, vor § 120 UrhG, marginal no. 45; with the same result *Stefan Mäger*, Der Schutz des Urhebers im internationalen Vertragsrecht, Berlin 1995, p. 286 (rather unconvincingly, cf. *my* book review in Archiv für Urheber-, Film-, Funk- und Theaterrecht [UFITA] 132 [1996] 310-315), *Loewenheim*, Rechtswahl bei Filmlizenzverträgen, Zeitschrift für Urheber- und Medienrecht [ZUM] 1999, 923-927, at p. 926. To the contrary,

misunderstands the basic principles of conflict of laws. Each and every mandatory rule of German law is not for that reason also an internationally mandatory rule under Art. 34 EGBGB. The privileged treatment of economically or socially motivated mandatory rules in Art. 34 EGBGB is a special case of the public policy exception (Art. 6 EGBGB), which must only be used with the utmost restraint. The foundation of conflict of laws is the equivalence of all legal systems, however different they may be in the individual case. Therefore, we generally have to start with the presumption that the foreign copyright law, made applicable by the German choice of law rules, has in store the necessary minimum of author-protecting rules.[22]

For §§ 32, 32a UrhG, the German legislator has enacted a special connecting rule, probably under the correct assumption that its newly created instrument to safeguard the adequate remuneration for the author finds no parallel in foreign copyright laws. As to all *other* author-protecting rules, however, the question of their international scope of application has been left open. An *argumentum e contrario* § 32b UrhG might be considered at most for the revocation right of the author, which has also been introduced by the recent copyright contracts law reform in § 34(3) second sentence UrhG in case the exploiter's enterprise has been sold. But a more convincing argument against any remote consequences of § 32b UrhG is that this rule was only added at the very last minute and should therefore address nothing other than the specific problem expressly mentioned.

Before thinking about any public policy exception in international copyright law, whether in the form of the general exception in Art. 6 or of the special connecting rule in Art. 34 EGBGB, one has to know to which choice of law rules the different connecting objects belong (characterization). While § 32 and § 32a UrhG concern only the amount of the promised quid pro quo and therefore clearly belong to the proper law of the contract, all the other mentioned connecting objects are in the borderland between the proper law of the contract and the law governing the transfer of the right. The (non-)transferability is an attribute of the right contracted for and thus a given for the proper law of the contract. The revocation rights, too, have an *in rem* aspect if exercising them leads to the lapse of the license, even if their root – as in § 34(3) second sentence UrhG or in the case of a revocation for non-exercise in § 41 UrhG – lies in a disturbance of the contractual relationship. The same applies for the *in rem* effects of legal termination rights as in § 40(3) UrhG.

---

and rightly so, *Hilty/Peukert* GRUR Int. 2002, 649 et seq.; *von Welser*, in *Wandtke/Bullinger* (*supra* note 11), § 32b UrhG, marginal no. 2, and in IPRax 2002, 365.

[22] Cf. *Schack*, UrhR, marginal no. 1148.

IV. Delimitation of the Proper Laws of the Copyright and the Contract

Therefore, the primary task is the delimitation of the respective scopes of application of the proper laws of the copyright and the contract. This conceptual distinction is self-evident in the international property law of physical things. It applies exactly the same way in the field of international *intellectual* property law, regardless of how one determines the governing copyright law. If, e.g., the relevant *lex rei sitae* (Art. 43[1] EGBGB) declares a religious or museum object to be a *res extra commercium,* the resulting non-transferability is governed exclusively by the law of the physical location of the object, and the parties are not free to leap over that result.[23] The same applies to restrictions on copyright transfers, especially as they would miss their function if they were at the disposal of the proper law of the contract. The latter is typically determined by the center of administration of the exploiter or by a choice of law clause favorable to him,[24] and is therefore hardly able to effectively protect the author.

Whether a transfer is dependent on – or, as in principle in German law, abstracted from[25] – the underlying contractual obligation, in any case both have to be neatly distinguished as a matter of conflicts law.[26] The transfer itself, the limits of transferability, and also the *in rem* effects of a revocation of exploitation rights[27] are all questions that fall under the proper law of the copyright and not of the contract.[28]

Where the law allows the author to terminate a licensing agreement after some specified time, as in the United States with the termination right after 35 years,[29] limiting the transfer in time is supposed to allow the author to regain

---

[23] Cf. *Schack*, Kunst und Recht, Cologne 2004, marginal no. 502.

[24] See *supra* I. and II.

[25] As to the (controversial) validity of the principle of the abstract nature of the transfer of real rights in German copyright law, cf. BGHZ 27, 90, 95 et seq. – Privatsekretärin; BGH GRUR 1982, 369, 371 – Allwetterbad; *Schack*, UrhR, marginal nos. 525 et seqq.; *Rehbinder*, Urheberrecht, 13th ed. Munich 2004, marginal no. 322(3).

[26] *Schack*, UrhR, marginal nos. 913, 1147; *von Welser*, in *Wandtke/Bullinger* (*supra* note 11), vor § 120 UrhG, marginal no. 22; *Andreas Wille*, Die Verfügung im internationalen Urheberrecht, Sinzheim 1997, pp. 101 et seq.

[27] Cf. §§ 41(5), 42(5) UrhG; as to § 34(3) second sentence UrhG, cf. *Koch-Sembdner*, Das Rückrufsrecht des Urhebers bei Unternehmensveräußerungen, Göttingen 2004, pp. 163 et seq.

[28] As in the text *Hausmann*, Festschrift Schwarz (*supra* note 9), pp. 64 et seq. Cf. also Art. 33(2) EGBGB and the corresponding Art. 12(2) of the Rome Convention.

[29] But under § 203(b)(5) Copyright Act 1976 limited to "grants that arise under this title" (17 U.S.C.), i.e., to exploitation acts in the United States; cf. *Patry*, Choice of Law in International Copyright, AmJCompL 48 (2000) 383-470, at p. 447. As to the German law *de lege ferenda* against such a territorial limitation of the termination right, *Clemens Kohnen*, Die Beendigung von Nutzungsrechten im US-amerikanischen und deutschen Urheberrecht, Göttingen 2004 (in print), ch. 3 B III 3 a aa. A similar termination right was discussed during the 2002 reform of the German copyright contracts law (cf. *Schack* ZUM 2001, 453, 460), but has as yet not been enacted into law.

control of his work. This aim is independent from the proper law of the contract and shows that the issue here – as with the split term of protection ("renewal") that has been replaced by the termination right in 1978 – is the content and transferability, i.e., questions of the proper law of copyright.[30]

The question of *how* the proper law of copyright shall be determined is much disputed in Germany. The still-prevailing opinion subjects the whole of copyright – its accrual, content, transfer, and extinction – to the law of the country for which protection is claimed (*lex loci protectionis*). This way the copyright decays into a bundle of independent national rights. It is most difficult and cumbersome to join all these mosaic pieces together for a coherent transnational exploitation. That's why a growing number of legal authors demand a differentiated copyright conflicts rule[31] which might eventually be extended to other informal IP rights.[32]

While the content and limitations of copyright are in unison subject to the law of the protecting country, the disputed but central preliminary questions of the accrual, transfer, and transferability of copyright must be determined consistently by the law of the country of origin (*lex originis*), i.e., in general, the country where the work was first published.[33] This stable connecting rule is finding more and more followers both in and outside Germany, not the least under the impression of worldwide exploitation of works in the Internet.[34] Unchangeably subject to the country of origin must be the central issues of the first ownership of the copyright[35] and especially the here interesting aspects of

---

[30] Differently *Kohnen* (preceding note), ch. 3 B III 7 b, who wants to enforce the propagated termination right against a foreign contract law by way of § 32b UrhG because the legal termination right supplements the author's claim to an adequate remuneration.

[31] For the foundation, see *Schack*, Zur Anknüpfung des Urheberrechts im internationalen Privatrecht, Berlin 1979; *idem*, UrhR, marginal nos. 887 et seqq.; *idem*, Internationale Urheber-, Marken- und Wettbewerbsrechtsverletzungen im Internet, MultiMedia und Recht [MMR] 2000, 59-65.

[32] Cf. *Ropohl*, Zur Anknüpfung der formlosen Markenrechte im Internationalen Privatrecht, Göttingen 2003.

[33] Cf. *Schack*, UrhR, marginal nos. 900-903.

[34] From this perspective for the universality principle, see *Intveen*, Internationales Urheberrecht und Internet, Baden-Baden 1999; *Muth*, Die Bestimmung des anwendbaren Rechts bei Urheberrechtsverletzungen im Internet, Frankfurt/Main 2000.

[35] *Schack*, UrhR, marginal no. 912; *Kegel*, in *Soergel*, Kommentar zum Bürgerlichen Gesetzbuch, vol. 10, 12th ed. Stuttgart 1996, nach Art. 12 EGBGB, marginal no. 29; *von Welser*, in *Wandtke/Bullinger* (*supra* note 11), vor § 120 UrhG, marginal no. 11, and in IPRax 2003, 441; *Michael Burian*, Audiovisuelle Werke im russischen und deutschen Urheberrecht, Baden-Baden 2003, pp. 266 et seqq., 277; *Fawcett/Torremans*, Intellectual Property and Private International Law, Oxford 1998, p. 512; *Torremans*, The Law Applicable to Copyright, Revue internationale du droit d'auteur [RIDA] 188 (2001) 37-115, at pp. 75, 83; Itar-Tass Russian News Agency v. Russian Kurier, Inc., 153 F.3d 82 (2d Cir. 1998) = GRUR Int. 1999, 639 with annotation *Schack*; *Patry* AmJCompL 48 (2000) 410 et seqq.; cf. also *Ginsburg*, Die Rolle des nationalen Urheberrechts im Zeitalter der internationalen Urheberrechtsnormen, GRUR Int. 2000, 97-110, at p. 107. – Contra BGHZ 136, 380, 387 = JZ 1998, 1015 with annotation *Schack* – Spielbankaffaire.

the transfer[36] and the transferability[37] of the copyright. Consequently, the proper law of transfer is that of the country of origin. This law also governs the presumptions in §§ 31(5), 88(1), 89(1), 92 UrhG on the scope of the transfer or the license,[38] insofar as the presumptions do not bear upon the contractual obligation but on the transfer as such. An important aspect of transferability is the prohibition in § 31(4) UrhG of licensing as-yet-unknown uses.[39]

Nevertheless, the prevailing opinion in Germany, as already noted, applies the law of the protecting country to the transfer[40] as well as to the transferability of the copyright.[41] That inescapably leads into the impasse of the mosaic concept. In view of the growing worldwide marketing of copyrights and licenses, this is untenable in any orderly system of conflict of laws.

Realizing this has tempted quite a number of adherents of the majority opinion to throw the most basic distinction between the proper laws of the contract and of the transfer overboard and to apply the law of the contract also to the transfer[42] and the transferability[43] of the copyright. It is true that this leads to only one law being uniformly applied, but the proper law of the contract is most inappropriate where, as in our case, the conflict of laws protection of the weaker party is at issue. If the law doesn't protect the author – in

---

[36] *Schack*, UrhR, marginal nos. 914 et seq., including its abstract nature, cf. *Schack*, Anknüpfung (*supra* note 31), no. 115; *Kohnen* (*supra* note 29), ch. 3 B III 3 a bb. For a case of reversion of rights under the German law of the country of origin see French Cour de cassation, chambre civile, RIDA 189 (2001) 357, 359 – Films sans frontières.

[37] *Schack*, UrhR, marginal no. 917; *Alfons Braun*, Die internationale Coproduktion von Filmen im IPR, Munich 1996, p. 187; *Patry* AmJCompL 48 (2000) 431 et seqq., 469 et seq.

[38] Cf. also Art. 11bis(3) first sentence of the Berne Convention (Paris revision of 1971).

[39] Contradictory *von Welser* IPRax 2002, pp. 365 and 366.

[40] *Mackensen*, Der Verlagsvertrag im internationalen Privatrecht, Munich 1965, pp. 65 et seqq.; *Knörzer*, Das Urheberrecht im deutschen IPR, (dissertation) Mannheim 1992, pp. 120 et seqq.; *Siehr*, Internationales Privatrecht, Heidelberg 2001, pp. 291 et seq.; OLG München ZUM 1999, 653, 655 et seq. – Eine Stadt sucht einen Mörder; cf. also BGHZ 118, 394, 397 – Alf (for an American licensor as the proper plaintiff).

[41] BGH GRUR 1988, 296, 298 – GEMA-Vermutung IV (to § 31[4] UrhG); BGHZ 136, 380, 387 – Spielbankaffaire (later decision in the same case: OLG München MMR 2002, 312, 314 with annotation *Haupt*); *Eugen Ulmer*, Die Immaterialgüterrechte im internationalen Privatrecht, Cologne 1975, no. 69; *Katzenberger* (*supra* note 11), p. 258; *Hausmann*, Festschrift Schwarz (*supra* note 9), p. 64; *Fawcett/Torremans* (*supra* note 35), pp. 515 et seq.; *Torremans* RIDA 188 (2001) 95.

[42] *Ulmer* (preceding note), no. 67; *Drobnig*, Originärer Erwerb und Übertragung von Immaterialgüterrechten im Kollisionsrecht, Rabels Zeitschrift für ausländisches und internationales Privatrecht [RabelsZ] 40 (1976) 195-208, at pp. 203 et seq.; *Walter* (*supra* note 11), § 57, marginal nos. 190 et seq.; *Loewenheim* ZUM 1999, 925; *Markus Junker*, Anwendbares Recht und internationale Zuständigkeit bei Urheberrechtsverletzungen im Internet, Kassel 2002, p. 188; *Nimmer*, Who is the Copyright Owner When Laws Conflict?, GRUR Int. 1973, 302, 303; OLG Frankfurt/Main GRUR 1998, 141, 142 – Mackintosh-Entwürfe. Same for the revocation rights of §§ 41, 42 UrhG *Katzenberger* (*supra* note 11), pp. 251, 258.

[43] *Nimmer* GRUR Int. 1973, 303.

contrast to consumers or employees[44] in Artt. 29, 30 EGBGB (= Artt. 5, 6 Rome Convention) – from the freedom of the stronger party to choose the applicable law, it is categorically impermissible to re-characterize the copyright rules of protection and hand them over just to the proper law of the contract.[45]

Behind the transferability restrictions stand important interests of author protection that can be realized only through the proper law of copyright which – regardless of how it is determined – is not at the parties' disposal. That is true not only for the unchangeable law of the country of origin but also for the *lex loci protectionis*. Here again, one must clearly distinguish the *lex loci protectionis* governing the content of the copyright from the *lex loci delicti* governing the consequences of its violation.[46] According to Art. 42 EGBGB, only the law of the tort is accessible to an *ex post* choice of law,[47] but not the content of the infringed right![48] But as the mosaic concept inherent in the *lex loci protectionis* is unacceptable for the parties and also for the courts which happen to be confronted with transborder copyright cases more and more often, the only way in conformity with the conflicts system is applying the law of the country of origin to all questions relating to the transfer of the right.

V. Solution

This qualification decision solves the problem: Beyond § 32b UrhG, the question is no longer about a special connecting rule in the meaning of Art. 34 EGBGB to impose German copyright law against a foreign proper law of the contract. At issue instead is simply the application of the proper law of copyright designated by the German conflict rules (subject to a *renvoi*, Art. 4[1] EGBGB). If this is a foreign copyright law, it will be applied unless it is "manifestly incompatible" with the public policy of the German forum (Art. 6 EGBGB). Such exceptional circumstances will be rare – and probably not less so than in international property law in general. As long as we apply the correct

---

[44] Art. 30 EGBGB applies also to salaried authors; cf. *Hilty/Peukert* GRUR Int. 2002, 648; *von Welser*, in *Wandtke/Bullinger* (*supra* note 11), § 32b UrhG, marginal nos. 6, 8; *Dreier/ Schulze* (*supra* note 12), § 32b UrhG, marginal no. 5 with further references. § 32b UrhG applies irrespective of the place of employment and therefore is neither redundant nor superseded by Art. 30 EGBGB as *lex specialis*; contra *Haas* (*supra* note 8), marginal no. 482.

[45] Cf. *Schack*, UrhR, marginal nos. 914, 917.

[46] Overlooked by *Strömholm*, The immovable lex loci delicti in international copyright law, in: Aufbruch nach Europa, 75 Jahre Max-Planck-Institut für Privatrecht, Tübingen 2001, 517-527, at pp. 523 et seqq. Not sufficiently clear, also Art. 8(1) of the proposal of July 22, 2003, of an EU Regulation on the law applicable to non-contractual obligations ("Rome II"), COM(2003) 427 final.

[47] Cf. *Schack*, UrhR, marginal no. 925 with further references; *Möhring/Nicolini-Hartmann* (*supra* note 21), vor § 120 UrhG, marginal no. 37; explicitly in Switzerland, Schweiz Art. 110(2) IPRG.

[48] Only insofar correct, BGHZ 136, 380, 386 = JZ 1998, 1015, with in other respects critical annotation *Schack* 1019 – Spielbankaffaire.

indiscriminate conflicts rule with good judgment we'll rarely have to turn to special connecting rules, which must necessarily disrupt the conformity of decisions in different jurisdictions and which, as the example of § 32b UrhG shows, may in practice not even attain the desired result. The fewer special connecting rules the better. This is also and especially true in the bewildering field of international IP law.

Discussion: Contractual Obligations

FRIEDRICH WENZEL BULST and CHRISTIAN A. HEINZE

Drexl's proposal to allow for free choice of law in many consumer contracts within the Internal Market was criticized for overestimating the extent and success of harmonization of consumer protection within the Community and for overemphasizing supplier interests. The law on unfair contract terms was used as an example of substantial differences among the laws of the Member States and their application despite harmonization. Furthermore, as the Brussels I Regulation provides for exclusive jurisdiction at the domicile of the consumer in the usual case, the availability of choice of law would frequently lead to the application of foreign law, which would make consumer litigation overly expensive. In addition, in the Internet context, application of the consumer's law may be regarded as the natural consequence of the supplier's decision to direct its business activity to consumers in all Member States. It was argued that the supplier could easily avoid this consequence by requiring consumers to disclose their country of origin and by only contracting with consumers residing in its home state. In addition, confidence of consumers in electronic commerce would be served best by application of the laws of their habitual residence. Many businesses were reported to have articulated their willingness to comply with this objective.

In defense of his initial proposal, *Drexl* invoked more recent consumer protection directives (e.g., consumer credit) which moved away from minimum harmonization, as well as the recent ECJ decision on tobacco advertising which emphasized the importance of the Internal Market. He also referred to small and medium-sized undertakings that would find it difficult to comply with 15 or more different consumer laws. He considered it unrealistic for businesses engaging in electronic commerce to limit their economic activity to consumers from certain jurisdictions. It should therefore be left to competition between enterprises whether or not they offer to apply the law of the consumer's origin to their contracts. The eBay system was proposed as a model for consumer dispute resolution without legislation, and the EC was encouraged to promote this kind of self-regulation. However, there was also a concern that eBay may not be typical of consumer disputes because of eBay's neutral role, for which there would be no equivalent in purely bilateral consumer-business relationships.

In the course of the discussion of *Metzger's* paper, it was agreed that the application of Article 4 of the Rome Convention to license agreements could be easily resolved only in cases where the sole duty of the licensee was to pay royalties. In that case, the law of the licensor ought to be applied because the situation is comparable to a sale of goods. For more complex contracts such as distribution agreements, no general solution was readily at hand. There was some disagreement as to how the debate over whether copyright is primarily based in natural law or part of national trade policy was to be resolved.

Part 3: Non-contractual Obligations

Community IP Rights and Conflict of Laws

WINFRIED TILMANN

I. Introduction

There are three existing Community IP Titles: Community Trademark (CTM), Community Design (CD), and Community Plant Breeders' Rights (CPBR). The international private law of Member States would refer to the Community Titles themselves for all relevant legal questions because the territory of protection is the Community. This would apply to the non-contractual legal questions regarding the transfer of rights, the rights on the IP, licenses, the scope of protection, and civil side questions.

However, the Community Titles do not contain rules for all those questions. They refer to national law solutions regarding quite a number of questions of that kind. Therefore, we have before us a "hybrid law situation": the legal answers are partly given by the Community Titles themselves, and partly by the national law to which they refer.

Regarding the extent of that mixture: The CTM (1993) and the CD (2001) are rather similar. Astonishingly, the CPBR (1994) is more advanced than the CD (seven years later). The Community Patent (CP, probably decided in 2004) goes even farther than the CPBR.

II. The Community Trademark (CTM)

Let us start with the CTM. In which questions can we notice a "hybrid situation"? It is true for the CTM as an object of transactions. It is further true for the desist order and the defense against that. It is particularly true for the other sanctions in case of infringement. And there is a general catch-all clause referring to national law. If a CTM court that is competent for the whole

Community is used (Art. 2 of the Brussels Regulation: the court at the seat of the defendant), that court may, in the case of a multi-state infringement, be forced to inform itself and apply the national law of quite a number of Member States.

For the CTM as an object of transactions, the CTM Regulation contains specific rules in Art. 17 to 23 on the change of rights, the rights on the CTM and, besides others, the license. If these specific rules do not cover the legal question, Art. 16 contains a catch-all clause. It refers to the law of the state where the CTM owner has his seat or residence. If he has no seat or residence within the Community, the law of Spain applies (the seat of the CTM Office).

Therefore, the CTM court may have to apply the law of another state. However (and this is an advantage), the court must apply only one foreign law, not the law of many states. Still, there may be problems because the seat may have changed or the law may have changed. The relevant factors are the seat and the law when the act concerning the CTM took place.

At first sight, the desist order does not seem to present a big problem. This order is regulated in Art. 98 I. However, the defendant may raise quite a number of private law defenses. Parts of these defenses are regulated in the CTM Regulation itself, such as the right to use a name or to use descriptive words (Art. 12) or the exhaustion of rights (Art. 13).

For all other defenses, Art. 14 refers to Title X and, by this, to Art. 98 II, which refers to the law of the infringement state, including its international private law. This is problematic because the court may be forced to apply many foreign laws in case of multi-state infringement.

The application of the enforcement rules for the sanctions is not a difficult job: Art. 98 II sentence 2 refers to the law of the CTM court itself.

As I said, CPBR is more advanced than the CTM: The CPBR Regulation also contains rules for the damage claim and for adequate remuneration (if there is no negligence on the part of the infringer). The compensation claim (regarding the time between publication of the application and the grant) and the claim for unlawful enrichment are not regulated. In both cases, the CPBR refers to the national law of the infringement state, not, however, to its international private law. Furthermore, the CPBR contains a rule that there would be no other referrals to national law. Therefore, the courts will have to decide on the regulated sanctions (example: damages) in all respects.

Now to the main problem: the unregulated sanctions, Art. 98 II. The CTM refers to the national law of the infringement state, including its international private law, forcing the court with a competence for the Community as a whole (Art. 2 Brussels Regulation: Court of the Seat of the Defendant) to apply a multitude of foreign laws in a multi-state infringement case. Some authors (Knaak, Festschrift Tilmann 2003, 373/378) have argued that the referral could be one regarding the general international law of torts, which would lead to the law of the country where the infringing *act* took place. I doubt whether this solution is viable. The referral in an IP text will certainly be a referral to the IP law of the other state. Furthermore, the solution does not help if the infringer himself *acts* in a multitude of states.

Can we expect an improvement on unregulated sanctions in the CTM Regulation by Art. 8 II of the draft Rome II Regulation (draft of July 22, 2003) which refers to the *act* of infringement in regard to Community Titles? This is the same solution that *Knaak* and others have proposed regarding the existing law. However, this solution does not help in cases where the infringer himself *acts* in a multitude of states (Leible/Engel, EuZW 2004, 7/13).

There will be a certain reduction of complexity if the draft Directive on Sanctions for IP Rights materializes. However, it will be a directive with a minimum standard allowing for stricter rules in Member States. Therefore, the differences of law will not be abolished. Still, the deviations from the minimum standard will be known to the courts of Member States rather soon, so they can serve as a kind of benchmark.

Regarding all other unregulated questions, the CTM Regulation refers to the law of the CTM court. If it is the court according to Art. 2 of the Brussels Regulation (seat of the defendant), it must apply its international private law, thus being forced to apply the rules of a multitude of other Member States if we have a multi-state infringement. There is no problem if the CTM court is used as the infringement court (Art. 5 No. 3 of the Brussels Regulation), because then the court will apply its own law.

If we try to evaluate the "hybrid situation" in the three existing Community Titles, the smallest problem seems to exist regarding the Community Titles as the object of legal actions (for instance: transferal, license). The Community Titles contain specific rules. They refer to national law only in the unregulated part, but only to one national law.

A different situation exists regarding the sanctions. Regarding the desist order, the private law defenses of the defendant are subject to national law (not to the Community Title). The unregulated sanctions also follow national law regarding multi-state infringements of a plurality of the law of Member States. In all these critical points, the Rome II draft will bring only a limited improvement. The same is true for the Directive on Sanctions.

III. Community Patent

The Community Patent Regulation (draft) seems to simplify the questions because it provides for a Central Court regarding infringement and the decision on validity. However, the opposite is true. There will be no national Community Patent Court that can be used as the referral point to apply national law. I will deal with four separate cases.

The first case concerns a European claim that will be decided upon by a national court. This is true for the inventor's vindication (Art. 5). However, it is a European claim, Art. 30, which describes the competence of the Central Court but does not contain a referral to Art. 5. This means that this claim must be decided by national courts.

The reason for this is that in many cases there are vindication claims of employees, and the laws regarding the inventions of employees are very different between Member States. This exclusion is certainly much too broad, since it excludes the competence of the Central Court for vindication claims of persons other than employees as well.

The law to be applied regarding inventions of employees is regulated in Art. 4 II in the same way as in Art. 60 EPC: The law of the state where the employee is working is applicable; if that is not given, the state where the employer entertains his enterprise will apply.

The second case is that the Central Court applies national law. This is true regarding the CP as object (Art. 14). Here we find the same rules that apply to the CTM (examples: transferal, license). If there is no rule in the CP Regulation, there is a referral to the law of the Member State where the patent owner has his seat or his residence; in the last order it is referred to Germany as the seat of the European Patent Office.

Who should decide on those national law rules? It should be the Central Court. Art. 30 does not contain jurisdiction for that; however, this competence is given implicitly because it is a part of the question of the right to sue. Otherwise, the Central Court would be blocked by defenses of that kind.

The third case is that national courts decide on national law. This is the normal case. An example: The claimant raises claims out of a license contract. The international private law side is covered by Rome I.

A problematic case four is marked by the specialty that European law and national law must be applied at the same time. The CTM Regulation regulates the sanctions in case of infringement. However, there may be a multitude of civil law side questions (for instance, regarding damages: Has the claim been fulfilled or not?) and of civil law defenses (Tilmann, GRUR Int. 2003, 381/386 f.).

How should the Central Court deal with these "hybrid situations" and the private law part of these situations? I believe that the Central Court (part of the European Court of Justice) will try to apply the private law common to all Member States in easy questions. If there are difficult questions, the Central Court must apply a national law. However, it is difficult to see which national law it should apply because there is no national CP court whose law could be addressed. There is no solution except, perhaps, applying the law of the seat of the EPA (German law). It is clear that this complex situation increases the pressure to promote the development of a Community private law.

IV. Conclusion

The territoriality principle regarding Community Titles does not render a practical solution, because the Community Titles do not contain private law solutions for all private law questions. Therefore, they must refer to the law of Member States, and in difficult cases they must refer to a multitude of laws of Member States.

The Community Patent Regulation makes things more difficult because for many questions there is no rule which tells us which law of which Member State must be applied. The draft Rome II and the Directive on Sanctions will improve the situation, but will not resolve its complexity.

The progress of the Community in the field of IP Community Titles is breathtaking, especially the creation of a Central Court to decide private law questions in the absence of Community private law. However, as in the past, IP law will force legislators – this time the Community legislators – to take steps to come to a civil law on the Community level.

Unfair Competition Law Protection Against Imitations: A Hybrid under the Future Art. 5 Rome II Regulation?

MATTHIAS LEISTNER*

I. Introduction

The Commission Proposal for a Regulation on the law applicable to non-contractual obligations (Rome II Proposal)[1] provides in its Art. 5 for an autonomous connection for actions for damage arising out of an act of unfair competition. Apart from its main field of application, i.e., the choice of law applicable to advertising practices, this provision will be of considerable relevance for the protection of intellectual property. This is because in most Member States, the case law on unfair competition (and sometimes even explicit statutory provisions in this field) provides for a protection of certain commercial products against unfair imitations by competitors. Art. 5 Rome II Proposal will be of particular practical importance in this field, as substantive law standards concerning "unfair imitations" differ considerably throughout Europe. However, Art. 5 Rome II Proposal in its present (amended) form shows a certain ambiguity regarding acts of unfair copying, as it remains unclear if these acts should be assessed under Art. 5 par. 1 or under Art. 5 par. 2 Rome II Proposal. The following considerations attempt to answer the question of how acts of unfair imitation should be qualified under Art. 5 Rome II Proposal. The

* The lecture form has been maintained, adding only some indispensable references.
[1] COM (2003) 427 final of July 22, 2003.

proposed solution shall be compared to the established principles in this particular field of private international law and shall be evaluated critically, taking into account the main objective of the Regulation, i.e., the completion of the internal market. With respect to this main objective, some points of more general interest regarding substantive law harmonization in the field of unfair competition can also be made as a result of the analysis of private international law.

The issue can hardly be discussed without a certain understanding of substantive law standards in the field of unfair competition in what follows. First, the legal situation regarding actions against unfair imitations in the Member States shall be outlined briefly (see *infra* II). Second, the development of Art. 5 Rome II Proposal in the legislative process will be analyzed and the resulting provision in its present form will be evaluated and compared to the private international principles regarding unfair competition in the national laws of the Member States (see *infra* III). This analysis provides the background for the discussion of how to interpret Art. 5 Rome II Proposal with respect to acts of unfair imitation (see *infra* IV). Finally, the proposed solution shall be evaluated regarding the objectives of the Rome II Proposal and some points of more general interest shall be made (see *infra* V).

II. Substantive Law Background

1. National Law of the Member States

In very general terms, it can be said that while in most continental European Member States a comprehensive concept of unfair competition including actions against unfair imitations by competitors is established, in the United Kingdom and in Ireland such a comprehensive concept does not exist. In part, however, unfair imitations can be actionable in these latter countries under the general tort of "passing off."

Taking Germany as an example for the continental European approach, it can be said that unfair imitations by competitors are assessed under the general clause of the German Unfair Competition Act. The act provides for a general prohibition of unfair commercial practices in order to protect the interests of competitors, collective interests of consumers, and the general public interest in undistorted competition.[2] However, according to traditional doctrine and case law – which is based on an e contrario argument on the grounds of the particular limits of the established instruments for exclusive IP protection, which in principle shall prevail over the more flexible unfair competition law assess-

---

[2] This threefold monistic purpose of unfair competition law has been established in case law; for an early example, cf. *Federal Supreme Court – "Suwa"*, 1957 GRUR 365, 367. The pending reform of the German Unfair Competition Act will lead to an explicit provision acknowledging this classic trinity of objectives of unfair competition law (§ 1 of the new Act).

ment – businesses in principle are free to imitate products of their competitors. Hence, supplementary protection under unfair competition law is restricted to protection against particularly unfair imitations. Therefore, such supplementary protection is (in theory) only granted if additional circumstances (beyond the mere fact of imitation itself) exist that qualify the behavior of the offender as particularly unfair.[3] Since the action against unfair imitations was originally rooted in the concept of protection against misrepresentation, the most important of these criteria are the question of possible customer confusion regarding the origin of a particular product, and the assessment of possible damage to the goodwill of a competitor.[4] Other criteria include the technique of imitation (namely slavish and direct imitations are treated very rigidly[5]), the substantiality of the investment of the claimant, the market position of the claimant's product, as well as the specific creative features of this product. However, despite all these assessment criteria and the principle of freedom of imitation in competition, unfair competition protection law has in fact been developed in case law in some fields – namely regarding the slavish and direct copying of aesthetic creations – into a proper supplementary protection instrument for original subject matter which does not qualify for exclusive IP protection. The most important examples from German case law include the protection of fashion novelties[6] and other designs,[7] such as the shape of a cosmetic box[8] or the design of a particular set of bedclothes,[9] but also the imitation of complex technical characteristics of a product.[10] In summary, while in principle unfair competition law protection is granted only against particularly unfair imitations, in practice in Germany, as in most of the continental European Member States, this action – particularly in cases of almost identical reproduction – has developed into a flexible protection system for creative products that do not qualify for exclusive IP protection. Particularly, even when no substantial confusion in the market is created regarding the origin of the product, the free-riding on the reputation of a competitor can trigger unfair competition protection against direct imitations.[11]

---

[3] Cf., for example, *Schricker,* Urheberrecht-Kommentar, 2nd ed. 1999, Einführung, pt. 36 et seq.

[4] See lately *Federal Supreme Court – "Les-Paul-Gitarren",* 1998 GRUR 830.

[5] In these cases, the *Federal Supreme Court* regards a possible free-riding on the reputation of a competitor as sufficient for triggering the unfair competition protection, even when no confusion in the market is created at all; cf. *Federal Supreme Court – "Les-Paul-Gitarren",* 1998 GRUR 830. Cf. also *infra* in the following text.

[6] Cf. *Federal Supreme Court – "Modeneuheit",* 1973 GRUR 478, *Federal Supreme Court – "Pullovermuster",* 1992 GRUR 448.

[7] Cf. *Federal Supreme Court – "Les-Paul-Gitarren",* 1998 GRUR 830.

[8] Cf. *Federal Supreme Court – "Ovalpuderdose",* 1976 WRP 370.

[9] Cf. *Federal Supreme Court – "Buntstreifensatin II",* 1969 GRUR 292.

[10] Cf. *Federal Supreme Court – "Rollstuhlnachbau",* Judgment of 17 June 1999 – I ZR 213/96.

[11] Cf. *Federal Supreme Court – "Les-Paul-Gitarren",* 1998 GRUR 830.

Contrast this with the legal situation in the United Kingdom and Ireland. No comprehensive concept of unfair competition exists in these countries. The continental European "general clause" of unfair competition is here functionally replaced by some specific actions of common law and equity, and (in the advertising law field) by a particularly highly developed system of self-regulation.[12] As for protection against imitations by competitors, the common law tort of passing off is particularly relevant. In its traditional form, this tort provides for the principle that "nobody has the right to represent his goods as the goods of somebody else."[13] Therefore, the three main elements of the traditional form of a passing off action are, first, goodwill or reputation attached to the product of the claimant; second, a misrepresentation by the defendant to the public leading or likely to lead the public to believe that products offered by him are products of the claimant; and third, this misrepresentation results or is likely to result in a damage to the claimant by reason of the erroneous belief of the public regarding the source of the defendant's products.[14] It can be seen clearly that the passing off action under English law is based much more clearly on misrepresentation than the broader form of unfair competition under continental European systems. However, common law has also developed an extended form of passing off. In this extended form, the action can apply more generally to acts of misrepresentation which injure another trader's goodwill or reputation.[15] While this paves the way for applying the tort of passing off to the protection of whole classes of products (as in the "Champagne" cases[16]) or even more generally to indications of origin (as in the "Swiss Chocolate" cases[17]), still the need for a misrepresentation to customers

---

[12] The main body of self-regulation is the so-called CAP (Committee of Advertising Practices) Code. Decisions upon complaints of competitors or customers under the CAP Code are made by the Advertising Standards Authority (ASA), which is composed proportionally with representatives of businesses and consumer associations. See further on the English self-regulation system *Jergolla,* Die Werbeselbstkontrolle in Großbritannien 2003.

[13] *Reddaway v. Benham* (1906) AC 199 HL.

[14] Cf. the reformulation of the "classic" definition of passing off per Lord Oliver in the *"Jif Lemon"* case, *Reckitt & Coleman v. Borden* [1990] RPC 341 HL.

[15] Cf. the authoritative modern formulation of passing off in the *"Advocaat"* case per Lord Diplock, *Warnink v. Townend* [1980] RPC 31: "*Spalding v. Gamage* and the later cases make it possible to identify five characteristics which must be present in order to create a valid cause of action for passing off: (1) a misrepresentation (2) made by a trader in the course of trade, (3) to prospective customers of his or ultimate consumers of goods or services supplied by him, (4) which is calculated to injure the business or goodwill of another trader (in the sense that it is a reasonably foreseeable consequence) and (5) which causes actual damage to a business or goodwill of the trader by whom the action is brought or (in a *quia timet* action) will probably do so."

[16] Cf. the *Spanish Champagne* cases, *Bollinger v. Costa Brava* [1960] RPC 16 and *Taittinger SA v. Allbev Ltd.* [1993] F.S.R. 641, CA; as well as the *English Sherry* case, *Vine Products v. Mackenzie,* [1969] RPC 1.

[17] *Chocosuisse v. Cadbury,* [1999] RPC 117 per Laddie J; followed by *Chocosuisse v. Cadbury* [1999] RPC 826 CA.

remains a crucial condition of a passing off action. Hence, although the action has been stretched into a somewhat broader concept of unfair competition as far as a more general protection against misleading of consumers which damages the goodwill of another trader is concerned, it has not developed – as in the continental European countries – into a general protection against the misappropriation of the investment and creations of competitors which is – at least in cases of slavish and direct imitations – to some extent independent from the existence of any form of misrepresentation.[18] Especially from the viewpoint of English lawyers, this is seen as a fundamental dividing line between the continental European and the English approach to unfair competition, which they believe should not be shifted in the direction of the more comprehensive approach of continental European systems.

2. *Level of European Harmonization*

Consequently, European harmonization in the fields of unfair competition law and of consumer protection law has always consciously avoided tackling the issue of the protection of competitors against acts of unfair competition.

For this reason, though the Misleading Advertisements Directive[19] established the monistic "trinity" of protection purposes (competitors, consumers, and the general public) of unfair competition law known from the continental European concepts, it neither extended protection against acts of unfair competition beyond the scope of misleading forms of advertising, nor did it provide for a real harmonization of the individual actions of competitors against misleading advertisements. Similarly, and even more remarkable, although the new Proposal of the Commission for a Directive concerning unfair business-to-consumer commercial practices in the internal market ("Unfair Commercial Practices Directive")[20] provides for a fairly comprehensive harmonization approach regarding unfair competition, it thoroughly avoids the issue

---

[18] Remarkably, the development in the United States in this respect differed somewhat from the development in the Commonwealth countries. Already in 1918, in the *INS* case (248 US 215 [1918]) the *Federal Supreme Court* developed a broader concept of unfair competition that covered *misappropriation* in addition to misrepresentation. This classic authority, however, has remained rather isolated, even in U.S. case law, and never been taken over by English or Australian courts. Cf. further on the impact and reception of the *INS* case *Ohly,* Richterrecht und Generalklausel im Recht des unlauteren Wettbewerbs, 1997, p. 81 et seq.

[19] Directive 84/450 of 10 September 1984, in the version of Directive 97/55 of October 6, 1997, OJ L 290 of 23.10.1997, p. 18 et seq.

[20] COM (2003) 356 final, for the Directive Proposal of 2003. Cf. also, most recently, European Parliament legislative resolution on the proposal for a European Parliament and Council directive concerning unfair business-to-consumer commercial practices in the Internal Market and amending Directives 84/450/EEC, 97/7/EC and 98/27/EC (the Unfair Commercial Practices Directive) (COM(2003) 356 – C5-0288/2003 – 2003/0134(COD)), Doc. P5_TA-PROV(2004)0298 of 20 April 2004; Political Agreement of the „Competitiveness" Council on the Unfair Commercial Practices Directive Proposal, 2003/0134 (COD) of 25 May 2004.

of protection of competitors against acts of unfair competition, consequently not covering protection against unfair imitations at all.[21] In summary, it can be held that no specific harmonization measures have yet been taken in this field. There are no concrete plans for harmonization either.

However, some instruments of Community law have a considerable indirect relevance for the area of unfair competition law protection against imitations. First, the European Regulation on Community Designs,[22] apart from introducing protection for registered designs, provides for broad, unitary, Community-wide, three-year protection for unregistered designs based on the mere substantive conditions of sufficient novelty and individual character. This Community right is additional to the potential supplementary unfair competition protection in most of the continental European laws. Actually, this effective protection instrument might well replace the comparably weaker supplementary unfair competition law protection in a long-term perspective, particularly because it seems capable of delivering a higher degree of legal certainty than the flexible concept of unfair competition. However, at present the relationship between these two instruments is still not completely clear; unfair competition law protection could well remain relevant as a "safety net" for creations below the individuality and novelty threshold of the Regulation. The remedy provided in the Regulation is injunctions and the usual accessory means. With respect to further ongoing national sanctions (i.e., damage claims), for the time being the choice of law question is left to the law of the Member States by Art. 89 (1) lit. d) Community Design Regulation. However, according to Article 8 (2) of the Rome II Proposal, the applicable substantive law in cases of infringements of Community rights under the future Rome II Regulation would be the law of the Member State in which the act of infringement is committed.

The second instrument that is worth mentioning is the E-Commerce Directive of 2000.[23] Although this Directive does not harmonize substantive law in the field of unfair competition, it provides for the application of the principle of mutual recognition in the whole coordinated area of the Directive, covering all provisions directly or indirectly relevant to commercial communications in the Internet, and particularly the field of unfair competition law as

---

[21] Unfair Commercial Practices Directive – Explanatory Memorandum, COM (2003) 356 final, par. 40. Critical to this limited approach, *Leistner,* Unfair Competition or Consumer Protection, in: *Cambridge Yearbook of European Studies,* Vol. 6 2004, forthcoming; now cf. also the statement of the German government preceding the Political Agreement of the „Competitiveness" Council on the Unfair Commercial Practices Directive Proposal, 2003/0134 (COD) of 25 May 2004, Annex 2.

[22] Council Regulation (EC) No. 6/2002 of December 12, 2001, on Community Designs, OJ L 3, of 5.1.2002, p. 1 et seq.

[23] Directive 2000/31/EC of the European Parliament and of the Council of June 8, 2000, on certain legal aspects of information society services, in particular electronic commerce, in the internal market, OJ EC 2000 L 178, p. 1-16.

far as Internet communications are concerned. The impact of this provision is twofold. On the one hand, regarding Internet marketing it provides businesses with the necessary legal certainty that they have to comply only with the standard of their country of origin. On the other hand, as far as the coordinated area of the E-Commerce Directive reaches, since there is no significant substantive law harmonization, it has been argued that the Directive could possibly lead to the danger of a race to the bottom between the Member States regarding substantive law standards. If this danger were real it would be of considerable significance in the field of unfair competition law protection against imitations because this area is not harmonized at all. Because the country-of-origin provision, as a second ("correction") step, will considerably influence the outcome of the application of the choice of law provision of Art. 5 Rome II Proposal,[24] this should be kept in mind as we move on to the analysis of the legislative development of Art. 5 and to the questions regarding its application to acts of unfair imitation.

III. Art. 5 Rome II Proposal – Legislative Development and General Evaluation

1. Legislative Development

Art. 6 of the Commission's Draft Proposal (the provision that has now become Art. 5 in the official Proposal) already provided for a choice of law rule essentially oriented at the market effects of an act of unfair competition. At the same time, this "market effects" rule already echoed the objectives of unfair competition law as they are laid down in the Misleading Advertisements Directive, namely the "horizontal" protection of the interests of competitors and the "vertical" protection of the interests of consumers in an undistorted competition:

> Art. 6 – Unfair competition and other unfair practices
> The law applicable to a non-contractual obligation arising from unfair competition or other unfair practices shall be the law of the country where the unfair competition or other practice affects competitive relations or the collective interests of consumers.

While the general reaction to Art. 6 Draft Proposal in the consultation process was very positive, some points of criticism regarding the formulation and the "fine tuning" of the provision were made. To start with the more technical points of criticism first, it was correctly observed that the wording of Art. 6 Draft Proposal as well as the formulation of the general principle in Art. 3 Draft Proposal (in remarkable difference to Art. 5 no. 3 Jurisdiction and Judgments

---

[24] Cf. further on the co-application of Art. 5 Rome II Proposal and the principles of mutual recognition in different acts of Community secondary law, *Leistner*, in: *Drexl/Kur* (ed.), IP and Private International Law – Heading for the Future (forthcoming 2004).

Regulation[25]) did not cover the possibility of *ex ante* injunctions.[26] Consequently, the Commission broadened the formulation of the new Art. 5 (1) in the official Rome II Proposal by including not only acts that affect competitive relations or the collective interests of consumers, but also acts that are *likely* to affect those relations and interests. This formulation now clearly includes *ex ante* injunctive relief, which aligns Art. 5 Rome II Proposal with the jurisdiction rule in Art. 5 no. 3 of the Jurisdiction and Judgments Regulation.[27]

Second, various commentators remarked that the choice of law criteria developed in different national laws to deal with so-called spill-over situations[28] – which all try to exclude, on the basis of a more or less objective (or subjective) standard, the application of the laws of countries where competition is not *substantially* affected[29] – could hardly be based on the original wording of the draft proposal which did not include such a limitation at all.[30] The present formulation of Art. 5 (1) of the official Rome II Proposal now allows at least the exclusion of insignificant influences on third countries in "traditional" media spill-over situations, where an act of unfair competition is neither (subjectively) directed nor (objectively) apt to influence a third market directly and substantially.[31]

---

[25] Council Regulation 44/2001 of December 22, 2000, on jurisdiction and the recognition and enforcements of judgments in civil and commercial matters, 2001 OJ EC L 12, p. 1.

[26] Cf. for example the Comments of the *Hamburg Group for Private International Law,* 2003 RabelsZ 2, at 19.

[27] A corresponding amendment has been made in Art. 3 (1) Rome II Proposal. Therefore, this gap, which also existed with respect to the general rule of Art. 3 of the original Draft Proposal, has now been closed in both provisions.

[28] As, for example, the different criteria (language, relevance of disclaimers, currency, and so forth) German jurisdiction and doctrine have considered in order to make the question of *substantial* market effect more operable. For a short overview with further references, cf. *Leistner,* Werberecht im Internet, in: *Bettinger/Leistner* (ed.), Werbung und Vertrieb im Internet, p. 5, at 48 et seq.

[29] Cf. from German case law, *Federal Supreme Court* – "*Tampax*", 1971 GRUR 153, at 154.

[30] Cf. as one example *Deutscher Rat für Internationales Privatrecht,* Stellungnahme der 2. Kommission des Deutschen Rates für Internationales Privatrecht zum Vorentwurf eines Vorschlags der Europäischen Kommission für eine Verordnung des Rates über das auf außervertragliche Schuldverhältnisse anzuwendende Recht, available at <http://europa.eu.int/comm/justice_home/news/consulting_public/rome_ii/deutscher_rat_internat_privatrecht_de.pdf> (visited February 5, 2004), p. 17 et seq.

[31] Presumably, the Art. 5 (1) "test," if an act "directly and substantially" influences a third market, will have to be interpreted objectively rather than focusing on the subjective intentions of the offender. With special respect to the two relevant strands of thought in German legal doctrine which either focus (subjectively) on the intentions of the offender or (objectively) on the substantiality of the market effect, and the substantially objective core of both approaches, cf. further *Leistner, supra* note 28, at 48 et seq.

These two very valuable points of criticismas well as some other refinements of formulation are now reflected in Art. 5 (1) of the official Rome II Proposal:[32]

> Art. 5 Unfair Competition
> (1) The law applicable to a non-contractual obligation arising out of an act of unfair competition shall be the law of the country where competitive relations or the collective interests of consumers are or are likely to be directly and substantially affected.
> (2) ..."

Additionally, one more fundamental amendment that is of particular interest for our topic was proposed successfully in the Consultation Process. It was remarked in the Consultation Process that the application of the "market effects" principle is not justified with respect to unfair practices that do not harm a competitor as a reflex of a market distortion but are rather aimed directly at a specific competitor and realize themselves exclusively in the relation to that specific competitor without reflexively distorting the market.[33] Examples of such actions could be the violation of a commercial secret through a competitor, or the enticement of another competitor's employees. In these cases, although a market effect may not always be entirely excluded, the object of the offence is no longer the market, or fair competition as such (*par conditio concurrentium*), but the offended competitor himself. Hence, a mandatory conflict rule in favor of the law of the affected market would be erroneous.[34] Rather, the competitor should have the benefit of the general rules of Art. 3 Rome II, namely its additional country of residence (seat) rule (Art. 3 (2) Rome II proposal), and the flexible opening clause (Art. 3 (3) Rome II proposal) which, for example, in the case of an enticement of employees of a competitor, would allow the *lex causae* to apply to the act of unfair competition , i.e., the law applicable to the employment contracts. The Commission has now adopted

[32] Of course, apart from these "successful" critical recommendations that were considered by the Commission in the amended official Rome II Proposal, many other valuable propositions have been made in the consultation process. Particularly, the proposition of the *Hamburg Group* to introduce an additional private international law country-of-origin rule for cases of inter-Community advertising deserves to be mentioned here. For a comprehensive (and critical) discussion of this particularly far-reaching proposition, see *Leistner,* in: *Drexl/Kur* (ed.), IP and Private International Law – Heading for the Future (forthcoming 2004).

[33] The modern private international law of Switzerland also makes this distinction in Art. 136 par. 2 Swiss Private International Law, and the same approach is taken by Art. 4 (2) of the Dutch Act on Private International Law of 2001. Similarly (with some subtle but significant differences as to German case law, to which we will have to come back, *infra* IV.2.) in Germany, Austria, and Spain it follows from case law that the specific markets effect principle (in Germany derived from case law, cf. *infra* IV.2.; cf. for Austria, § 48 par. 2 Austrian Private International Law; for Spain Art. 4 Ley de la Competencia Desleal) does not apply to acts that target a specific competitor. Cf. *Dethloff,* Europäisierung des Wettbewerbsrechts, 2001, p. 70 et seq.; cf. also Rome II Regulation proposal – Explanatory Memorandum, p. 16; cf. also *Deutscher Rat für Internationales Privatrecht, supra* note 30, p. 26.

[34] Cf. *infra* III.2.

this view in its official Rome II Proposal, and has formulated a new paragraph 2 of Art. 5 which provides for the applicability of Art. 3 (2) and (3) where an act of unfair competition exclusively affects the interests of a specific competitor:

> Art. 5 Unfair Competition
> (1) ... .
> (2) Where an act of unfair competition affects exclusively the interests of a specific competitor, Art. 3 (2) and (3) shall apply.

This provision, quite obviously, is of direct relevance for the question of how to assess acts of unfair imitation under Art. 5 Rome II Proposal, as these cases appear to be on the borderline between acts that merely affect the interests of a specific competitor and acts that result in a significant distortion of the market. Therefore, from the wording it seems far from clear under which paragraph of the new Art. 5 Rome II Proposal acts of unfair imitation (and acts of slavish imitation in particular) should be dealt with. Before this question is discussed, Art. 5 Rome II Proposal shall be briefly evaluated in a more general sense.

2. *General Evaluation*

The market effects principle laid down in Art. 5 (1) Rome II Proposal[35] is by and large in accordance with the choice of law practice in most of the continental European Member States. However, a specific provision to this end exists only in Austria, Spain, and Switzerland (the latter shall be mentioned here although it is not an EU or EEA Member State).[36] In the other Member States, the same result is reached in case law on the grounds of the application and adaptation of the general Private International Law Rule on the *lex loci delicti.*[37]

---

[35] Cf. even clearer Recital 11: "... connection to the law of the relevant market. ..."

[36] Cf. § 48 par. 2 Austrian Private International Law; Art. 4 Ley de la Competencia Desleal; Art. 136 par. 1 Swiss Private International Law. For details, cf. *Dethloff,* Europäisierung des Wettbewerbsrechts, 2001, p. 59 et seq. Cf. also Explanatory Memorandum, p. 16.

[37] The dogmatic method of attaining this result differs from Member State to Member State, and often even within one Member State's legal doctrine. Either it is assumed that with respect to the general rule of the *lec loci delicti,* in cases of acts of unfair competition, the place where the harmful act occurred and the place where the loss is sustained fall together at the place of market effect. Or it is accepted that, concerning acts of unfair competition, only the place where the harmful act occurred is relevant, which then again is assumed to be the place where the action of the defendant directly influences the market. Also, the third possibility has been submitted – to rely upon the place where the direct damage is sustained as the connecting factor under the general rule of *lex loci delicti,* which then again typically would be the place of market effect (where the direct sales losses are sustained by the claimant). For further details, cf. *Dethloff,* Europäisierung des Wettbewerbsrechts, 2001, p. 59 et seq. with comprehensive references. Cf. also Explanatory Memorandum, p. 16.

In quite general terms, in the United Kingdom the guiding principles under the Private International Law Act 1995[38] are essentially the same, although the situation is considerably more complicated because of the characterization problem that arises from the substantive law difference between the much narrower tort of passing off[39] and the broader conceptions of unfair competition in the continental European Member States.[40] Presumably, both *passing off actions* and *unfair competition actions* (the latter on the basis, for example, of some foreign law with a comprehensive unfair competition concept) in general would be dealt with by the English courts under sec. 11 Act 1995, which provides for the *lex loci delicti*. According to sec. 11, the crucial test would then be to determine where the elements of the respective action on which the claimant bases his case have taken place, *i.e.* in the case of *passing off*, where a

---

[38] In the following, reference is made only to the statutory provisions of Part III ("Choice of law in tort and delict") of the Private International Law (Miscellaneous Provisions) Act 1995 (Act 1995), whereas the old common law choice of law rules are not discussed. Although Part III Act 1995, according to sec. 14 (2) and sec. 10 (a) Act 1995, is limited in its scope to the abolition of those common law tort choice of law rules that required double actionability (in both the law of the forum and the law of another country) for the purpose of determining whether a tort was actionable, this condition is fulfilled for the old common law choice of law rules in both areas of substantive law which are of interest here, namely the tort of passing off and the law of unfair competition. This is because in common law, the double actionability rule was applied to cases of passing off (cf. *James Borrough Distillers plc v Speymalt Whisky Distributors Ltd,* 1989 SLT 561), and equally to cases which involved unfair competition under continental European substantive laws (cf. *Alfred Dunhill v Synoptic SA,* [1979] FSR 337). Therefore, the former common law tort choice of law rules in this field are no longer of relevance. Cf. *Fawcett/Torremans,* Intellectual Property in Private International Law, 1998, p. 616 et seq., 653 et seq. and 682.

[39] The actions of *malicious falsehood* and *defamation* shall not be discussed here. Although they might in some fields functionally overlap with continental European unfair competition law actions, they are not particularly relevant for the topic discussed here. For more on English tort choice of law rules in these fields, cf. *Fawcett/Torremans,* Intellectual Property in Private International Law, 1998, p. 669 et seq., 672 et seq.

[40] When an action against an act of unfair imitation is brought before the English courts, essentially three possibilities exist. The case may be pleaded straightforwardly as a case of passing off. In this situation it is to be characterized as an action in passing off with the consequence that sec. 11 Act 1995 applies. The two other possibilities concern situations in which the claimant relies upon foreign unfair competition law, in which case his action may or may not take the (narrower) form of passing off. The latter case is, again, quite straightforward: if the claimant relies upon parts of unfair competition law that are broader than the passing off action, his action is to be characterized as unfair competition. If the claimant, however, relies on a part of unfair competition protection against imitations that take the form of passing off (i.e., when an element of misrepresentation is present), the situation is more difficult. However, it is submitted that even in such cases the better arguments are in favor of characterizing the action as an unfair competition law action. Ultimately, unfair competition in England will presumably also be dealt with under the general tort rule of sec. 11 Act 1995, although the application of this provision in unfair competition actions might differ in nuance from the application of sec. 11 with respect to passing off actions. Cf. comprehensively *Fawcett/Torremans,* Intellectual Property in Private International Law, 1998, p. 652 et seq., 678 et seq.

misrepresentation was made to the customers, where the goodwill of the claimant existed, and where the direct damage was sustained by the claimant. Under the *passing off action*, in the overwhelming majority of cases these three elements will occur in one single country, namely the country where the market is directly influenced by the marketing and sales of the imitations.[41] According to sec. 11 (1) Act 1995, the law of this (market) country would then be applied.[42] With respect to *unfair competition actions* (brought before the English courts on the basis of the substantive law of some other Member State with a comprehensive unfair competition law concept), again, in most cases the elements of the action will all occur in the same country, namely the country where the imitated products or services are marketed. Accordingly, sec. 11(1) Act 1995 would equally lead to the application of the law of the country where the direct effect on the market occurs.[43] In summary, the new English statutory choice of law rules lead in practice to pretty much the same result as the principle in Art. 5 (1) Rome II Proposal.[44] Hence, in summary, it can be held that the principle in Art. 5 (1) Rome II Proposal (for the moment without regard to the displacement rule in Art. 5 (2)) is essentially in line with the choice of law rules in the Member States of the European Union.

---

[41] For the solution in the rare cases of real multi-country passing off, which should be dealt with under the "most significant element rule" of sec. 11 (2) (c) Act 1995, cf. *Fawcett/Torremans,* Intellectual Property in Private International Law, 1998, p. 659 et seq.

[42] It is submitted that this result remains essentially the same, even when a single act of the defendant leads to a multi-state infringement of the claimant, such as when the infringer uses imitated elements on his Internet website for Europe-wide marketing purposes (as for the correction of this result through Art. 3 E-Commerce-Directive, cf. *infra* V). In these cases, the influence on the several national markets would have to be regarded as a series of separate torts of passing off. The elements of the action – a misrepresentation to customers, goodwill of the claimant, and damage – are equally given in all the countries where the market is directly influenced by the activity of the defendant. Cf. further *Fawcett/Torremans,* Intellectual Property in Private International Law, 1998, p. 658 et seq.

[43] Cf. *Fawcett/Torremans,* Intellectual Property in Private International Law, 1998, p. 684 et seq. Equally in the (rare) cases of real multi-country unfair competition, when Art. 11 (2) (c) Act 1995 should be applied, it is submitted that the most significant element of an unfair competition law action would presumably be the direct economic loss to the victim. According to Art. 11 (2) (c) Act 1995, consequently the law of the country(ies) where the direct loss is sustained (namely the loss of sales in the case of the marketing of unlawful imitations) would have to be applied. Cf. for further discussion on that issue (even the application of Art. 11 (2) (b) Act 1995 in such cases has been proposed in English doctrine on the grounds of the doubtful approach that the basis of unfair competition was a property right of the claimant to compete freely [which is quite contentious even in Germany, where this old doctrine was developed originally and has remained a minority opinion, cf. for example *Baumbach-Hefermehl,* Wettbewerbsrecht, 2001, Einl UWG at para 44 et seq.]) *Fawcett/Torremans,* Intellectual Property in Private International Law, 1998, p. 685 et seq.

[44] Additionally, the practice of the main self-regulation institution, the Advertising Standards Authority (ASA), strongly supports this legal viewpoint since the ASA usually renders decisions under the CAP Code on the condition that a marketing measure reaches the English market, without regard to the origin of the advertising company. Cf. *Jergolla,* Die Werbeselbstkontrolle in Großbritannien, 2003, p. 13 et seq.

In European Union law itself, Art. 5 (1) finds a certain precedence in the case law of the European Court of Justice (ECJ) regarding the extraterritorial application of Art. 81 EC. The leading decision of the ECJ in this field provides in effect for a market effects principle comparable to the principle in Art. 5 (1), although not explicitly formulating it.[45] Moreover, as mentioned earlier on, the particular formulation of Art. 5 (1) – taking into account the competitive relations as well as the interests of the customer side of the market – is consistent with the modern institutional approach of the existing European Union directives in the field of unfair competition law, which follow the triple objective of protecting the interests of competitors, consumers, and the public in general in an undistorted competition.[46]

In the systematic context of the future Rome II Regulation, the market effects principle could presumably also be based on the general rule of Art. 3. This is because the country "in which the damage arises or is likely to arise" in unfair competition law is the country where the competitive interests collide;[47] however, this correct interpretation of the *lex loci delicti* is hardly clearly enough established in all the Member States to provide the necessary legal certainty.[48] In this systematic context, Art. 5 (1) Rome II Proposal could be regarded as a necessary and mandatory clarification as to the *lex loci delicti* in cases of non-contractual obligations arising out of an act of unfair competition.[49] Even more importantly, Art. 5 Rome II Proposal was necessary in order

---

[45] *ECJ "Woodpulp" case,* joined cases 89/85, [1988] ECR V-5193. The ECJ calls its test an "implementation" test rather than a market effects test. However, the results of the "implementation" doctrine seem to be essentially the same as under the "market effects" principle.

[46] Cf. Sales Promotion Regulation proposal – Explanatory Memorandum, p. 15.

[47] Consequently, most of the continental European Member States reach the result (of applying the law of the country in which the market is distorted) through a respective interpretation of the *lex loci delicti,* cf. Explanatory Memorandum, p. 16; *Dethloff,* Europäisierung des Wettbewerbsrechts, 2001, p. 59 et seq. Cf. for further details *supra* note 37.

[48] Cf. Explanatory Memorandum, *loc. cit.;* as for the considerable differences in detail, cf. *supra* note 37.

[49] At the same time this makes clear that the new provision in Art. 5 (1) Rome II Proposal would be essentially in line with the jurisdiction rules of the Jurisdiction and Judgments Regulation (*supra* note 25). Apart from the basic jurisdiction of the courts for the place of the defendant's habitual residence, Art. 5 no. 3 Jurisdiction and Judgments Regulation provides for the jurisdiction of the "courts for the place where the harmful event occurred ..." (cf. for the applicability of Art. 5 no. 3 Jurisdiction and Judgments Regulation to individual or collective actions for injunctions in the Unfair Competition and Consumer Protection law field, *ECJ "Henkel",* decision of October 1, 2002, Case C-167/2000, [2002] ECR nyr, available at <www.curia.eu.int>). Although the ECJ has always held that Art. 5 no. 3 Jurisdiction and Judgments Regulation provides for jurisdiction at both the place where the harmful act occurred and the place where the loss is sustained, when these two places are not the same (cf. *ECJ "Mines de Potasse d'Alsace",* decision of November 30, 1976, Case 21/76, [1976] ECR 1735), in case of acts of unfair competition, in a correct interpretation these places would almost always fall together in one place, namely the place where the direct loss (in sales) is sustained by the claimant, i.e., where the market is influenced by the defendant. Cf. for further details *supra* note 37.

to guarantee the mandatory and conclusionary character of the "market effects" rule. Because of the inevitable involvement of the multiple different interests of *all* the competitors and consumers on a given market, as a matter of principle the "market effects" rule should not be subjected to the same exceptions (regarding the law of the common place of residence and the general displacement possibility) as the general rule; these exceptions only make sense in an essentially bilateral relationship. In this respect the new provision will hopefully provide considerable clarification as compared to the national laws of some Member States. Only when acts of unfair competition target a specific competitor without directly affecting the market at all (i.e., in cases of acts which target the operative interests of the competitor without having a direct impact on the market, such as enticement of employees and the like) can the exceptions be applied reasonably.[50] This is exactly the solution which shall presumably be obtained by the two paragraphs of Art. 5 Rome II Proposal, because Art. 5 (2) provides for the applicability of Art. 3 (2) and (3) in essentially bilateral cases. The formulation of this exception, however, leaves considerable room for interpretation, and therefore has to be analyzed more closely.[51] For the moment, nonetheless, it can be held that in principle, the bifurcated provision of Art. 5 Rome II Proposal should be met with approval. However, the reference to Art. 3 (2) and (3) Rome II Proposal should be amended to include the general rule of Art. 3 (1) as well. For acts that exclusively target the operative interests of a competitor and have no direct impact on the market at all, the correct choice of law approach would be to characterize such acts as parts of general tort law rather than to regard them as unfair competition, and therefore the whole provision of Art. 3 Rome II Proposal should be applied.[52]

But what does this mean for acts of unfair imitation in competition? Particularly, do Artt. 5 (2), 3 (2) Rome II Proposal apply to situations of export competition as a displacement rule with the consequence that when both competitors have their seat in the same Member State, but the situation to be assessed regards their competition in another Member State, nonetheless the law of the state of origin can be applied instead of the market law? Here the vague formulation of Art. 5 (2) Rome II Proposal, and particularly some ambiguous comments in the Explanatory Memorandum, lead to considerable legal uncertainty as to the scope of Art. 5 (2). This is of utmost relevance for cases of unfair copying. The matter shall be discussed now.

---

[50] Cf. *supra* III.1.

[51] Cf. *infra* IV.

[52] This shortcoming of Art. 5 (2) Rome II Proposal in its present form has been underlined by *Prof. Peter Mankowski* in the discussion of this paper at the Hamburg Conference.

IV. Unfair Imitations Under Art. 5 Rome II Proposal

1. Autonomous Interpretation of Art. 5 Rome II Proposal

From the wording of Art. 5 (2) Rome II Proposal, it seems at first glance that acts of unfair imitation are not covered by this provision because typically they do not exclusively affect only the interests of a specific competitor, but also have an impact on the interests of customers. Hence the market effect rule would always prevail with respect to acts of unfair imitation. However, this line of reasoning is quite contentious. Particularly in cases of slavish imitation, if there is no clear misrepresentation involved, i.e., if customers typically know that the product is imitated,[53] it could as well be argued that such acts exclusively affect the interests of a specific competitor, namely the producer of the original product.

The systematic comparison with another proposed instrument of substantive Community secondary law, the Unfair Commercial Practices Directive Proposal (concerning unfair business-to-consumer commercial practices in the internal market),[54] reflects a similar approach in substantive unfair competition law. This Directive proposal, as mentioned earlier, although it contains a proper general clause of unfair competition, is merely concerned with business-to-consumer situations and consequently (for reasons which cannot be further specified here[55]) is quite thoroughly limited in its scope and purpose to the protection of consumer interests. Regarding slavish imitations, the Explanatory Memorandum clarifies: "The Directive is concerned only with matters affecting consumers' economic interests. ... [This] also means that acts which constitute unfair competition in some Member States but which do not harm the economic interests of consumers, such as slavish imitation (i.e., copying independently of any likelihood of consumer confusion) ... are outside the scope of the Directive."[56] This seems to imply that slavish imitations do not have an impact on consumer interests at all if no element of misrepresentation is involved. Consequently, regarding Art. 5 Rome II Proposal they would have to be qualified as exclusively affecting the interests of competitors, and therefore be dealt with under Art. 5 (2). Hence, in cases of export competition and slavish imitations, when both competitors have their seat in the same Member State,

---

[53] Cf. for an example of this group of slavish imitations *Federal Supreme Court – "Tchibo/Rolex I"*, 1985 GRUR 876; cf. critically *Beater*, Unlauterer Wettbewerb, 2002, p. 586 et seq.

[54] Proposal for a Directive of the European Parliament and of the Council concerning unfair business-to-consumer commercial practices in the internal market and amending Directives 84/450 EEC, 97/7/EC and 98/27/EC (the Unfair Commercial Practices Directive), Doc. COM (2003) 356 final.

[55] Cf. on this issue *Leistner*, Unfair Competition or Consumer Protection, in: *Cambridge Yearbook of European Studies*, Vol. 6 2004, forthcoming.

[56] Cf. Unfair Commercial Practices Directive – Explanatory Memorandum, COM (2003) 356 final, par. 39 and 40.

the law of this Member State could be applied instead of the market law. However, the test as to whether an element of misrepresentation exists in a certain case of unfair imitation seems quite uncertain because this question can only be answered on normative grounds. Whenever an act of unfair competition (such as unfair imitation) realizes itself via *directly* affecting the market, it will not only have an impact on a specific competitor's interests; it will also inevitably influence the market order on the foreign market (the *par conditio concurrentium*) as such, and hence touch the collective interests of consumers. Therefore, the Art. 5 (2) test in these cases could no longer be such as to ask whether an act of unfair competition has no impact on consumers' interests at all; instead, it would require an assessment of whether the collective interests of consumers are *sufficiently* affected to require the market law to be applied.

The Explanatory Memorandum of the Rome II Proposal sees this problem and delivers a solution by explaining that Art. 5 par. 2 Rome II Proposal "deals with situations where an act of unfair competition *targets* a specific competitor... . It is not entirely excluded that such conduct may also have a negative impact on a given market, but these are situations that have to be regarded as bilateral."[57] However, this is a test quite different from the test as to whether an act of unfair competition affects *only the interests* of a specific competitor. Quite to the contrary, it is acknowledged that an act of unfair competition necessarily almost always has an impact on the interests of competitors *and* of consumers because it influences (either directly or indirectly) the conditions on a given market. Therefore, the Art. 5 (2) test as to whether an act of unfair competition affects *exclusively* the interests of competitors apparently cannot work on such grounds if it is applied at face value.

One alternative would be to interpret Art. 5 (2) in such a way that it applies already if an act of unfair competition affects *mainly* the interests of a competitor, for example, because the act is targeted at a specific competitor. However, this re-interpreted condition would be based heavily upon normative considerations which seem to lack the necessary legal certainty to serve as a reliable choice of law principle. Moreover, it seems to overstretch the scope of the exception to the main principle in Art. 5 (1) Rome II Proposal.[58]

However, the Explanatory Memorandum also suggests a further alternative reading of Art. 5 (2) Rome II Proposal which could provide for the necessary legal certainty. As the formulation cited above shows, the Explanatory Memorandum seems to assume that the crucial condition of the application of Art. 5 (2) Rome II Proposal should be that the situation in question is essentially a *bilateral* situation. With regard to acts of unfair competition, this can only be the case when an act of unfair competition is targeted *directly* at the operational interests of the claimant, and consequently also realizes itself

---

[57] Cf. Explanatory Memorandum, p. 16, emphasis by the author.

[58] Cf. on the predominating rule of the principle in Art. 5 (1) Rome II Proposal, namely Recital 11.

directly in the bilateral relationship between the two competitors, instead of first affecting the customer side of the market and then only *indirectly* damaging the competitor. Hence, Art. 5 (2) Rome II Proposal would have to be read in the sense that the exceptions apply when the *direct* effects of an act of unfair competition prejudice exclusively the interests of a specific competitor, without at the same time influencing the customer side of the market.

The Explanatory Memorandum as well as the formulation of Art. 5 (2) Rome II Proposal show a certain ambiguity as to these two straightforwardly different approaches, either the "predominant interest/specific target" approach or the "exclusive operative interests/direct bilaterality" approach. Both solutions could probably be based on the actual wording of Art. 5 (2) Rome II Proposal, although the formulation of this provision arguably rather points in the direction of the "exclusive operative interest/direct bilaterality" approach. However, even the examples given in the Explanatory Memorandum for essentially bilateral situations, namely "enticing away a competitor's staff, corruption, industrial espionage, disclosure of business secrets, or inducing breach of contract" reflect both approaches. Although the examples do mainly describe situations in which an act of unfair competition directly and exclusively concerns a specific competitor without at the same time influencing the other market side, they also contain one exception to that trend. In the case of inducing another competitor's customers to breach their contracts, the impact on the customer side of the market cannot be denied. Therefore, the examples, although showing a clear trend toward the "exclusive interest/direct bilaterality" approach, are not entirely clear in that point. Besides this ambiguity, however, it is remarkable for our topic that the list of examples does not cover slavish imitations.

Actually, the question of whether Art. 5 (2) Rome II Proposal with its exceptions from the market effects principle – namely the application of the law of the common place of residence – applies to acts of slavish imitation crucially depends on which of the two outlined approaches to the interpretation of that provision is chosen. On the grounds of the "prevailing interest/specific target" approach, the substance of the test would be to examine to what extent an element of misrepresentation is involved. On the basis of this rather uncertain normative test, it would be decided whether Art. 5 (2) applies to a situation of slavish imitation, i.e., Art. 5 (2) would apply if no sufficient element of misrepresentation was found in a particular case to assume that consumers' interests are substantially affected. The "exclusive operative interest/direct bilaterality" test, on the other hand, would straightforwardly lead to the exclusion of unfair imitations of all kinds from the scope of the Art. 5 (2) exceptions because acts of unfair (even of slavish) imitation always realize themselves by influencing the other (customer) side of the market first, which then only indirectly leads to the damage of the interests of the competitor. Hence, on the basis of this approach, the market law would always govern acts of unfair imitation, even in cases of pure export competition between two competitors from the same Member State.

The question is which of these two approaches should be preferred. Actually, although the private international laws of some Member States, on which Art. 5 (2) Rome II Proposal was modeled,[59] reflect exactly the same ambiguity that can be perceived in Art. 5 (2) Rome II Proposal, they do give some guidance as to the question of which interpretation of Art. 5 (2) should prevail.

2. *Exceptions from the Market Effects Principle in Private International Laws of the Member States*

The Explanatory Memorandum mentions as the models of Art. 5 (2) Rome II Proposal the provisions in section 4 (2) of the Dutch Act on Private International Law of 2001, and section 136 (2) of the Swiss Act on Private International Law, as well as the comparable approach in German case law. Additionally, the similar provisions in Austria (§ 48 (2) Austrian Act on Private International Law) and Spain (Art. 4 Ley de la Competencia Desleal) could also be mentioned. The Explanatory Memorandum suggests that all these approaches more or less resemble each other.[60] However, at second glance, exactly the same ambiguity which characterizes Art. 5 (2) Rome II Proposal also distinguishes these national approaches from each other.

While the explicit provisions in Switzerland, Austria, the Netherlands, and Spain quite clearly focus on the question of whether an act of unfair competition affects *directly* and exclusively the *operational* interests of the business of a competitor – i.e., whether an act of unfair competition directly targets the operational sequences of another competitor's business – German case law is straightforwardly different from that approach. In a general way, it can be said that while the statutory approaches in the former countries could be categorized as representatives of the "exclusive operative interest/direct bilaterality" test, the approach of German case law represents the "predominant interest/specific target" theory, or is at least ambiguous in this field.[61]

In German law, the Federal Supreme Court, after having established the "market effect" principle (remarkably in a case concerning unfair imitations),[62]

---

[59] Cf. Explanatory Memorandum, p. 16; cf. further *infra* IV.2.

[60] Cf. *loc cit.*: "The German courts take the same approach".

[61] Cf. with comprehensive references in this field *Dethloff*, Europäisierung des Wettbewerbsrechts, 2001, p. 70 et seq.

[62] *Federal Supreme Court – "Kindersaugflaschen"*, 1962 GRUR 243. In this decision the *Federal Supreme Court* made it clear that mere preparatory acts in Germany, in a case where a German business competed with the "imitated" products on the U.S. American market, were not a sufficient connecting factor for the application of German law. The substance of the teleological argument of the Court was that otherwise, when competition on a foreign market was concerned, German competitors would be severely disadvantaged in comparison to their

on several (not very many) occasions dealt with the question of whether the exception relating to the common residence of the parties, also known to German law,[63] should apply in cases of unfair competition. The first such decision was the *"Stahlexport"* case of 1963.[64] The case concerned a German competitor's free-riding on the distinguished reputation of another German steel product business in the French market. In other words, the case was concerned with a situation of pure export competition between two German competitors. According to the Federal Supreme Court, German law applies in such situations when either the two German competitors are *the only* competitors on the foreign market,[65] or when the act of unfair competition exclusively affects the individual interests of a specific competitor at which it is specifically targeted. Now it seems quite surprising that in the actual case – a case of defamation which also included an alleged free-riding in marketing activities on another competitor's goodwill – the Federal Supreme Court would assume that the act *exclusively* affected a specific competitor's interests. And, indeed, the line of reasoning of the Federal Supreme Court continues with a subtle difference, stressing that the interests of consumers to be protected against confusion were *predominated* in such a case by the main impact of the act of unfair competition, namely the damage to the interests of the competitor. Obviously, this argument is no longer based on the *exclusive* effect on a specific competitor's interest but rather on the predominance of the damage to the competitor's interests over the effects on the interests of consumers. This predominance in the case in question seems far from clear, however. Instead, the gist of the argument of the Federal Supreme Court seems to be that because of the *specific targeting* of a single competitor, the interests of this competitor prevail over the undoubtedly (and possibly equally) affected interests of the consumer side of the market. Within the categorization developed above, the Federal Supreme

---

foreign competitors through the application of the stricter German unfair competition law standards to their activities on the mere basis of preparatory acts in Germany. In other words, the gist of the argument was that in order to maintain the principle of *par conditio concurrentium* in international cases, a business activity on a foreign market should be governed by the law of that foreign market.

[63] At the time of the classic Federal Supreme Court authorities discussed here, this exception was based on § 1 par. 1 of the "*Verordnung des Ministerrates für die Reichsverteidigung über die Rechtsanwendung bei Schädigungen deutscher Staatsangehöriger außerhalb des Reichsgebiets*," of December 7, 1942, a statutory instrument governing the law applicable to obligations arising out of general tort law. Outside the scope of this provision (which covered only claims for damages), the possible exception was based on the old *Nußbaum* principle of the *Reichsgericht*. Today, the exception in German law is explicitly provided for in Art. 40 par. 2 EGBGB (German Private International Law Act for Civil Matters), although again restricted in scope to damages claims.

[64] *Federal Supreme Court – "Stahlexport"*, 40 BGHZ 391.

[65] This first alternative will practically never be relevant (especially when potential competition is taken into account), and can therefore be neglected for our present purpose. Cf. further *Köhler/Piper*, UWG, 3rd edition 2002, § 1 par. 99.

Court's *"Stahlexport"* case would therefore have to be regarded as an application of the "predominant interest/specific target" approach.[66]

Contrast this with the *"Domgarten Brand"* case. In this case the Federal Supreme Court[67] had to deal with misleading denominations of a product by a German trader that merely affected export competition, targeted at the English market, between this trader and another German competitor. Here, the Federal Supreme Court denied a specific targeting of the other German competitor, and consequently assumed that the public interest to prevent a misrepresentation to English customers prevailed over the damage to the interests of the competitor with the result that (English) market law had to be applied.

Actually, it seems quite unclear why the balance of the collective interests of the consumer side of the market and the interests of a specific competitor in such a case shall be different from the balance of interests in the *"Stahlexport"* case. The Federal Supreme Court seems to assume that the balance of interests depends on the question of whether an act of unfair competition *targets* a *specific* competitor. However, this test of "specific targeting" is irrelevant as to the potential of an act of unfair competition to affect the collective interests of consumers on a given market. The reason why a misleading product denomination in this respect should be more weighty than in a case of defamation or passing off remains obscure.[68] Again, it is doubtful whether the "predominating interest/specific target" approach can deliver the degree of legal certainty that is necessary for a clear-cut choice of law test.

Therefore, the classic German authorities in this field quite neatly illustrate the limits of the "predominating interest/specific target" approach. Particularly concerning slavish imitations, the outcome of the application of this test would be rather unpredictable. Either the fact that slavish imitations are typically targeted at a specific competitor would lead to the applicability of Art. 5 (2) Rome II Proposal straightforwardly (with the result that the law of the common

[66] However, a crucial difference between Art. 5 (2) Rome II Proposal and German case law in this field remains even on the basis of the "predominant interest/specific target" understanding of Art. 5 (2) Rome II Proposal. This is because the *Federal Supreme Court* in the *"Ein Champagner unter den Mineralwässern"* case, 1988 NJW 644 (actually a German "champagne" case quite comparable to the cases in which the English courts *inter alia* developed the extended form of passing off) clearly refused to apply the *"Stahlexport"* principles to competition of two foreign competitors (from the same country) on the German market. Hence, while Art. 5 (2) Rome II Proposal would lead to the application of the law of the country of common residence, assuming that the necessary specific targeting was given, German case law refuses this reversed application of the *"Stahlexport"* principle, instead applying German law to such cases. Actually there seems to be no convincing reasons for this half-sided approach of German private international law in this field, except for the general tendency of courts to apply the *lex fori;* cf. *Dethloff,* Europäisierung des Wettbewerbsrechts, 2001, p. 71. Insofar Art. 5 (2) Rome II Proposal even in its "prevailing interest/specific target" interpretation would bring an approvable change to German private international law by making the application of the *"Stahlexport"* principle more coherent.

[67] *Federal Supreme Court – "Domgarten-Brand",* 1983 IPRax 118.

[68] Cf. *Dethloff,* Die Europäisierung des Wettbewerbsrechts, 2001, p. 73.

place of residence could be applied optionally); or it would have to be assessed in each single case whether there is a sufficient element of misrepresentation involved to let the consumers' interests prevail (with the result in a mandatory application of market law).

Moreover, there is a reason in principle why the exceptions of Artt. 5 (2), 3 (2), and (3) Rome II Proposal (i.e., the common place of residence exception and the general displacement possibility) should not be applied to situations where the competitors' interests merely prevail over the consumers' interests, which are likewise touched. This reason follows from the very objective of the market effects principle in unfair competition law, as it has been established, for example, by the "*Kindersaugflaschen*" case concerning slavish imitations, and as it is acknowledged in European law by the Rome II Proposal.[69] This main objective of the market effects principle is to ascertain the equal protection of the interests of competitors, consumers, and the general public in an undistorted competition.[70] Therefore, in order to maintain and protect the *par conditio concurrentium* (the same conditions for every competitor) on a given national market, in principle the law of the market country has to apply whenever an act of unfair competition directly influences the customer side of this market.[71] Only when an act of unfair competition is limited to directly damaging a competitor without at the same time directly influencing the other market side on the foreign market (though of course an indirect effect on competition may also ultimately result from such bilateral acts), the exception in favor of a possible application of the law of the country of common residence can apply. Otherwise, the market conduct on a given national market of two competitors both having their seat in another Member State would be possibly assessed differently, as compared to the market actions of their competitors from the market country or from third countries. It is precisely the resulting distortion of competition which Art. 5 (1) Rome II Proposal is meant to prevent. Hence, a broader interpretation of the exception of Art. 5 (2) Rome II Proposal along the lines of the "predominant interests/specific target" approach, besides leading into considerable legal uncertainty, would seriously undermine the market effects principle and the very purpose of Art. 5 Rome II Proposal. Therefore, the principle of *effet utile* in Community law interpretation also argues for the narrower interpretation of Art. 5 (2) Rome II Proposal in the sense of an "exclusive operative interest/direct bilaterality" approach.

To summarize the result from this analysis of the private international law provisions of the Member States on which Art. 5 Rome II Proposal, and namely par. 2 of this provision, was modeled, it can be said that the better reasons

---

[69] Cf. *supra* note 62; Explanatory Memorandum, p. 16; and specifically Recital 11 of the Rome II Proposal.

[70] Cf. specifically Recital 11 of the Rome II Proposal.

[71] Cf., for example, *Sack*, Die kollisionsrechtliche Beurteilung grenzüberschreitender Werbe- und Absatztätigkeit nach deutschem Recht, 1988 GRUR Int. 320, 326; cf. also *Dethloff*, Die Europäisierung des Wettbewerbsrechts, 2001, p. 73 et seq.

argue in favor of applying Art. 5 Rome II Proposal in the straight sense of an "exclusive operative interest/direct bilaterality" test. This is the interpretation as it follows from Swiss, Austrian, Spanish, and Dutch statutory provisions rather than from the more ambiguous German case law in this field. This interpretation is not only in line with the main objective of Art. 5 Rome II Proposal in its entirety,[72] but also seems to be more coherent with the wording of this provision and with most of the examples in the Explanatory Memorandum.[73] Hence, according to Art. 5 (2) Rome II Proposal, the exceptions of Art. 3 (2) and (3) can only be applied when an act of unfair competition is directly bilateral, i.e., affects only and exclusively the business operations of a specific competitor without directly influencing the other side of the market at all.

Because they only realize themselves via the influence on the other (consumer) side of the market, it follows that acts of unfair or slavish imitations fall straightforwardly out of the scope of Art. 5 (2) Rome II Proposal. To such acts, the principle of Art. 5 (1) Rome II Proposal applies without exceptions. Hence, under the future Rome II Regulation, acts of unfair imitation will have to be assessed under the law of the country(ies) where they directly and substantially affect (or are likely to affect) competitive relations or the collective interests of consumers, namely under the law of the countries in which they are marketed.

To be sure, at this point the attained result is only based upon a rather continental European perspective on the proper interpretation of the possible future Rome II Regulation. However, as it shall be briefly outlined in the following part, the result is essentially the same when assessing acts of unfair imitations under an English perspective on the possible new Rome II Regulation. This convergence of national perspectives will probably be of substantial importance for the practical application of the possible future Rome II Regulation in this field, because in view of the relative scarcity of cases regarding this specific question, an ECJ decision clarifying these issues cannot be expected in a short-term perspective.

3. *A UK Perspective on Unfair Imitations under the Rome II Regulation Proposal*

As has been described above, the only instrument[74] that can essentially apply to "unfair" imitations in competition under English substantive law is the common law tort of passing off, namely in its extended form.[75] Although much narrower

---

[72] As it follows from Recital 11 Rome II Proposal, for example.

[73] Cf. Explanatory Memorandum, p. 16.

[74] Some other actions, such as *breach of confidence,* for example, may also have a certain bearing in cases of unfair competition, but can be neglected for our present purposes. Cf. also *supra* II.1.

[75] Cf. *supra* II.1.

than the continental European approach in this field, it might at least provide for an action against another competitor's copying of products when a misrepresentation to customers follows from the marketing of the imitated products.[76]

However, given the fact that this action is part of general tort law in the United Kingdom, and keeping in mind the general reluctance of common law judges to acknowledge a concept of unfair competition,[77] from an English perspective it seems not entirely certain whether cases of unfair imitation would be characterized at all as a part of unfair competition law to be dealt with under Art. 5 Rome II Proposal. This correct characterization cannot be seriously in doubt (even from an English perspective) when the claimant pleads the case as an unfair competition case under the substantive law of a foreign country. In this case, Art. 5 Rome II Proposal would presumably be applied straightforwardly. But when the action is brought before the English courts as a passing off action under English substantive law, the question seems to be more difficult.[78] From an English law standpoint, the obvious alternative would then be to characterize the obligations arising out of that passing off action as a part of general tort law, and consequently to apply the general principle of Art. 3 Rome II Proposal.

Hence, the crucial question to be discussed here is whether common law judges, in applying the future Rome II Regulation, would characterize passing off actions as cases under Art. 3 or as cases under Art. 5 Rome II Regulation. Given the method of autonomous interpretation of European law, and taking into account the examples for Art. 5 cases in the Explanatory Memorandum to the Rome II Proposal which particularly include "acts that exploit a competitor's value *(passing off and the like),*"[79] the answer seems to be that cases of unfair imitation – even when they are brought before the English courts as a passing off case – would presumably be dealt with under Art. 5 Rome II Proposal. Besides, the notion (although not the comprehensive concept) of unfair competition is far more common to English judges than it might seem at first sight. The most visible example of this is the *obiter dictum* on passing off per Clarke LJ. in the "*Arsenal*" case,[80] which was mainly concerned (of course) with the trademark law assessment of imitations of official "Arsenal F.C." symbols, crests, and the like: "... the cause of action traditionally called passing

---

[76] This is shown clearly in the cases concerning so-called look-alike products, which at first glance imitate the "get-up" of another more reputed product in order to mislead customers. Cf. the *"Jif Lemon"* case (*supra* note 14), and the *"Penguin Puffin"* case, *United Biscuits v. Asda* [1997] RPC 513.

[77] Cf. comprehensively *Ohly,* Richterrecht und Generalklausel im Recht des unlauteren Wettbewerbs, 1997, p. 73 et seq

[78] Cf. for this characterization problem *supra* III.2. Cf. further on that issue *Fawcett/Torremans,* Intellectual Property in Private International Law, 1998, p. 652 et seq.

[79] Explanatory Memorandum, p. 15; emphasis by the author.

[80] [2003] RPC 39.

off, *perhaps best referred to as unfair competition.*"[81] Hence, English judges, although reluctant to develop a general *action* of unfair competition, are quite aware of the fact that the passing off action (especially in its extended form) covers an area of law that is seen as part of unfair competition law in European law.[82] Consequently, Art. 5 Rome II Proposal would presumably be applied to obligations arising out of acts of unfair imitation as far as these are actionable under the extended form of passing off.

The subsequent question as to whether the Art. 5 (2) Rome II Proposal exception would be applied to acts of unfair imitation seems not much easier to answer. This is because the *action* of passing off is usually not understood, in common law, as an instrument of consumer protection. Therefore, from a common law perspective, it seems not unimaginable that Art. 5 (2) Rome II Proposal would be applied to such an action on the basis that the passing off action only (i.e., "exclusively") deals with the interests of the specific competitor that is affected by the act of imitation.[83] However, given the fact that successful passing off actions always require a substantial misrepresentation to the *customer side* of the market, the element of protecting collective consumers' interests, although not actionable itself and not the direct objective of the action, is much more substantial to a passing off action than it is to the broader continental European concept of slavish imitations. The requirement of a substantial market confusion makes it clear that the interest of the public in undistorted competition is inevitably affected by any *act* of passing off. Under these circumstances (without regard to the objective of the action), *acts* of passing off could hardly be seen as "exclusively [affecting] the interests of a specific competitor" in the sense of Art. 5 (2) Rome II Proposal. Hence, it is submitted that from an English law perspective, Art. 5 (1) Rome II Proposal would be applied to acts of passing off, without granting the possible exceptions of Art. 5 (2).

---

[81] Emphasis by the author; for comprehensive examples regarding the use of the notion in more recent English case law, cf. *Ohly,* Richterrecht und Generalklausel im Recht des unlauteren Wettbewerbs, 1997, namely p. 86 et seq. (citing *inter alia* the *"Advocaat"* case, and the *"Spanish Champagne"* case, as seen in the *"British Sherry"* case per Cross J.: "[I]t uncovered a piece of common law or equity which had till then escaped notice. ... In truth the decision went beyond the well-trodden paths of passing off into the unmapped area of 'unfair trading' or 'unfair competition'").

[82] Cf. *supra* (note 81); cf. also *Cornish,* Intellectual Property, 2003, para 1-13 et seq., at para 1-21.

[83] For the current English statutory provision with respect to displacement of the general choice of law principle of tort law, cf. sec. 12 Act 1995; and specifically on the application of this provision to actions of passing off and unfair competition, *Fawcett/Torremans,* Intellectual Property in Private International Law, 1998, p. 664 et seq., 687 et seq. Especially in cases of pure export competition of two competitors having their seat in England, the application of the general displacement rule of sec. 12 (1) Act 1995 would probably lead to the application of English substantive law. Cf. also the Scots case of *William Grant & Sons Ltd. v Glen Catrine Bonded Warehouse Ltd,* 1995 SLT 936.

In summary, the outlined English law perspective on the future Rome II Regulation with regard to acts of unfair imitation acknowledges the result obtained above. Until the ECJ by way of a preliminary reference decision possibly clarifies the matter, Art. 5 (2) Rome II should not apply to any case of unfair imitation in competition. Instead, Art. 5 (1) Rome II Proposal should apply without exceptions. Hence, even in cases of pure export competition between two national competitors, only the law of the country where the marketing of the imitations directly and substantially affects the market should be applicable. This is the solution of the statutory provisions in Swiss, Austrian, Spanish, and Dutch law. For German private international law as well as for English choice of law rules,[84] this solution will possibly bring about some smaller changes, or at least a considerable clarification with respect to cases of export competition, as has been made clear above (IV.2.).

The last part of these considerations shall discuss whether this result is essentially in line with the main objective of the Regulation, namely the harmonization of conflict rules and the boosting of legal certainty as to the applicable law, which is aimed at completing a European area of justice in order to guarantee *the proper functioning of the internal market.*[85] On these grounds, Art. 5 Rome II Proposal can be evaluated conclusively, and, moreover, some lessons for substantive European law in the unfair competition law field can be derived from the analysis of the choice of law rule.

V. Evaluation and Conclusion

Especially regarding the internal market objective of the future Regulation, it could be doubted at first glance that the approach to unfair imitations under Art. 5 Rome II Proposal, as it has been brought forward here, leads to the most effective result.

Particularly in cases of Europe-wide multi-state marketing (of imitated products or services), the narrow understanding of the Art. 5 (2) Rome II Proposal exception could lead to additional uncertainty regarding the substantive law standards that apply to actions on the different national Member States' markets. An example may illustrate the problem. In a situation where two competitors from Germany engage in Europe-wide competition, the application of Art. 5 (1) Rome II Proposal to obligations arising from acts of unfair (slavish) imitation would lead to the typical mosaic approach of private international law in this field. According to Art. 5 (1) Rome II Proposal, it would be mandatory to assess the lawfulness of the imitations regarding both actions for injunctions and actions for damages on a case-by-case basis under

[84] Cf. note 83 above.

[85] Cf. the Explanatory Memorandum, and specifically the legal basis for the Regulation Proposal, Art. 65 (b): "... insofar as necessary for the proper functioning of the internal market. ..."

the laws of each of the different Member States where the imitating products are marketed. Naturally, the application of Art. 5 (2) Rome II Proposal would lead to a considerable simplification in such a case. The common law of residence of the two German competitors could be uniformly applied to settle the matter throughout Europe. Although at first glance this result may seem more effective than the mosaic approach under Art. 5 (1) Rome II Proposal, in fact it would lead to considerable distortions of competition, and therefore rather hamper the proper functioning of the internal market.

This is because such a solution would ignore the inner connection of uniform European choice of law rules with the underlying level of harmonization of substantive law in particular fields of law; moreover, with the principle of mutual recognition as it follows from ECJ case law and – even broader and more effective – from some acts of Community secondary law, such as the "TV without Frontiers" Directive and the E-Commerce Directive. In the field of complementary unfair competition law protection against imitations through competitors, as has been said, no substantial level of harmonization has been reached yet. Hence, the application of Art. 5 (2) Rome II Proposal in cases such as the case described above would lead to the problem that the defendant from Germany (the producer of the imitations), in his market conduct on, e.g., the English market (and all the other national markets of the Member States with more liberal standards than Germany), would be treated differently from other competitors (having their seat in any third Member State instead of Germany). Namely, while the third country or English competitors could freely imitate the products of the German claimant (the producer of the original products) on the English market (and on all other more liberal national markets under the more liberal "market effects" law, i.e., the law of the countries where the products are marketed), the German defendant could not even do so on these more liberal markets. This would considerably distort competition on the markets of all the Member States with more liberal standards than Germany to the disadvantage of the German defendant, and hence lead to exactly the situation which Art. 5 (1) Rome II Proposal is intended to prevent. Therefore, in principle, the mosaic approach is, at present, the only reasonable choice of law option for Europe-wide multi-state situations with regard to unfair imitations.[86]

Given the present piecemeal harmonization of substantive unfair competition law, this point can be generalized for the whole field of unfair competition, and therefore the narrower interpretation of Art. 5 (2) Rome II Proposal, such as to open the market effects rule to exceptions only in cases of purely bilateral acts of competitors which have no direct effects on the customer side of the market at all, is the only solution that is coherent with the present level of harmonization in substantive law. Therefore, in the overwhelming majority of cases,

[86] However, in favor of a country-of-origin rule in such situations, *Dethloff,* Europäisierung des Wettbewerbsrechts, 2001, p. 284 et seq. with respect to unfair competition choice of law in general.

the market effects rule provision of Art. 5 (1) Rome II Proposal will prevail over Art. 5 (2). Only in purely bilateral cases without any direct impact on the customer side of the market will the exceptions of Art. 3 (2) and (3) Rome II Proposal apply.

The market effects rule leads, admittedly, to considerable legal uncertainty for Europe-wide advertising and marketing campaigns with respect to the standards in substantive law in the different Member States.[87] This uncertainty, in turn, can lead to substantial search costs regarding the necessary assessment of the substantive law standards in all the different Member States, therefore hampering the proper functioning of the internal market. The problem is particularly relevant with respect to marketing in cross-border media such as television and the Internet. However, with respect to these most problematic environments, the internal market provision of the "TV without Frontiers" Directive – as far as the scope of this Directive reaches – and the considerably broader internal market provision in the E-Commerce Directive provide for the application of the European principle of mutual recognition ("country-of-origin" rules), and therefore considerably reduce the problematic effects of the mosaic approach in private international law for the functioning of the internal market. Additionally, the Sales Promotion Directive Proposal[88] as well as the Unfair Commercial Practices Directive proposal[89] foresee even further-reaching provisions on mutual recognition for the areas of law which these Directives would substantially harmonize.[90] For the moment, therefore, the logic of European harmonization in unfair competition law seems to combine a harmonized market effects choice of law rule with specific European Secondary law provisions harmonizing certain fields of substantive unfair competition law, and underpinning harmonization in these "coordinated" fields with correspondent "internal market" provisions providing for the specific applicability of the principle of mutual recognition ("country-of-origin rules") in the harmonized fields of law. Outside the scope of these special instruments, Europe-wide marketing and distribution by European traders remains governed by the ECJ case law regarding Art. 28 EC.

---

87 Cf. already the comments of the *Hamburg Group for Private International Law,* 2003 RabelsZ 2, at 20.

88 Amended Proposal for a Regulation concerning sales promotions in the internal market, Doc. COM (2002) 585 final (hereafter referred to as Sales Promotions Regulation Proposal).

89 Proposal for a Directive concerning unfair business-to-consumer commercial practices in the internal market (the Unfair Commercial Practices Directive), Doc. COM (2003) 356 final (hereafter referred to as [Unfair Commercial Practices] Directive Proposal). Cf. also note 20 above.

90 However, the most recent version of the proposed Unfair Commercial Practices Directive, i.e. the version of the political agreement in the "Competitiveness" Council of 25 May 2004, 2003/0134 (COD), Annex 1, no longer contains an express "country of origin"-rule. The reason given for the cancellation of the "country of origin"-rule is that because of the full harmonisation, achieved through the Directive, such a clause would be unnecessary.

Art. 5 Rome II Proposal in its present form, and in the interpretation proposed here, fits well into such a framework of harmonization. How the co-application of the choice of law rule in private international law and the European secondary law provisions on mutual recognition would have to be carried out in practice in order to obtain the ideal result for the further development of the internal market has been outlined elsewhere.[91] For the moment, suffice it to say that, in the field of unfair competition law protection against imitations by competitors, neither substantive harmonization nor the introduction of a principle of mutual recognition (apart from Art. 3 E-Commerce-Directive for electronic communications) can be expected for the near future. Hence, Art. 5 (1) Rome II Proposal will apply in this field and provide for the choice of the law of the market country in virtually all practical cases, apart from imitations in electronic communications.

The interpretation brought forward here reduces the role of the displacement clause in Art. 5 (2) Rome II Proposal to cases where an act of unfair competition exclusively affects the interests of another competitor in the unhampered pursuit of his business operations, without directly affecting the customer side of the market at all. The broader interpretation of Art. 5 (2) Rome II Proposal, which would include situations where a competitor is specifically targeted by another competitor's action *on the market*, would ignore that in such cases the impact of this single and unitary market action on the interests of the consumer side of the market cannot be separated from – much less be balanced against – the effect of the interests of the competitor.

Actually, this is a more general lesson that can be learned from the analysis of Art. 5 Rome II Proposal for the further development of the pending Unfair Commercial Practices Directive Proposal. The Unfair Commercial Practices Directive Proposal tries to limit its scope and main objective to the prevention of commercial practices that affect the interests *of consumers,* while the interests of competitors and businesses in general shall not be protected. Therefore, the proposal excludes from its scope (besides straightforward B2B situations) the whole field of non-confusing comparative advertising, where the comparison itself is misleading, and some other substantial fields of unfair competition law, probably because all these fields are seen as fields predominated by the objective to protect competitors against each other.[92] Such a "separation" approach can hardly work, as the analysis of Art. 5 (2) Rome II Proposal has shown.[93] Quite to the contrary, Art. 5 Rome II Proposal in its entirety underlines the importance of the monistic trinity of protection purposes

[91] Cf. *Leistner,* in: *Drexl/Kur* (ed.), IP and Private International Law – Heading for the Future (forthcoming 2004).

[92] Cf. critically, *Köhler/Lettl,* Das geltende europäische Lauterkeitsrecht, der Vorschlag für eine EG-Richtlinie über unlautere Geschäftspraktiken und die UWG Reform, 2003 WRP 1019 at 1031 et seq.; *Leistner,* Unfair Competition or Consumer Protection, in: *Cambridge Yearbook of European Studies,* Vol. 6 2004, forthcoming.

[93] Cf. also note 21 above.

in unfair competition law from the perspective of a choice of law rule. Whenever an act of unfair competition realizes itself via influencing the customer side of the market, its effects on the interests of competitors can no longer be separated from – much less prevail over – its impact on the collective interests of consumers and on the public interest in an undistorted competition, which have to be equally taken into account. This monistic trinity of protection purposes is clearly acknowledged by Art. 5 of the future Rome II Regulation. This is the lesson from private international law for the substantive law harmonization in the field of unfair competition: The monistic trinity of protection purposes cannot and should not be separated in European unfair competition law.

Patent Infringement, Choice of Laws, and the Forthcoming Rome II Regulation

M. PERTEGÁS SENDER

I. Introduction

A presentation on the law applicable to patent infringement disputes takes for granted that a court may accept jurisdiction over disputes concerning the enforcement of foreign patent rights.

Supranational enforcement of cross-border patent infringement cases is still an aspiration that may eventually become legal reality.[1] In the meantime, national courts have increasingly tackled the intricacies of cross-border enforcement of patent rights. Emergent case law has presented evidence of major difficulties in applying private international rules to cross-border patent enforcement. The debate has principally focused on the highly controversial application of the current European jurisdictional instruments[2] to cross-border patent enforcement cases.[3] The issue of the applicable law has so far been given less attention than it deserves.

---

[1] Cf. the contribution by Winfried Tilmann to this book (p. 123 et seq.).

[2] In chronological order, these instruments are the 1968 Brussels Convention on Jurisdiction and the Enforcement of Judgments on Civil and Commercial Matters, O.J. C 27, January 26, 1998, 1, (consolidated version); the 1988 Lugano Convention on Jurisdiction and the Enforcement of Judgments in Civil and Commercial Matters, O.J. L 319, November 25, 1988, 9; and Council Regulation nr. 44/2001 of December 22, 2000, O.J. L 12, January 16, 2001, 1.

[3] It is expected that the European Court of Justice (ECJ) will take the opportunity to clarify a number of crucial issues when dealing with two pending cases on the application of the Brussels Convention to cross-border patent enforcement (status: July 2004). Cf. Case C-4/03, (*GAT/Luk Lamellen*), O.J. C 55, March 8, 2003, 14 and Case C-539/03, (*Roche Nederland/ Primus*), O.J. C 59, March 6, 2004, 11.

This contribution attempts to examine how choice of law rules deal with patent enforcement. Attention needs to be drawn in the first place to the national solutions that currently determine which law governs cross-border patent enforcement cases. We will then turn to the Commission Proposal on Rome II,[4] in particular to its Article 8. It is important to assess to which extent the proposed rule should be preferred to the current mosaic of national choice of law rules.

II. Comparative Approach[5]

In the current state of law, the applicable law to cross-border patent infringement cases is determined by the choice of law rules of the state where the proceedings are conducted. It is incorrect to assume that the international conventions in the patent area ensure the application of the law of the state of protection (*lex loci protectionis*) as the only possible choice of law rule (*infra* 1.). Furthermore, a comparative overview shows that the law of the state of protection is not the only feasible choice of law rule for patent infringement disputes. Other connecting factors have been put forward in this specific area (*infra* 2.).

1. International Conventions in the Patent Area

It has been argued that the principle of national treatment enhanced by *inter alia* Article 3(1) TRIPs Agreement, Article 2 Paris Industrial Property Convention, or Article 64(3) European Patent Convention (EPC) can be interpreted as an indication in favor of the *lex loci protectionis* as the choice of law rule.

Article 64(3) of the EPC states that "any infringement of a European patent shall be dealt with by national law." The question arises as to how "national law" will be determined: Should we assume that this law is necessarily the law

---

The Swiss Supreme Court has acknowledged the possibility of cross-border patent enforcement in the framework of the 1988 Lugano Convention. Cf., for instance, Swiss Supreme Court, October 7, 2002, (*Test Cassettes*), *GRUR Int.* 2003, 561; *I.I.C.* 2004, 206; Swiss Supreme Court, February 21, 2003, case 370/2002, available at <http://www.bger.ch>.

[4] Proposal for a Regulation on the Law Applicable to Non-Contractual Obligations ("Rome II"), COM (2003) 427 final, not yet published in the O.J., hereafter "Rome II Proposal." The text has not yet been discussed by the European Parliament in Plenary (status: July 2004). Cf. the report presented by Ms. Wallis MEP, Rapporteur of the Committee on Legal Affairs and the Internal Market on April 5, 2004. With respect to Article 8, the Rapporteur proposes amending the Commission Proposal in order to apply "the law of the country in which the act of infringement is committed" to IP infringements.

[5] This part is based upon Chapter 5 of my book on *Cross-border enforcement of patent rights*, Oxford, OUP, 2002, 209-271.

of the protecting country[6] or does it refer to the law designated by the choice of law rules of the state where legal proceedings are pending?

It is submitted that the second interpretation is more in conformity with the text and purpose of Article 64(3) of the EPC. In the first place, reference is made to "national law" and not to "substantive" or "internal" law. In order to exclude the working of the choice of law rules, international conventions generally refer to the expression "internal law",[7] or state that the term "law" does not include choice of law rules.[8] In the absence of an express indication to the contrary, there is no reason to interpret Article 64(3) of the EPC as excluding the use of private international rules in order to determine the relevant substantive rules.

Furthermore, the harmonization of the choice of law rules of the EPC Member States clearly goes beyond the *ratio* of Article 64(3) of the EPC. Indeed, this provision must be read in combination with Article 64(1) of the EPC, which provides that the European patent is to have the effects of a national patent in the designated states.[9] Article 64(3) of the EPC ensures that the post-grant life of a European patent is ruled by national law in the same way as a national patent. The private international law rules of the forum apply in disputes concerning the enforcement of national patents, and hence the same rules must apply in cases involving European patents.

It is far from clear that the international conventions in the patent area impose a given choice of law rule. The national treatment requirement that can be inferred from those international conventions is met by applying the same choice of law rule to all patentees, regardless of their nationality. Accordingly,

---

[6] As stated, among others, by Sandrock, O., "Verletzung von gewerblichen Schutzrechten und Urheberrechten," in: von Caemmerer, E., *Vorschläge und Gutachten zur Reform des deutschen internationalen Privatrechts der außervertraglichen Schuldverhältnisse*, Tübingen, J.C.B. Mohr (Paul Siebeck), 1983, 396.

See, similarly, in *obiter*, Court of Appeals, January 21, 1999, (*Pearce/Ove Arup*), *All E.R.* 1999, 769; *GRUR Int.* 1999, 787 (summary in German and commentary by M. Zigann), where the Court of Appeals held that "'national law' in the context of Article 64 EPC, means the law of the state in respect of which the patent is granted – see Article 64(1)." See, extensively, Arnold, R., "Cross-border Enforcement: The Latest Chapter", *I.P.Q.* 1999, 393-400.

[7] See, for instance, Articles 4 and 5 of the 1973 Hague Convention on the law applicable to products liability, concluded on October 2, 1973, or Articles 5 and 6 of the 1978 Hague Convention on the law applicable to agency, concluded on October 19, 1996, available at: <http://www.hcch.net>.

[8] See, for instance, Article 21(1) of the 1996 Hague Convention on jurisdiction, applicable law, recognition, enforcement, and co-operation in respect of parental responsibility and measures for the protection of children, concluded on October 19, 1996, available at: <http://www.hcch.net>.

According to Article 21(1), "in this Chapter the term 'law' means the law in force in a State other than its choice of law rules."

[9] Tritton, G., *Intellectual property in Europe*, 2nd ed., London, Sweet & Maxwell, 2002, 79: "Once granted, the issues of validity and infringement post-grant are matters for the national courts who theoretically will uniformly apply the substantive law of the EPC (as enacted into domestic patent laws)."

the only private international implication of Article 64(3) EPC (and similar provisions in the TRIPs Agreement and the PIPC) is that nationality cannot be used as a connecting factor because this may lead to a different degree of protection granted to national and foreign patentees. It follows that such a partial choice of law rule must be completed by the choice of law rule of the state in which infringement proceedings are pending.

2. *Relevant Choice of Law Rules*

In the absence of a uniform set of choice of law rules at the international level, the determination of the applicable law depends upon three factors. The first issue to be considered is the relevant choice of law rules of the state where the plaintiff attempts to enforce its patent rights. Accordingly, the point of departure in the determination of the applicable law is the place where the parties are involved in infringement proceedings. This all depends on the jurisdictional system applicable to the dispute. Second, one must identify which specific choice of law rule is applicable to patent infringement disputes. While in some legal orders a specific choice of law rule applies to patent (infringement) disputes, in others the applicable law must be inferred by reference to more general choice of law rules, such as those applicable to torts. Last but not least, it must be considered which interpretation is to be given to the relevant choice of law rule where cross-border patent protection is requested. There is generally a need to "adapt" the relevant choice of law rules in the light of the particularities of these cases.

Based upon a comparative study of a number of states, it is possible to identify two major tendencies. Both the law of the protecting state (*lex loci protectionis*) and the law of the place of infringement (*lex loci delicti*) co-exist in the current private international mosaic.

a) The Law of the Protecting State

Patent infringement is regulated by the *lex loci protectionis* or law of the protecting state in several jurisdictions across Europe. The Swiss Private International Law Act and the Belgian Private International Law Draft Act may be used as examples.

The 1987 Swiss private international law codification is generally considered to be a source of inspiration for other codification attempts across Europe. Its influence is noticeable in later codifications such as the Italian 1995 Private International Law Act and the German partial codification of tort and property choice of law rules. It follows that Italian and German choice of law rules rely as well on the *locus protectionis* as a connecting factor for patent infringements.

aa) Switzerland

The choice of law rule applicable to patent infringement disputes brought before the Swiss courts may be qualified as a realistic and progressive solution that combines the classical *lex loci protectionis* rule and a limited freedom of the parties to choose the law applicable to the dispute.

According to Article 110(1) of the Swiss PIL,[10] "rights in intellectual property are governed by the law of the country for which protection of those rights is sought" ("les droits de la propriété intellectuelle sont régis par le droit de l'Etat pour lequel la protection de la protection intellectuelle est revendiquée"). Article 110(2) of the Swiss PIL allows the parties to choose the application of the law of the forum (that is, Swiss law) to infringement disputes: "for claims arising out of a harmful event, the parties may agree, at any time after the damage occurred, that the law at the place of the court applies" ("en ce qui concerne les prétentions consécutives à un acte illicite, les parties peuvent toujour convenir, après l'événement dommageable, de l'application du droit du for").

The general rule (Article 110(1) of the Swiss PIL) refers to the law of the state in which the plaintiff claims to have patent protection.[11] Accordingly, two or more laws will apply if the plaintiff claims that parallel infringements have occurred in different states. The law of each state is relied upon with regard to the alleged infringement of the local national patent right. Accordingly, the law of each protecting state will determine whether an infringement occurred within its territory. Where a particular national law claims extraterritorial application – for instance, where it allows redress for patent infringement committed abroad – the exception of public order (Article 17 of the Swiss PIL) or the general exception clause in Article 15[12] may be invoked.

bb) Belgium

In recent years, Belgium has become a well-known jurisdiction for patent practitioners. Its courts have shamefully been associated with *mala fide* prac-

---

[10] Swiss Private International Law Statute of 18 December 1987, published *inter alia* in Dutoit, B., *Commentaire de la loi fédérale du 18 décembre 1987*, Basel, Helbing & Lichtenhahn, 1997.

[11] Vischer, F., "Das Internationale Privatrecht des Immaterialgüterrechtes nach dem schweizerischem IPR Gesetzenentwurf," *GRUR Int.* 1987, 678; Novier, M., *La propriété intellectuelle en droit international privé suisse*, Lausanne, Chabloz, 1996, 147; Dutoit, B., *Commentaire de la loi fédérale du 18 décembre 1987*, Basel, Helbing & Lichtenhahn, 1997, 292.

For an application of Article 110(1) Swiss PIL, see Swiss Supreme Court, January 13, 1998, *GRUR* 1998, 1009.

[12] Article 15(1) Swiss PIL: "The law designated by this Statute is, by way of exception, not applicable if, under all the circumstances, the case clearly only has a slight connection with the designated law, and has a much closer connection with another law."

tices of alleged patent infringers that filed for a cross-border negative declaration of infringement. It was expected that the lengthy proceedings before the Belgian courts would block any enforcement attempts by the patent holder by means of the rules on parallel proceedings set out by the European instruments on international jurisdiction.[13] It must be emphasized, however, that the outcome of the so-called "Belgian torpedoes" has been mitigated by a wise application of the jurisdiction rules by the Belgian courts. Despite increasing cross-border patent litigation before the Belgian courts,[14] the issue of the applicable law to such litigation remains rather unexplored.

Belgium is about to codify its private international rules. The Private International Law Act[15] has a specific provision concerning the law governing intellectual property disputes. Its Article 93 states that: (translation)

> 1. Intellectual property rights are governed by the law of the state for whose territory protection is claimed.
> 2. However, the issue of the original ownership of an industrial property right is governed by the law of the state with the closest connections to the intellectual activity. When this activity is performed in the framework of a contractual relationship, it is presumed that this state is the one whose law applies to this relationship.

With the introduction of such a choice of law, Belgium joins the majority of European states backing the *lex loci protectionis* as the choice of law rule for patent litigation. It is expected that the adoption of a specific choice of law rule for intellectual property will contribute to increasing the attention in judicial circles on choice of law problems in this specific area.

b) The Law of the Place of Infringement

Despite the predominance of the *lex loci protectionis*, there is room for alternative approaches to the issue of the applicable law to patent litigation. Austria and the Netherlands are here taken as examples of the application of the *lex loci delicti* to patent enforcement.

aa) Austria

Austrian private international law[16] seems to provide the clearest example of a choice of law system which applies the tort choice of law rules to intellectual

[13] Cf. note 2.

[14] For an overview, cf. Roox, K., *Grensoverschrijdende maatregelen in octrooizaken: Overzicht van Belgische rechtspraak* (1997-2002), *I.R.D.I.* 2002, 257-274.

[15] The Belgian PIL Act, available at <www.ipr.be>, is expected to be adopted in July 2004. It will enter into force three months after publication in the Official Journal (i.e. most probably before the end of 2004).

[16] Austrian Private International Law Statute of June 15, 1978, published *inter alia* in Schwimann, M., *Internationales Privatrecht, einschließlich Europarecht*, Vienna, Manz'sche Verlags- und Universitätsbuchhandlung, 1999.

property infringement cases. According to Article 34(1) of the Austrian PIL, "the creation, scope, and termination of intellectual property rights is determined by the law of the state where the act of exploitation or the act of infringement occurred" ("sind das Entstehen, der Inhalt und das Erlöschen von Immaterialgüterrechten nach dem Recht des Staates zu beurteilen, in dem eine Benützungs- oder Verletzungshandlung gesetzt wird"). According to the official commentary to the Austrian PIL, the intent is – for instance – for Dutch law to apply where an alleged act of infringement is committed in the Netherlands; indeed, protection will be denied if no patent protection has been granted in the Netherlands.[17]

However, both the Austrian doctrine[18] and the case law of the Austrian Supreme Court have interpreted this choice of law rule as referring to the law of the state for which protection is claimed ("für dessen Gebiet der Schutz begehrt/beansprucht wird"), at least with respect to trademark[19] and copyright[20] infringements. This interpretation has been confirmed by *inter alia* the judgment of the Austrian Supreme Court in the *Adolf Loos-Werke II* case, where an action for copyright infringement was filed against a publishing company which marketed the allegedly infringing books in German-speaking countries. The Austrian Supreme Court held that (translation):[21]

> "According to Article 34(1) of the Austrian PIL, the creation, scope and termination of intellectual property rights is determined by the law of the state where the act of exploitation or the act of infringement occurred. Accordingly, the legislator has chosen

[17] This example is given by Sandrock: see Sandrock, O., "Verletzung von gewerblichen Schutzrechten und Urheberrechten," in: von Caemerer, E., *Vorschläge und Gutachten zur Reform des deutschen internationalen Privatrechts der außervertraglichen Schuldverhältnisse*, Tübingen, J.C.B. Mohr (Paul Siebeck), 1983, 415.

[18] Mänhardt, F. & Posch, W., *Internationales Privatrecht, Privatrechtsvergleichung, Einheitsprivatrecht*, Vienna, Springer-Verlag, 1995, 41; Schwimann, M., *Internationales Privatrecht, einschließlich Europarecht*, Vienna, Manzsche Verlags- und Universitätsbuchhandlung, 1999, 112.

[19] Austrian Supreme Court, July 28, 1983, (*Attco*), *GRUR Int.* 1984, 453, comm. H. Wirner (Austrian law applies to determine whether an Austrian trademark has been infringed; besides, Austria was the "Handlungsort," that is, the place where the infringing act occurred); Austrian Supreme Court, January 14, 1986 (*Sacher Hotel*), *GRUR Int.* 1986, 735 (German law applies to decide whether the manufacturing in Germany of "Wieners Sachers Kaffee" infringed the German trademark and the commercial name held by the Sacher Hotel). In fact, in those two cases, the literal interpretation of Article 34(1) Austrian PIL would have resulted in the application of the same substantive law.

[20] Austrian Supreme Court, June 17, 1986, (*Hotel-Video*), *GRUR Int.* 1986, 728 (Austrian law applies because the plaintiff claims to have copyright protection in Austria); Austrian Supreme Court, September, 18, 1990 (*Sachverständigenprüfung*), *GRUR Int.* 1991, 650 (a distributive application of Article 34(1) Austrian PIL leads to the application of German and Austrian copyright law).

[21] Austrian Supreme Court, September 28, 1993, *GRUR Int.* 1994, 638 (it is necessary for the plaintiff to adduce evidence as to the allegedly infringed rights; *in casu*, the plaintiff claimed to be entitled to cross-border protection against acts constituting copyright infringement).

the law of the protecting state as a connecting factor (...). The protecting state is not the state where the proceedings are pending. If the plaintiff claims that the defendant has infringed all or some of the rights that the former holds in several states, the alleged infringement shall be assessed in each state on the basis of the law of the state where the infringement took place (unless renvoi applies)."

On a balance, it is interesting to note that the Austrian Supreme Court has explicitly confirmed that a distributive application of the choice of law rule is the most appropriate solution in a cross-border infringement situation. It is submitted that this solution should and probably will be adopted by other European jurisdictions faced with similar cross-border cases.

bb) The Netherlands

The Dutch Private International Statute on Torts[22] does not contain any reference to infringements of intellectual property. In the absence of a specific choice of law rule for infringement of intellectual property rights, resort to the general choice of law rule, i.e., the *lex loci delicti*, appears to be possible. The Dutch Supreme Court explicitly confirmed in the *Bigott/Doucal* case that a copyright infringement falls within the scope of the tort choice of law rule.[23] It follows that the same rule applies in patent or trademark cases.

According to Article 3(1) of Dutch PIL, the law governing torts is the *lex loci delicti*.[24] However, a number of exceptions, such as the choice of law by the parties or the law of the common domicile, are available under Dutch PIL.[25] It is questionable whether these exceptions are compatible with the particularities of patent enforcement.[26]

It is interesting to note that the Dutch courts – which for a number of years now have been willing to take jurisdiction over cross-border patent infringement disputes – do not seem to have devoted much attention to the thorny issue of the law applicable to the dispute. The fact that patent litigation generally

---

[22] Statute on the Law Applicable to Torts of April 11, 2001, hereafter "Dutch PIL," available in English in *NILR* (*Netherlands International Law Review*), 2003, 222-224. For a German translation and thorough commentary on the Statute, cf. Kadner Graziano, T., "Das niederländische 'Gesetz zum Kollisionsrecht der unerlaubten Handlung' (Wet conflictenrecht onrechtmatige daad) – Ein Vergleich mit der deutschen Kodifikation und dem europäischen Rechtszustand," *IPRax* 2004, 137-145 and 157-158.

[23] Dutch Supreme Court, January 27, 1995, (*Bigott/Doucal*), *N.I.P.R.* 1995, 388 (whether infringement exists is determined by the law of the place where the alleged acts of infringement have been committed). See, similarly, Court of Appeals Arnhem, June 26, 1993, *B.I.E.* 1995, 44; *N.I.P.R.* 1995, 555 (the acts of infringement committed outside Dutch territory fall within the scope of the respective *lex loci delicti*).

[24] This provision confirms the case law of the Dutch *Hoge Raad* (cf. Dutch Supreme Court, November 19, 1993, (*COVA/Banque Générale du Luxembourg*), *N.J.* 1994, nr. 622, 2901).

[25] Cf. Strikwerda, L., *Inleiding tot het Nederlandse Internationaal Privaatrecht*, 7th ed., Deventer, Kluwer, 2002, 182-188.

[26] Cf. Pontier, J.A., *Onrechtmatige daad*, in: Praktijkreeks IPR nr. 16, Deventer, Kluwer, 2001, 95-96.

forms the object of interlocutory proceedings (*kort geding*) probably explains why the issue of which law is applied to the infringement courts has remained latent in a number of cases.

Only a few decisions have confirmed that an alleged patent infringement must be governed by the *lex loci delicti* and that, if jurisdiction is taken over infringement in different states, the law of each state must be applied. For instance, in an (unpublished) judgment in *Foster/Cargo Handling Systems*, the president of the District Court of the Hague stated that it was necessary to take into consideration the German and British interpretation of the doctrine of equivalents, as the plaintiff had requested a cross-border injunction covering Germany and the United Kingdom.[27] Another example is given in the *Rhône Poulenc/Prographarm* judgment (translation):[28]

> "It is not disputed by Pharmachemie c.s. in the current kort geding proceedings that the activities carried out by defendants 2 to 5 in France should be governed by French law in order to determine whether the rights of Rhône Poulenc SA have been infringed."

Although it is generally accepted that the *lex loci delicti* applies to the question of the existence or non-existence of a patent infringement, whether in *kort geding* or final proceedings, it is submitted that the practical difficulties resulting from the multiplicity of applicable laws have contributed to doctrinal disagreement as to two essential issues in patent infringement cases. First, it has been pointed out that *kort geding* proceedings may not be the appropriate tool to try complicated patent cases. Second, it has been questioned whether the remedies available for patent infringement – and, in particular, the grant of an interim injunction – fall within the scope of the *lex loci delicti* or must be determined by the *lex fori* as the law applicable to procedural matters. To anticipate an argument to be made below (p. 169 *et seq.*), it would seem appropriate to tackle those issues in the course of the legislative decision-making process toward a Rome II Regulation.

3. *An Envisaged Codification of the Lex Loci Protectionis*

If the Rome II Proposal were to be adopted in its current version, Article 8 would consolidate the position of the *lex loci protectionis* as the specialized choice of law rule for infringements of intellectual property rights.

Article 8 of the Rome II Proposal reads as follows:

---

[27] This judgment is reported by J. Brinkhof. Cf. "Het grensoverschrijdend verbod in kort geding," *in* Boele-Woelki, K. and Grosheide, F.-W., (eds.), *Europees Privaatrecht*, Molengrafica, Lelystad, 1995, 242.

[28] President District Court The Hague, January 5, 1993, (*Rhône Poulenc/Prographarm*), *I.E.R.* 1993, 61. In the same vein. District Court The Hague, August 13, 2003, (*SmithKline Beecham/Synthon*), unpublished.

> Infringement of intellectual property rights
> 1. The law applicable to a non-contractual obligation arising from an infringement of an intellectual property right shall be the law of the country for which protection is sought.
> 2. In the case of a non-contractual obligation arising from an infringement of a unitary Community industrial property right, the relevant Community instrument shall apply. For any question that is not governed by that instrument, the applicable law shall be the law of the Member State in which the act of infringement is committed.

As Community rights are discussed elsewhere in this book,[29] what follows is an analysis of Article 8 Rome II Proposal from the perspective of the enforcement of national patent rights (generally arising out of a European or PCT patent application).

a) The Need for a Specialized Choice of Law Rule

The Commission acknowledges that the general rules contained in Articles 10 and 3 of the Rome II Proposal are incompatible with the specific requirements in the field of intellectual property. Indeed, neither party autonomy nor the closest connection with the tort (as identified on the basis of Article 3) are habitual connecting factors in choice of law rules applicable to infringements of intellectual property rights, or patent rights in particular.

Which connecting factor should be preferred within the IP infringement category? The Commission's choice for the *lex loci protectionis* is, to my mind, not only justified from a comparative point of view but also from the perspective of policy considerations. First, it needs to be recalled that recent codifications in Switzerland and Italy (and possibly Belgium) have adopted a similar connecting factor. Besides, some countries using the *lex loci delicti* rule advocate a peculiar interpretation of this choice of law rule in the specific area of infringement of intellectual property rights – for instance, Austria. Third, from the perspective of policy considerations, it is important to note that the *locus protectionis* is easily ascertainable and hence facilitates the task of determining the applicable law. It could be argued that using the *locus delicti* as a connecting factor presents the same advantage. However, the determination of the *locus delicti* may give rise to some difficulty because each national law has a different notion of what an act of infringement entails for the purposes of determining the governing law.[30] Where, for example, is the infringement place when a corporation manufactures an alleged infringing product in State A and sells it in States B and C through a local distributor? It appears that ascertaining the place where patent protection is claimed gives rise to fewer difficulties. Another argument in favor of the proposed rule is that it not only applies to

---

[29] Cf. the contribution of Winfried Tilmann (p. 123 et seq).

[30] Jiménez Blanco, P., *El derecho aplicable a la protección internacional de las patentes*, Granada, Comares, 1998, 78-79.

infringement cases but obviously also to issues related to the creation and validity of intellectual property rights. Accordingly, in patent infringement disputes where the patent validity is challenged, there is no need to distinguish between tortious and validity issues for the purposes of determining the applicable law. It follows that, in patent enforcement, it seems appropriate to deviate from the general rule for torts – the *lex loci delicti* – in favor of the specific *lex loci protectionis*.

b) Scope of Application of the *Lex Loci Protectionis*

Despite the growing consensus on the *lex loci protectionis* as the most consistent solution for the treatment of cross-border patent disputes, it is likely that the application of Article 8 Rome II Proposal will encounter important practical difficulties.

In particular, attention should be drawn to the scope of the *lex loci protectionis* from a material and territorial point of view.

aa) Material Scope of Application

According to Article 11 of the Rome II Proposal, the *lex loci protectionis* governs (in cross-border patent enforcement) *inter alia,* "the conditions and extent of liability ... and, *within the limits of its powers*, the measures which a court has power to take under its procedural law to prevent or terminate injury or damage or to ensure the provision of compensation"(emphasis added, MPS).

The references to the procedural law as the framework for the operation of Article 8 of the Rome II Proposal may give rise to problems of qualification. In fact, certain issues arising in the context of patent infringement disputes cannot be qualified as being inherent to patents as such, and accordingly fall outside the scope of application of the *lex loci protectionis*. It is important in order to define the scope of the choice of law rule to distinguish the issues being treated as part of the patent right from those that may be qualified as being procedural and hence falling under the *lex fori*.

Based upon the very wide function that Article 11 Rome II Proposal confers to the *lex loci protectionis*, it is debated whether, *inter alia*, the availability of remedies in interlocutory proceedings or the measure of damages have a procedural or a substantive nature. What follows is a personal interpretation of how to draw the dividing line between the *lex loci protectionis* and the *lex fori* as law applicable to procedural matters.[31]

On the one hand, there seems to be a well-established rule that issues relating to the *enforcement* of a patent right have a substantive nature. This

---

[31] Cf. Pertegás Sender, M., *Cross-border enforcement of patent rights*, Oxford, OUP, 2002; 264-269.

refers not only to the exact scope of patent rights but also to the actionability of those rights, that is, the remedies that patent holders can invoke against third parties. Accordingly, the *lex loci protectionis* determines the content and limitations of the *ius prohibendi* and, in particular, the availability of injunctions and damages to restrain further infringement of the monopoly right conferred by the patent. More to the point, if the plaintiff requests a cross-border injunction covering countries A, B, and C, it is necessary that the laws of these three countries recognize such a remedy for a patent infringement. Although there may be a practical problem when it comes to adducing evidence of this foreign law, it can be assumed that the law of most states will foresee such injunctive relief for patent infringement as required by the international enforcement regime.[32] As for damages, the *lex loci protectionis* should apply only to ascertain whether monetary compensation may generally be awarded to remedy infringement. If the question is answered affirmatively, the amount of the monetary awards may be established according to the *lex fori*.

On the other hand, matters related to procedure are governed by the law of the forum. Of particular importance to patent infringement disputes is the classification of the rules of evidence, the available procedures, and the measure of damages as procedural matters and, hence, outside the scope of the *lex loci protectionis*.

It follows that a distinction should be made between the availability of a given remedy – generally, injunctive relief and/or damages – and the procedure(s) available to the plaintiff to request those remedies. It is submitted that only the latter is governed by the law of the forum.

Accordingly, the thorny question of the applicable law to an action for interim injunctive relief is twofold. The court must base the awarded remedy on the *lex loci protectionis* but, on the other hand, it shall apply its own procedural rules to determine whether shortened and/or accelerated proceedings are available to the plaintiff.

If this interpretation of Article 11(d) Rome II Proposal is followed, there would be an incentive for *forum shopping* in states which provide for effective quick-fix procedures. Consider, for instance, the *Fort Dodge/Akzo Nobel* case.[33] In a case where 99 percent of the allegedly infringing activities had taken place in the United Kingdom, the plaintiff sought interim injunctive relief through a *kort geding* brought before the Dutch courts. The alleged infringer considered that it was vexatious that the plaintiff – a Dutch multinational – asked "a home court to interrupt a business which is well established in a foreign market, namely the United Kingdom, on an interlocutory basis and adopting principles which are alien to those which would have been applied by a British court."

32 See, for instance, Article 41 TRIPs Agreement.

33 Court of Appeals, *Fort Dodge v. Akzo Nobel*, *F.S.R.* 1998, 222.

Irrespective of the jurisdictional issue of whether a foreign defendant may be brought before the Dutch courts, it is submitted that it is indeed for Dutch law as the law of the forum to decide upon the availability of shortened procedures in the particular circumstances of the dispute.

In short, despite the adoption of a common European choice rule for infringement of intellectual property rights, the law applicable to the enforcement of patent rights is likely to remain a source of legal debate for the future. Referral to the *lex fori* for vital issues in patent infringement disputes such as the procedures for obtaining remedies and the lack of harmonization for such procedural matters may still lead to inconsistent case law after the entering into force of Rome II.

bb) Territorial Scope of *lex loci protectionis*

Once it has been established that the law of the protecting country applies to patent infringement disputes, the courts must be prepared to accept that different sets of rules may have to be applied to a cross-border patent infringement dispute. Indeed, an action of infringement based on parallel patents granted in different states requires a distributive application of the choice of law rule, and hence the application of the law(s) of the country for which protection is requested. If, for instance, a Belgian company invokes its European patent designating Belgium, the Netherlands, Germany, and France against an Italian competitor, the court needs to examine whether the alleged infringing acts fall within the scope of protection conferred by the law of each state for which protection is claimed.

It is striking that neither Article 8 itself nor explicitly the Commission Explanatory Memorandum acknowledges that a distributive application of the connecting factor is indeed the most appropriate solution to conflicts of patent laws. It is, however, submitted that the Commission favors a distributive application of Article 8(1) Rome II proposal. The Explanatory Memorandum refers indeed to the territorial scope of patent protection and concludes that "this rule, also known as the 'territorial principle,' enables each country to apply its own law to an infringement of an intellectual property right which is in force in its territory: counterfeiting an industrial property right is governed by the law of the country in which the patent was issued (…). This solution confirms that the rights held in each country are independent."[34]

It would be preferable for the definitive Rome II Regulation to explicitly acknowledge that several laws shall apply if protection is claimed for the territory of several states. Consequently, in cases where infringement takes place in several countries, it is not possible to apply the most protective of the

34 Rome II Proposal, p. 20.

laws of the different protecting states.[35] Neither is it possible to select the law of the state where the infringing effects are the most noticeable in order to avoid the distributive application of the choice of law rule.

It has been pointed out by several commentators[36] that a distributive application of the choice of law rule results in an increasing number of cases where the courts will have to deal with foreign law. Is it realistic to take it for granted that the judges' expertise in patent law covers not only their own legal system but also those of other countries for which protection is claimed?

Admittedly, litigation on the basis of foreign law is complicated and time-consuming. However, one should not overestimate the complexities arising from a distributive application of the choice of law rule. It is submitted that there will be many cases in which the allegedly infringing acts or products will indeed fall squarely within the patent claims, howsoever interpreted, and, consequently, the acts of the alleged infringer will be prohibited.[37] In other words, the application of a multiplicity of laws will lead to the same substantive result as to whether or not an infringement was committed.[38] However, it is not unthinkable for the court to be confronted with *Epilady* situations, that is, borderline infringement cases that may result in a finding of infringement according to one national law and a finding of non-infringement according to another national law. Consequently, a court should be prepared to explore the different interpretations granted to Article 69 of the EPC in the countries for which protection is claimed. The differences in interpretation of the patent claims and the divergent application of the doctrine of equivalents by the national courts may result, in exceptional cases, in a finding of infringement according to the law of one country, while there appears to be no infringement

---

35 Compare Geller, P.E., "International Intellectual Property, Conflicts of Laws and Internet Remedies," *E.I.P.R.* 2000, 130 (the localization of the infringing acts may take into consideration the (high) standard of protection set up by the TRIPs Agreement).

36 Brinkhof, J.J., "Beslechting van octrooigeschillen in Europa. Er moet nu echt wat gebeuren," in: Verkade, D.W.F. en Visser, D.J.G., (eds.), *Intellectuele eigenaardigheden: Opstellen aangeboden aan mr. Theo R. Bremer*, Deventer, Kluwer, 1998, 42. Similarly, O'Sullivan, G., "*Cross-border jurisdiction in patent infringement proceedings*," *E.I.P.R.* 1996, 661.

37 The courts have often relied on the presumption that, on the basis of the EPC and its Protocol on Interpretation, patent claims will be given a harmonized interpretation in the different EPC Contracting States. See, for instance, President District Court The Hague, April 9, 1996, (*Washington Research Foundation/Thamer e.a.*) *B.I.E.* 1998, 418; President District Court The Hague, May 22, 1995, (*Raychem/Thermon*), *B.I.E.* 1996, 130 (parallel patents not originating in European patent grant); President District Court The Hague, May 3, 1995, (*Bard/TD Medical*) *B.I.E.* 1996, 300.

38 For instance, the District Court Düsseldorf was seized with a case related to a patent licensing agreement covering Germany, France, the United Kingdom, Italy, and Sweden. The defendant refused to pay the agreed fees because it claimed that it had not used the plaintiff's patents. The main question was whether the products manufactured by the defendant fell within the patent's scope of protection. The German court answered in the affirmative by referring to the substantive law of each protecting state. See District Court Düsseldorf, September 22, 1998, (*Sonnenblende II*), *GRUR Int.* 1999, 458.

under the law of another country. It is a fact that such inconsistencies can only be avoided through a complete unification of substantive law.

The scarce case law on this issue shows that national courts tend to adopt a rather pragmatic view. In cases where (the national parts of a) European patent have been allegedly infringed, the court could get around the difficulty of having to apply different national laws through Article 69 of the EPC and the Protocol on the Interpretation of Article 69 of the Convention.[39] If infringement has been established on the basis of the local law, and unless evidence to the contrary is presented, a court could presume that there is no difference between forum and foreign law on the scope of protection conferred by the different patent rights. Especially in interlocutory proceedings, the investigation on foreign laws appears to be rather superficial.[40]

III. Concluding Remarks: What Is the Added Value of Rome II?

Taking the current predominance of the *lex loci protectionis* into consideration, one could argue that the added value of Article 8 of the Rome II Proposal, if adopted, is rather limited. Is it necessary to include a provision on the infringement of IP rights within the envisaged Rome II Regulation?

Several reasons may be adduced for a positive answer.

First, it is likely that an increasing number of patent disputes will be of a multinational nature. Cross-border litigation is a swifter, more effective way for the claimant to tackle a cross-border infringement. While the discussion has focused so far on the allocation of international jurisdiction, it may be expected that the debate on the applicable law will rapidly gain the attention it deserves. However, in the absence of clear guidelines, the debate on the applicable law may seriously affect the emerging cross-border patent enforcement strategies.

---

[39] Article 69 EPC provides that: "The extent of the protection conferred by a European patent or a European patent application shall be determined by the terms of the claims. Nevertheless, the description and drawings shall be used to interpret the claims."

The Protocol on the Interpretation of Article 69 EPC further specifies that this provision "should not be interpreted in the sense that the extent of the protection conferred by a European patent is to be understood as that defined by the strict, literal meaning of the wording used in the claims, the description and drawings being employed only for the purpose of resolving an ambiguity found in the claims. Neither should it be interpreted in the sense that the claims serve only as a guideline and that the actual protection conferred may extend to what, from a consideration of the description and drawings by a person skilled in the art, the patentee has contemplated. On the contrary, it is to be interpreted as defining a position between these extremes which combines a fair protection for the patentee with a reasonable degree of certainty for third parties."

[40] Cf. Pres. District Court Brussels, September 14, 2001, (*Colgate/Unilever*), *I.E.R.* 2002, 34. In that decision, the court granted a cross-border preliminary injunction without apparently devoting any attention to foreign patent law.

Second, there is at present no general consensus that the law of the protecting state should be the relevant choice of law rule. This may constitute an incentive for forum shopping. Furthermore, there is virtually no case law on how to ascertain and apply the relevant choice of law rule to cross-border patent enforcement cases. Due to the growing interest of litigants and doctrinal writers in cross-border patent enforcement, it would be desirable to introduce a uniform choice of law rule at the European level.

Third, the general regime in Rome II is not compatible with the territorial nature of patent rights. Accordingly, it would be inappropriate to unify the choice of law rules for non-contractual obligations without specifically taking the specific nature of tort disputes involving patent rights into consideration.

This contribution has highlighted some issues which need further consideration in the course of the legislative decision-making with regard to Rome II. First, it has been suggested to explicitly acknowledge that a situation of multiple infringements occurring in different countries shall be governed by the respective law of the state for which protection is invoked. Second, one should be aware of the added complications of a piecemeal application of patent laws. Although such complications cannot be underestimated, it is important to keep in mind that only substantive issues arising out of patent infringement litigation will be governed by the *lex loci protectionis*. Vital issues in infringement disputes such as the procedures for obtaining remedies are qualified as procedural matters and, consequently, do not fall under the scope of Article 8 of the forthcoming Rome II.

On the whole, a uniform choice of law rule along the lines of Article 8 of the Rome II Proposal is to be welcomed. The application of the current choice of law rules is a source of increasing unpredictability for cross-border patent strategies. A uniform choice of law rule – guaranteeing a distributive application of the law of the state of protection – constitutes an essential step in the "ongoing process"[41] toward coherent and predictable cross-border patent enforcement.

[41] In the words of Barbosa, C.R., "From Brussels to The Hague – The Ongoing Process Towards Effective Multinational Patent Enforcement," *I.I.C.* 2001, 729-763.

Trademark Conflicts on the Internet: Territoriality Redefined?

Annette Kur

I. Introduction

As was pointed out by Ansgar *Ohly* in his presentation at the Frauenchiemsee Conference in July 2003,[1] the problems we face in transborder trademark infringement cases typically result from a conflict of rights rather than from conflict of laws.[2] This applies in particular to the situation within the European

---

[1] The conference entitled "Jurisdiction and Choice of Law in Intellectual Property Matters – Perspectives for the Future" was arranged by the Max Planck Institute for Intellectual Property, Competition, and Tax Law. A. *Ohly*'s contribution under the title "Choice of Law in the Digital Environment – Problems and Possible Solutions" will be published in Drexl/Kur (eds.), IP and Private International Law – Heading for the Future (forthcoming).

[2] Although it is a consequence of the territoriality principle that governs all types of intellectual property rights, the problem is particularly acute in trademark law. In patent law, the fact that global novelty is normally required as a precondition for protection leaves only small chances for the acquisition by an independent inventor of a valid, parallel right in another territory than that where the patent was first obtained. In copyright, the legal structure is essentially different from trademark (and patent) law anyway, as the act of creation brings into existence one right which is universal in its nature, notwithstanding the fact that it is territorial in the sense that according to Art. 5.2 of the Berne Convention, content and scope of the right depend on the legal situation in the country where protection is sought. Another important difference between copyright and trademark (as well as patent) law concerns the fact that copyright does not confer a barring effect, as the right is not infringed by another independent creation, irrespective of the territory where it is conceived or used. Hence the problems arising in connection with Internet use of content protected by copyright usually are genuine choice of law problems in the sense that they result from differences in national

Union, where the substantive law applying to registered trademarks is fully harmonized.[3] Classical choice of law problems are therefore mostly confined to the area of sanctions, and this in particular with regard to Community trademarks, as has been explained in the contribution by *Tilmann*.[4] However, even after full substantive harmonization, national trademark rights remain subject to the basic principle of territoriality; this implies the possibility that the same or very similar marks, protected for the same or similar goods or services, belong to different owners in different member states, with the result that a conflict arises between them if any of them engages in transborder activities.

As a matter of principle, the situation is neither unknown in the world of intellectual property nor does it entail serious problems, as long as the transborder activities are carried out in the real or analogue world. If a trademark right belonging to X exists in state A, X will be in a position to sue any other person using the same or a similar mark for the same or similar goods or services, regardless of the fact that the alleged infringer may be the legitimate holder of that mark in state B. With the advent of the Internet, however, the scenario has become more complicated. As is frequently observed, it is hard to reconcile the global space created by digital communication media with the basic structure of territoriality, on which intellectual property, in particular industrial property rights, so heavily rely. This has given rise to (partly antagonistic) fears and misgivings which may be summarized as follows: As it is not possible any longer to confine the use of trademarks to individual territories, their presence on the Internet would necessarily and severely jeopardize the principle of territorial exclusivity. On the other hand, if exclusivity were to be enforced in a rigid manner even vis-à-vis use on the Internet, this would make commercial use of the Internet extremely hazardous or even impossible for trademark holders, as they could never be sure whether posting their signs in cyberspace would lead head-on into a conflict with a right existing somewhere in the world, in any country where computers have access to the Internet.

When reviewing the first alarmed reactions to the emerging difficulties, it comes as a pleasant surprise that it has been possible within a rather short time to pave the way for a pragmatic solution. The outlines of that approach are set forth in the "WIPO Joint Recommendation Concerning Provisions on the Protection of Marks, and Other Industrial Property Rights in Signs, on the

---

copyright laws, in particular regarding the limitations of copyright, rather than from a conflict of parallel rights existing in different territories.

[3] On the basis of the First Council Directive 89/104/EEC of December 21, 1988, to approximate the laws of the Member States relating to trademarks OJ EC L 40/1. However, material differences may prevail between European trademark law and the trademark law of non-EU countries, e.g., between Switzerland and the EU, with respect to regional vs. global exhaustion of trademark rights; see the example given *infra* III.4.

[4] This volume, at p. 123 *et seq*.

Internet"[5] that was elaborated in the framework of the WIPO SCT ("Standing Committee on the Law of Trademarks, Industrial Design and Geographical Indications") and has met with unanimous approval by the Assemblies of WIPO and Paris Convention Member States in their meeting of autumn 2001. A brief account of its contents will be given in the following.[6]

II. The WIPO Recommendation

The essential element in the Joint Recommendation is the rule that a sign which is used on the Internet shall only be considered as being used in a specific country if it has *commercial effect* there. This principle is contained in Art. 2, which reads as follows:

> "Use of a sign on the Internet shall constitute use in a Member State for the purpose of these provisions only if the use has a commercial effect in that Member State as described in Art. 3."

Art. 3 encompasses a comprehensive list of factors to be taken into account when assessing the presence of commercial effect in a given country. It is emphasized in the text that the list is non-exclusive, but that all relevant circumstances have to be taken into consideration by the competent authorities.

The factors themselves are divided in several subgroups. These relate to (a) circumstances indicating that the user is doing or seriously intends to do business in the Member State, (b) the level and character of commercial activity of the user in relation to the Member State, (c) the connection of an offer of goods or services on the Internet with the Member State, (d) the connection of the manner of use of goods or services on the Internet with the Member State, and finally, (e) the relation of the use of the sign on the Internet with a right in that sign in the Member State. All subgroups – apart from (a) – are further exemplified by making reference to situations which are indicative of specific modes of commercial use. For instance, when assessing the level and character of commercial activity in relation to the Member State according to (b), it would be decisive whether the user has actually served customers in the state concerned, or whether he offers post-sale activities there, etc.

---

[5] Adopted by the Assembly of the Paris Union for the Protection of Industrial Property and the General Assembly of the World Intellectual Property Organization (WIPO) at the Thirty-Sixth Series of Meetings of the Assemblies of the Member States of WIPO September 24–October 3, 2001, published on the WIPO website at <http://www.wipo.int/about-ip/en/development_iplaw/pub845.htm>.

[6] For more details, see *Wichard*, The Joint Recommendation Concerning Protection of Marks, and Other Industrial Property Rights in Signs, on the Internet, in: Drexl/Kur (*supra* note 1); see also *Kur*, Use of Trademarks on the Internet – The WIPO Recommendations, 33 IIC 41-47 (2002); *Ohly*, Kennzeichenkonflikte im Internet, in: Leible (ed.), Die Bedeutung des internationalen Privatrechts im Zeitalter der neuen Medien, 2003, p. 135, at 141 *et seq.*

Another important feature in the Joint Recommendation is the so-called "notice and avoidance of conflict" mechanism embedded in Artt. 9 *et seq*. The background is as follows:

The WIPO Recommendation relies on the general principle that two equally legitimate users of a protected sign should be allowed to co-exist on the Internet, if and to the extent that they both try their best to avoid a commercial effect in the country where the other person has a better right. This leaves the question as to what consequences might result from the use made of a sign on the Internet *before* any of the parties was aware of the conflict, and before the necessary safeguarding measures have been taken against evoking a commercial effect in the country or countries where the conflict exists. According to the clear majority opinion voiced during the negotiations in the SCT, the solution should be that a good-faith user could not be held liable for the violation of a right existing in another territory, before having been notified of the existence of that right in a certain prescribed manner. Hence the principle is set out in Art. 9 that the ordinary remedies for trademark infringement and unfair competition shall only apply if, and after, the user has failed to react in an adequate manner to the notice given to him, e.g., by adding a disclaimer, or by otherwise changing the text of the website or his or her commercial conduct.

The provisions following Art. 9 contain further details on the procedure. Pursuant to Art. 10, the user must explain to the rightholder why the use of the sign is legitimate in principle. Furthermore, and most important, the user must expeditiously undertake reasonable measures in order to avoid a commercial effect that would result in an infringement in the Member State where the conflicting right exists. Art. 11 regulates the way in which the notification must be given. Art. 12 sets out as a matter of principle that Member States must accept, *inter alia*, disclaimers as a reasonable measure to avoid a conflict, and it regulates in some detail which requirements must be fulfilled so that a statement can be acknowledged as constituting a disclaimer that is legally efficient.

In its last part, Artt. 13-15, the Recommendation deals with remedies. As a general principle, it is set out that remedies must be proportionate to the commercial effect of the use in a particular country, and that the legitimate user of a sign must be given the opportunity to adopt safeguarding measures – e.g., to add disclaimers to the text of his website or by creating gateway pages – in order to avoid a conflict with another sign in the territory where that sign is protected.[7]

---

[7] It is interesting to note in this context that although Art. 15 in principle stipulates that a national court should, wherever possible, try to avoid sanctions that would prohibit any future use of the sign on the Internet, it also confirms at least indirectly that a possibility exists for courts to impose injunctions with a global effect. However, a "global injunction," as it may be called, should never be imposed when the user of a sign is permitted to make that use under the law of a Member State to which he has a close connection, and when he uses the sign in good faith.

It will be obvious from these brief outlines that the WIPO Recommendation offers a common-sense-inspired compromise solution rather than seeking to preserve the territoriality principle in its pure form. Although the general rule is maintained that trademarks do possess a privileged position within the territory where their owner enjoys priority, it will be impossible in case of a genuine conflict of rights to claim of one's adversary 100 percent abstention from interference with a national right if that results from contents posted in cyberspace. While this principle appears to be acceptable – and accepted – as a point of departure, it entails a number of issues to be considered regarding its legal nature and its practical implications.

III. Issues to Consider

1. Legal Nature of the Market Impact Rule

The first question to be posed under the heading of this conference concerns the legal qualification of the Recommendation, in particular its basic rule that trademark use on the Internet does not infringe a right existing in a particular territory unless it has commercial effect there (in the following: market impact rule.) Is this a new kind of choice of law rule? The general and – in my view – correct opinion answers this in the negative.[8] The market impact rule as embedded in the WIPO Recommendation is not a rule determining the applicable law, but rather a rule pertaining to substantive law that serves to define and delimit the notion of infringement as occurring in a particular country.[9]

This result is sustained by examples from case law,[10] where courts faced with conflicts resulting from Internet use of trademarks have followed a similar route. For instance, when the French Tribunal de Grande Instance[11] held that

---

[8] See in particular *Wichard*, in Drexl/Kur (*supra* note 1); *Ohly*, in Drexl/Kur (*supra* note 1). It may, however, be relevant, at least indirectly, for ascertaining jurisdiction; see *infra*.

[9] For an in-depth analysis of the relation between choice of law and substantive law with respect to the territoriality principle, see *Fentiman,* Choice of Law and Intellectual Property, in Drexl/Kur (*supra* note 1). That a solution in Internet trademark infringement cases had to found on the level of substantive rather than in rules on jurisdiction or applicable law had already been argued at an early stage by *Bettinger & Thum*, Territorial Trademark Rights in The Global Village – International Jurisdiction, Choice of Law and and Substantive Law for Trademark Disputes on the Internet, 31 IIC 162, 285.

[10] In addition to the cases referred to in the following text, see Karlsruhe Court of Appeals, MMR 2002, 814 (case note *Mankowski*, at 817 *et seq.*); see also decisions by the London High Court, *1-800 Flowers Inc. v. Phonenames Ltd.*, [2002] F.S.R. 697, confirmed on appeal, [2002] F.S.R. 12, and *Euromarket Designs v. Peters and Crate & Barrel Ltd.*, [2001] F.S.R. 20.

[11] *SA BD Multimedia v. Joachim H.*, decision of March 11, 2003 reported in 05/03 BNA World Business & IP Report, 9. A different approach had been taken in the oft-cited decision by the Nanterre Court of Appeal in the Brokat (payline) case, decision of October 13, 1996, *SG 2 v. Brokat Informationssysteme GmbH.* The court found that the mere presence on the Internet

the use made by a German-based company of the domain name "domina.net" did not infringe the trademark "domina" which is registered and used by the plaintiff in France and several other countries, it certainly did not apply any foreign law, e.g., German law as the law where the allegedly infringing domain name was most likely having commercial effect. Instead, the claim was dismissed *inter alia* on the ground that absent a showing of actual harm, there was no trademark infringement under French law. The same applies to the *Hotel Maritime* case decided by the Hamburg Court of Appeals[12] concerning the advertising of a Danish hotel that allegedly infringed on the German trademark "Maritim". To apply Danish law as the law of the country to which the allegedly infringing advertisement for hotel services was primarily directed,[13] and where the services were actually rendered, was never even considered. German law was applied as a matter of self-evidence, and the claim was dismissed for lack of sufficient connection with the domestic market (*fehlender Inlandsbezug*).

Having said this, the legal basis in substantive law for such decisions must be identified. It is obvious that referring to the WIPO Recommendation would not account for a sufficient answer. Although having received the unanimous support by the Governing Assemblies and thus being backed by a strong political will, the WIPO Recommendation remains soft law. Hence, its role is confined at best to influencing the interpretation of the law as it stands unless a national legislature decides to introduce relevant changes; however, there is no obligation to do so.

Therefore, the sole legal basis for the assessment of cross-border trademark conflicts in EU Member States remains the national laws that have been harmonized on the basis of the trademark directive, or, when it comes to conflicts with a Community trademark, the Community Trademark Regulation (CTMR). Neither the directive, the CTMR, or any of the national laws have incorporated an express rule stating that in case of use of a conflicting mark on the Internet, infringement can only be found if commercial effect, or a similar criterion like actual harm, can be established. It has therefore been argued that in order to meet the challenges posed by trademark use on the Internet, the trademark directive as well as the CTMR should be changed.[14]

As sensible and understandable as this advice may be, the prospects for it to be followed in the near future appear minimal at best. Other arguments must be employed in order to sustain the common sense-induced results which have

---

of a German trademark on a website addressing German customers in the German language was sufficient to establish infringement of a French mark; see also *infra* 4.

[12] Hanseatisches OLG, MMR 2002, 822 – hotel-maritime.dk. The case is discussed in detail by *Ohly*, in Drexl/Kur (*supra* note 1).

[13] The hotel also tried to attract German customers by offering text in German on its website and distributing brochures in German. However, the decisive aspect was that the services offered were rendered in Denmark only.

[14] *Bettinger & Thum* (*supra* note 9), at 295 *et seq.*

been found by the courts in the decisions cited above. Indeed, it should not be difficult to reach consensus that the notion of "use in commerce" set out in European trademark law does imply a territorial element insofar as use of a mark is only deemed to be legally relevant if it is made in *domestic* commerce.[15] From there, it is only a small step to conclude that use in a ubiquitous medium only takes place in domestic commerce if it actually has effect on, or is targeted at, the national market. It is then just consequent to assume that infringing use in domestic commerce does not occur if a person takes reasonable steps to avoid interference to the best possible degree.

Another question arising in the context concerns the extent to which these matters have to be considered for the purpose of establishing national jurisdiction on the basis of the *locus delicti commissi* rule. It was repeatedly argued in the literature[16] that it is desirable in principle to apply certain qualifying criteria in order to rule out that mere availability on the Internet of potentially conflicting signs will be held sufficient to establish jurisdiction of courts in any country where the conflict exists. Resolving the issue in the framework of substantive law might indeed appear detrimental for the interests of the defendant, as the possibility would persist that legal proceedings would be commenced against the defendant in a foreign court.[17] In practice, however, the differences resulting from one or the other approach will most probably be less profound than it seems at first sight. Even if the case actually turns upon the jurisdiction issue, potential defendants must be aware that it may be necessary for them to appear before court and answer the claim if the case gives rise to issues of law or fact which the court does not take up or decide on its own motion. Depending on procedural rules and practice in the country concerned, this situation may not differ substantially from a full trial when the court decides on the merits. Even worse, what the defendant gets after pursuing the case through the courts may be nothing more than a ruling on (lacking) jurisdiction, instead of a judgment rejecting the infringement claim as such.[18] Vice versa, if it is clear from the beginning that, in spite of the court assuming jurisdiction, the case will be lost because the market impact rule is applied in

---

[15] The argumentation is developed in more detail by *Kur*, Territorialität versus Globalität – Kennzeichenkonflikte im Internet,WRP 2000, 935, at 937 ff.

[16] Early comments in the German literature concerning Internet trademark (domain name) conflicts were mostly focused on issues of jurisdiction rather than substantive law; see, e.g., *Kuner,* Internationale Zuständigkeitskonflikte im Internet, CR 1996, 453; *Bettinger*, Kennzeichenrecht im Cyberspace: Der Kampf um die Domain-Namen, GRUR Int. 1997, 402, 416; *Ubber*, Rechtsschutz bei Mißbrauch von Internet-Domains, WRP 497, 502; *Omsels*, Die Kennzeichenrechte im Internet, GRUR 1997, 328, 336; *Kur*, Internet und Kennzeichenrecht, in Loewenheim & Koch (eds.), Praxis des Online-Rechts, 1998, 325, 375. See also *Schack*, Internationale Urheber-, Marken- und Wettbewerbsverletzungen im Internet, MMR 2000, 135, 138, arguing in favor of a wide assumption of jurisidiction.

[17] See in particular the critical remarks by *Mankowski*, (*supra* note 10), at 818.

[18] For a thorough development of these arguments, see in particular *Bettinger/Thum* (*supra* note 9).

the framework of substantive law, the temptation for a plaintiff to initiate proceedings before that court may not be so great after all.[19]

Nevertheless, it cannot and should not be generally precluded that the market impact rule is already taken into account for the purpose of establishing jurisdiction.[20] Whether a full and definite evaluation is already made at that stage of the proceedings, or (as a rule) only afterward, when the court assesses the merits of the case, is largely a matter of convenience and/or of national traditions and procedural law.[21] With that background, it can be concluded that for Germany – and probably also for other (continental) European countries – it seems correct to assume that the market impact rule is a matter of "double relevance," meaning that although it has an impact for jurisdiction, it will be fully tried only in the framework of assessing substantive infringement.[22] This means in practice that courts will deny their competence on the basis of Art. 5.3 of the Brussels Regulation only in exceptional situations, i.e., when it is obvious from the pleadings that there is no plausible case at all for an infringement occurring in that country. In case of doubt – as in the French and German cases referred to above[23] – courts will regularly assume jurisdiction, with the final outcome to be founded on a comprehensive analysis of the issues posed under substantive law, including the territorial aspects of "use in commerce."

2. *Should the Rule Be Incorporated in Instruments Dealing with Choice of Law?*

As is generally known, Art. 8 of the proposed Rome II regulation[24] establishes the country of protection principle with respect to all intellectual property infringements, without mentioning the market impact rule in any form.[25] From

---

[19] However, this will depend on the specifics of national law, e.g., the question of whether the losing party will have to bear the full costs of the proceedings, etc.

[20] The proposals for international jurisidiction rules presently under discussion, i.e., the draft IP principles elaborated in the framework of a project conducted by the American Law Institute (*infra* note 26) as well as the proposal elaborated by the (Munich) MPI working group and presented in Drexl/Kur (*supra* note 1) do therefore contain rules that are similar to the WIPO Recommendation.

[21] For instance, according to U.S. procedural law, a full evaluation of these matters will have to have already occurred at the jurisdiction stage in order to ensure compliance with the principle of due process; see, e.g., *Besusan Restaurant Corp. v. King*, 937 F.Supp. 295 (S.D.N.Y. 1996).

[22] See *Ohly* (*supra* note 6) at 145 *et seq.*; *Bettinger & Thum* (*supra* note 9), at 175 *et seq.*; *Kur* (*supra* note 15), at 936; critical on this point: *Mankowski* (*supra* note 10).

[23] *Supra* notes 11, 12.

[24] Commission Proposal of July 22, 2003 for a Regulation of the European Parliament and the Council on the law applicable to non-contractual obligations ("Rome II"), COM (2003) 427 final.

[25] The provision was inserted into the proposal of July 2003 following the recommendation by the Hamburg Group for Private International Law.

the analysis in the previous section, leading to the conclusion that the market impact rule pertains to substantive law rather than to choice of law issues, the consequence can be drawn that this does not interfere with the option for courts to take the aspect of commercial effect into account when assessing whether an alleged infringement has actually occurred in the country of protection whose law is to be applied in the case. From that point of view, there is no need to change Art. 8 of the proposed Rome II regulation in order to encompass a satisfactory solution for Internet trademark infringement cases.

However, while this solution may be sufficient on the European level, the problems raised by Internet communication are by no means confined to the European Union; they are typically of a global nature. In view of this larger environment, it would indeed appear advisable to anchor the market impact rule in the context of internationally accepted provisions or principles on choice of law (and international jurisdiction), given that the manner and extent to which the rule can be relied upon as forming part of national trademark laws all over the world is still unclear in spite of its acceptance by WIPO and Paris Convention Member States in the Joint Recommendation.

An attempt in that direction seems to have been made in the ALI preliminary draft Principles on Jurisdiction and Choice of Law in Transborder Disputes (in the following: draft IP principles).[26] Sec. 301, the basic provision on determination of the applicable law with respect to existence and scope of intellectual property rights, comprises in its second paragraph a rule according to which the law applicable to determine the existence, validity, and scope of (unregistered) intellectual property rights and the remedies for their infringement is the law of any country where the alleged infringing act has or will significantly impact the market for the work or subject matter at issue.[27] This proviso is identified by its wording as a genuine choice of law rule. Quite importantly, however, it applies to unregistered intellectual property rights only, whereas for registered rights, Sec. 301 paragraph 1 establishes the rule that the law applicable to determine the existence, validity, and scope of such rights is the law of each country of registration (which is by definition also the country of protection[28]).

---

[26] Intellectual Property – Principles Governing Jurisdiction, Choice of Law, and Judgments in Transnational Disputes; reporters: Rochelle *Dreyfuss*, Jane *Ginsburg*, and François *Dessemontet*. For details and an evaluation of the project as it stands at present, see the contribution by Catherine *Kessedjian*, this volume at p. 19 *et seq*.

[27] Draft IP principles, preliminary draft No. 2 (January 2004).

[28] The fact that Art 8.1 of the proposed Rome II regulation refers (in accordance with Art. 5.2 2nd sentence of the Berne Convention, but with a clearer wording) to the country for which protection is sought, whereas the draft IP principles (with regard to registered rights) refer to the country of registration, may therefore appear negligible. However, the phrase "country for which protection is sought" has specific merits which are lost when reference is made instead to the country of registration, namely that it emphasizes the aspect that the court, guided by the plaintiff's claims, must actually identify and specify those countries in its judgment. It should not be forgotten that for reasons of national sovereignty, the power of a

The distinction between registered and unregistered rights introduced by the draft IP principles is of relevance most of all for copyright, which is beyond the topic covered by this contribution.[29] However, it also discriminates between registered and unregistered trademarks and other kinds of distinctive signs, to the effect that with regard to the former, the market impact rule is not mentioned at all (and therefore only applies as a part of substantive law, if national law so permits), whereas it governs choice of law in conflicts involving the latter. As the legal situation is not so different in both types of cases – it being understood that unregistered marks and distinctive signs are territorial IP rights as well,[30] the act of registration only being replaced by other requirements imposed by national law for the protection of such signs[31] – this result appears somewhat puzzling.[32]

One possible argument in favor of the discrimination might be that in the kind of conflicts covered by Sec. 301 2nd paragraph of the draft IP principles, reverting to the law of the country of market impact makes choice of law easier than under the country of protection approach. For instance, when a person entitled to claim goodwill in an unregistered trademark in the United Kingdom claims infringement of his right by a German firm offering services to German customers over the Internet, a choice of law rule based on market impact will most likely point to German law only, with the result that the claim will be dismissed if the plaintiff cannot establish the existence of his right in Germany. On the basis of the country of protection approach, it might be unclear whether

court to issue a legally binding verdict is confined to its own territory, and that in order for this power to be extended, with the judgment having to be observed also by courts and authorities abroad, specific requirements must be met which must be clearly stated and evaluated in the decision. In a world where decisions having extraterritorial effect are becoming more and more frequent, but also potentially more contentious, courts as well as the parties involved should not be given too much leeway to issue sweeping decisions in matters involving multiterritorial IP infringement without clearly indicating their territorial range. Consequently, the phrase "country for which protection is sought" should not be abandoned, but rather be taken seriously, making it a genuine and, in principle, indispensable task for the plaintiff to declare and explain which countries' protection is actually sought, and for the court to state explicitly for which countries the verdict is granted, in the meaning that it shall become legally effective with respect to infringements that are carried out in, and/or being directed to, that country.

[29] On copyright and choice of law problems, see the contribution by Graeme *Dinwoodie*, this volume at p. 195 et seq.

[30] The legal situation would be different if unregistered marks and other distinctive signs were to be protected only on the basis of rules against unfair competition (see Art. 5 of the proposed Rome II convention, as opposed to Art. 8). However, at least in the EU, it is generally acknowledged that those signs do have the quality of genuine IP rights.

[31] Like use in domestic commerce, often with the use having to result in a specific degree of public awareness.

[32] The explanation given for the different treatment of registered and unregistered rights in Sec. 301 of the draft IP principles by François *Dessemontet* was that it had been the intention at the time of drafting to follow the "European" structure of Art. 3 of the (then) preliminary draft proposal for the Rome II regulation. See also *infra* note 38.

protection is sought for Germany, the United Kingdom, or for both.[33] The latter solution would imply the necessity to apply both German and British law with respect to the infringement possibly occurring in each of those countries.[34]

However, that advantage – if it is considered to be one[35] – is relatively small in those cases where a commercial effect is felt in a larger number of countries, such as, typically, when copyright is infringed by making protected content available on the Internet. In those situations, it will not be possible to identify, on the basis of the market impact rule, one single national law applying to the infringement in its entirety.[36] This is not to say that the market impact rule becomes irrelevant in these cases. However, the function it performs is no different from what was pointed out above on the need to introduce a market-oriented approach toward multiterritorial infringement of (registered) trademarks, namely to ensure that the alleged infringer will not be held liable with respect to countries where the dissemination of content did not have any, or only minimal, commercial effect.[37] This parallelism underlines what has been said before, i.e., that there hardly seem to be any plausible reasons[38] for making a general distinction between registered and unregistered rights in the provision

---

[33] It is worth pointing out again in this context that it is for the plaintiff, possibly assisted by the court, to define the country or countries for which protection is sought as precisely as possible in the claims; see also *supra* note 28.

[34] This would not change the outcome: for the UK, an unregistered right would be assertable, but no infringement has taken place because of lacking market impact; and for Germany, the situation is the same as pointed out in the text above.

[35] The fact that the country of protection rule (in the wording embedded in Art. 8 of the proposed Rome II regulation) when applied as a point of departure to multiterritorial infringement cases may tend to enhance the complexity of matters instead of reducing it should be considered a virtue rather than a drawback, as it helps to raise the awareness of courts and parties to the fact that certain cases do have legal implications for more than one country. Only if this is properly understood will it become clear how cautiously one must proceed to not too readily impose remedies that have been set out in national law with a view to monoterritorial conflicts only.

[36] With a view to these situations, Sec. 302 of the draft IP principles contains additional options, allowing for the application of a single set of legal rules; see *infra* 3.

[37] It is true that in addition to limiting the number of countries in which the alleged infringer can be held liable, the market impact rule would also make it clear that the law of countries where no or only minimal impact is shown cannot be invoked as a defense, e.g., by pointing out that the conduct at stake in the proceedings would be legitimate under the law of that country. However, these matters can be better dealt with in the framework of the following provision that regulates infringements carried out in ubiquitous media, than in the general rule contained in Sec. 301.

[38] François *Dessemontet*'s explanation of the background for the wording of Sec. 301 paragraph 2, namely that it was founded on Art. 3.1 of the Rome II (preliminary draft) proposal, can also hardly be taken for a convincing argument. The distinction made in tort law between "act" and "effect," as reflected in Art. 3 of the proposed Rome II regulation, is not helpful in intellectual property matters anyway, as the only relevant question is whether the right is infringed, no matter whether the behavior constituting infringement would have to be qualified as "act" or "effect" in terms of tort law.

establishing the fundamental rule for choice of law concerning the existence and scope of intellectual property rights.[39]

As a conclusion, it is suggested that it is neither necessary nor advisable to deviate from the country of protection approach as the basic rule for determining the law applicable for determining the existence and scope of trademark (and other intellectual property) rights in transborder conflicts,[40] whether the rights are registered or not. Furthermore, in order to arrive at sensible and practicable results in an international environment, it should be ensured that the notion of infringement occurring in a particular territory is adequately limited by the market impact rule. A recommendable approach would be to combine the two principles, as might be done in the following manner:[41]

a) The principle of *lex protectionis* (in a clearly defined form, as in Art. 8 of proposed Rome II regulation) is adopted as a general rule for the determination of existence and scope of all IP rights;
b) it is clarified in the provision what "country of protection" means with respect to (i) existence and (ii) infringement of IP rights – in the latter case, it means "country where the infringement occurs or is threatening to occur, and where the judgment shall take effect";

---

[39] This is different for the issue of initial ownership, where industrial property on the one hand and copyright on the other do pose different questions.

[40] As was remarked by Haimo *Schack* during the conference, the country of protection rule should not comprise the sanctions to be imposed where the possibility should persist for the parties to make an *ex-post* choice of the law to be applied. Likewise, it does not comprise the issue of initial ownership, which is in any case less problematic for trademarks than it is in copyright. However, it might be discussed whether in the case of a trademark right resulting from a contractual relationship, the issue of initial ownership should be determined according to the law governing the contract. This solution is endorsed in the second version of the draft IP principles (Jan. 2004).

[41] A provision in this vein, which follows the numbering and to some extent also the structure of the draft IP principles, could read as follows:

§ 301

General Rule

(1) As a general rule, the law applicable to determine the existence, validity, and scope of intellectual property rights is the law of the country for which protection is sought.

(2) The country for which protection is sought is

(a) …

(b) the country [each country] in which the alleged infringement occurs or is threatening to occur, and where, or in regard of which, the remedies claimed in the proceedings shall become effective.

(3) For the application of paragraph (2) (b) in transborder conflicts, an alleged infringement shall only be held to occur in a country if it has [commercial effect] [substantial impact on the market] in that country.

(4) Notwithstanding paragraph (3), an alleged violation of a personal right shall be held to occur in a country where the right is substantially affected.

c) it is stated that in transborder infringement cases, an infringement is only held to occur in a particular country if it has (substantial) commercial impact on the market there, which includes targeting of the market.[42]

3. Modification of the Basic Rule in Multiterritorial Infringement Cases

Having endorsed *lex protectionis* as the basic rule to be applied for determining the law governing existence and scope of trademark (as well as other IP) rights, it has to be conceded that for the assessment of infringements occurring on a global scale, it will be impossible to abide by a strict application of the country of protection principle, even if supplemented by a market impact rule. In addition to establishing a general rule like the one proposed above, the task remains therefore to promulgate provisions that are capable of coping with those extraordinary situations. In the present version of the draft IP principles, this task is assumed by Sec. 302. In exceptional cases, e.g., when it is unduly burdensome for the court to decide on the basis of all the laws of the territories involved, or when the content of the applicable substantive law cannot be ascertained,[43] the court shall identify the law most suitable to be applied in the case, preferably the law of the country with the closest connection to the dispute. As factors to be taken into account for choosing the appropriate law, the provision refers to the center of gravity of the alleged infringer's business undertaking as well as to the extent of the activities and the investment of the rightholder. Furthermore, attention shall be paid to "the degree to which the desirability of such regulation is generally accepted as evidenced by the TRIPS and successive international laws." As a default rule, the law of the forum shall apply.

The issues raised by the provision are too complex to be discussed here in detail, apart from the fact that their main impact will be in copyright rather than in trademark law. Nevertheless, the following aspects shall be highlighted. As a starting point, it must be remembered that even in the age of cyberspace, the importance and wisdom of the objectives underlying the territoriality principle should not be forgotten or underestimated; it is essential for safeguarding the individual states' sovereign decisions on how intellectual property should be regulated in their own country. There is no doubt that the *lex protectionis* rule as the principle presently dominating in private international IP law is best

[42] A reservation has to be made for personal rights and *droits moraux*, which may be affected even in the absence of commercial impact; see § 301. 3 of the draft IP principles and paragraph four of the provision proposed in the previous note.

[43] § 302 of the draft IP principles (Preliminary Draft No. 2, January 2004). Deviation from the country of protection principle shall also be possible if "it is clear from all the circumstances of the case that it is more closely connected to the law of another country," or if "there is a preexisting relationship between the parties that is closely connected with the claims in issue."

suited to ensure that the territoriality principle and its political implications are respected internationally.[44] It follows that each deviation from this rule must be motivated carefully, should be restricted to those cases when it is actually necessary, and should be phrased as precisely as possible regarding both the prerequisites for its application and its legal consequences.

It is highly doubtful that a rule like the one presently proposed in the draft IP principles lives up to these requirements. There is an obvious risk that courts, when applying these rules, will too easily resort to simplifying strategies whenever they find it too burdensome to apply foreign law, possibly with quite critical consequences.[45] In order to control such tendencies, the exceptional character of the rule should be established beyond doubt. It should be stated in an unmistakable fashion that the *lex protectionis* principle (supplemented by the market impact rule) must be observed as long as the foreign countries for which protection is sought are individually specified in the claims, and if the judgment shall become valid with respect to acts taken out within, or being (exclusively) targeted to, those countries.[46] By contrast, the use of simplifying strategies should be allowed for, and should be reserved to, cases concerned with an alleged infringement that is ubiquitous in the meaning that it occurs, or may occur, in an indefinite number of countries, so that individual specification in the claims is not possible, i.e., infringements carried out on the Internet or by comparable means.[47]

In the latter cases, the most sensible solution would indeed be to apply the law of the country having the closest connection to the infringement in its entirety. Pending further deliberations on how the determination should be made, it is foreseeable that the primary choice will often be between the country where the harmful effect of the infringement is felt most and the country from

---

[44] For an in-depth analysis of the issue, see *Fentiman*, in Drexl/Kur (*supra* note 1).

[45] As an example illustrating the mechanism of Sec. 302, the example is mentioned in the comments to the draft IP principles that two American companies use conflicting marks in a multitude of countries. Based on the factors listed in Sec. 302, the result is endorsed that "U.S. law will control issues of infringement around the world." Hence, the losing party would be hindered from doing further business in a country where, according to domestic law, using the mark would be perfectly legal. It would probably be a matter of (U.S.) constitutional law to decide whether this regulation is compatible with the general principle of freedom of citizens to engage in legitimate business abroad.

[46] In order to encompass possible difficulties that may accrue with respect to ascertaining the contents of the law in a given country, this rule could be qualified by a presumption stating that the substantive law in that country (a) does not differ substantially from the law of other countries whose law is applied in the proceedings and (b) complies with international conventions applicable in the field concerned. However, if those aspects do not furnish a sufficient basis for a presumption, the court should dismiss the claim regarding the country or countries whose law cannot be ascertained.

[47] It should be clear that a judgment based on that provision would only take effect against acts taken out in the same way – i.e., in ubiquitous media – and would not entail a prohibition of acts taken out in an ordinary, analogue fashion in a country whose law, in consequence of the application of a simplifying strategy, has not been taken into account for the decision.

which the infringement originates. This will typically coincide with the rightholder's and the defendant's main places of business respectively.[48] The key problem resulting from this constellation concerns the fact that if the legal situation in both countries differs materially with respect to an issue that is decisive for the judgment, the choice between the two sets of rules will be very difficult and risks becoming arbitrary. It cannot be ignored that in such a situation there will be a strong tendency to favor the *lex fori*. According to the structure of international principles currently under debate, the choice of forum is made by the rightholder[49] with a possible option to consolidate worldwide proceedings before the courts in his or her home country,[50] so the negative consequences this may entail for the defendant must be taken very seriously. It is therefore proposed that instead of making a decision in favor of one law to be applied and completely disregarding the other(s), the court must find a compromise solution, either by limiting the injunction to certain territories (if that is possible), or by otherwise taking account of the principle that remedies should be proportionate to the harm actually caused, and should not unduly interfere with legitimate business carried out in other countries. Also in that respect, the WIPO Recommendation, in particular Articles 13 to 15, may serve as a guideline.[51]

4. *Application of the Market Impact Rule: Practical Problems*

Notwithstanding issues of legal qualification and possible codification in instruments dealing with choice of law, the market impact rule as a general approach toward transborder trademark infringement cases seems to meet with general approval. This does not mean, however, that the problems to which the rule can give rise in practice have already been conquered. For instance, it is still unclear whether and to what extent the line of reasoning reflected in the German and French court decisions referred to above will also be followed by others. It should not be forgotten that not too long ago, another French court

---

48 This corresponds to the factors mentioned in the draft IP principles, *supra* 2.

49 In that respect, the draft IP principles as well as the MPI proposal (presented in Drexl/Kur, *supra* note 1) follow the structure set out in the 1999 DHJC (Draft Hague Jurisdiction Convention). It is for the plaintiff to choose the forum. However, if an alleged infringer claims for declaration of non-infringement, a subsequent claim by the rightholder for substantive remedies will prevail. Hence, for all practical purposes, it is always the rightholder who has the choice of forum.

50 This applies to the draft IP principles, and it would also result from Art. 10.4 last half-sentence of the 1999 DHJC. By contrast, the options for a rightholder to consolidate proceedings in his or her home country are considerably more restricted in the MPI proposal. See *Kur*, in Drexl/Kur (*supra* note 1), and in Principles Governing Jurisidiction, Choice of Law and Judgments in Transnational Disputes: A European Perspective, CRi 2003, 65, at 69.

51 For a compromise proposal based on the WIPO Recommendation, see *Kur*, CRi 2003 (*supra* note 50), at 72.

decided that visibility in France of a German trademark displayed in Internet advertisements directed to German customers amounted to infringement of the same mark belonging to a different owner in France.[52] And even if it should be generally agreed by now that this view is too strict and should no longer be applied, it remains an open question how far the zone of tolerance admitted for Internet use of trademarks can be extended without clashing with cogent provisions of European trademark law. Is it really compatible with the principle that trademarks can claim protection against any use of an infringing sign if, as suggested by the Tribunal de Grande Instance in the *domina* case referred to above, the owner must prove actual delivery of products into the country where he enjoys priority? It is ultimately for the European Court of Justice to decide on these and other issues.

The full range of practical problems to be considered cannot possibly be depicted here. The following examples are only meant to furnish some additional illustration, starting with a relatively straightforward case:

A Swiss chain of drugstores advertises, *inter alia* over the Internet, cheap but genuine Dior products it has acquired via "gray import" from Hong Kong. The languages are German, Italian, and French. The prices are indicated in Swiss francs, but the customer is offered the opportunity, by clicking a hyperlink, to transform them into other currencies, including Euro. The company offers mail order services for those who do not have a drugstore market in their vicinity. The legal situation is basically clear: The offering and advertising for sale of the products is legal in Switzerland,[53] whereas EU trademark law prohibits such conduct for products imported, without authorization by the rightful owner, from non-EU (including EEA) countries.[54] Hence, Dior may claim violation of its (national) trademark rights separately before the courts in Germany, France, and Italy, the basis being Art. 5.3 of the Lugano Convention.[55] Even better, Dior may claim violation of its Community trademark before the Community trademark court located in the country where the company has its seat, and claim sanctions for the infringement as a whole, the basis being Art. 93.2 CTMR. Taking account of the principles set out in the WIPO Recommendation,[56] the competent court(s) will have to assess whether the use of the mark made on the Internet has commercial impact in (the individual

[52] Nanterre Court of Appeals, decision of October 13, 1996, *SG 2 v. Brokat Informationssysteme GmbH*.

[53] See Swiss Federal Court, 23.10.1996, BGE III 469 – Chanel; for a German decision in a similar vein, see KG Berlin (Court of Appeals), 1997 CR 685 – concert concept.

[54] This follows from Art. 7.1 of the trademark directive, according to ECJ C-335/96, ECR 1998 I-4799 – Silhouette/Hartlauer.

[55] An alternative option, though possibly not as favorable for Dior, would be to commence consolidated proceedings in Switzerland, based on Art. 2 Lugano Convention.

[56] As was pointed out *supra* 1., the WIPO Recommendation cannot provide the legal basis for the assessment, which remains European trademark law. They can only influence the interpretation of those rules, in particular the meaning of "use in (domestic) commerce."

countries or) the Community, which it certainly has. The question would then arise whether and to what extent the court would be obliged to impose only proportionate sanctions, and to avoid interference with legitimate business carried out in other countries. If account is taken of these matters, the court will not be in a position to issue a general, unqualified prohibitive injunction against advertising on the Internet, or against any offering of mail order services. Instead, the judgment would probably have to be restricted to ordering that the website must contain a disclaimer with respect to delivery of the products to customers domiciled in the EU. It is unclear whether additional measures might be imposed, e.g., to delete the device enabling transformation of prices indicated in Swiss francs into Euro. In the aftermath of such a decision, the burden would be on the plaintiff to monitor whether the disclaimer posted on the website is actually followed (e.g., by test purchases).

Monitoring of decisions implying, but not expressly regulating, prohibition of use of a sign on the Internet may raise more complicated issues, as is shown by the following example: A Swedish company – the branch of an international company – has been enjoined by a court decision from using a particular sign in Sweden. The company stops marketing its products in Sweden under that sign and removes all advertisements from its website. However, products under the sign are still displayed as generally available, without Sweden being excluded, on the website of the foreign-based parent company which can be accessed through a hyperlink posted on the website of the Swedish company. Is the Swedish company liable to pay the fine imposed for violation of the judgment unless it removes the link to its mother company?

IV. Summary and Conclusions

The specific problems raised by trademark infringement resulting from Internet use of conflicting signs are best resolved by using a market impact approach, as is set out in the WIPO Recommendation of 2001, and which is also reflected in recent court decisions, e.g., in Germany and France. There is general agreement that the rule does not concern the law to be applied, but that it pertains to substantive law, defining the notion of infringement as occurring in a particular country. The fact that the rule is not included in (international) legal instruments dealing with choice of law issues, such as the proposed Rome II regulation, does not therefore mean that it cannot be applied by national courts, it being submitted that the law of the country of protection as the law to be applied in trademark infringement cases does provide a sufficient legal basis for limiting the notion of infringement accordingly.

Notwithstanding the legal qualification of the market impact rule as forming part of substantive law, it would certainly serve the interests of legal security and transparency in international relations if the rule were embedded in future principles or conventions dealing with choice of law. In that regard, however, it does not appear feasible to replace the country of protection principle by the market impact rule, and/or to distinguish in that respect between registered and unregistered rights. A preferable approach would be to combine both rules, with the country of protection principle governing choice of law concerning existence and scope of rights, and the market impact rule ensuring that in cases of transborder conflicts, an infringement is not deemed to occur in a country where it does not have any, or only marginal, market effect.[57]

In addition to that basic rule, special provisions must be drafted in order to take account of infringements with potentially global impact. It would be impossible in such cases to abide by a strict application of the country of protection principle, even if it is supplemented by a market impact rule. The simplifying strategies to be applied in such a situation should, however, be restricted to those cases when this is actually necessary. Furthermore, it should be ensured that the legitimate interests of both parties are adequately taken into account when remedies are imposed. The WIPO Recommendation may also serve as a guideline in that respect.

Lastly, it must be observed that even though general agreement seems to prevail with respect to the desirability and feasibility of a market impact rule in transborder (trademark) infringement cases, the implementation of that rule in practice will give rise to intricate problems. When faced with conflicts involving use of marks on the Internet, the deciding courts will have to get used to formulating their decisions as precisely as possible in order to limit the legal consequences to those elements of the behavior which are actually infringing without interfering with legitimate use in, or directed to, other countries that are not comprised by the judgment. However, in consequence of the specific character of the communication medium, it may sometimes be very difficult or even impossible to anticipate problems that may occur on the enforcement stage. Hence, even if courts and parties undertake their best effort to take possible extraterritorial effects of the judgment into account, and to phrase and/or limit the decision accordingly, this will often not be sufficient to dissolve doubts as to how and in which future actions the judgment shall be enforced.

This leads to the closing remark. Even with the market impact rule being relatively securely anchored in present law, and possibly even expressly comprised in future international conventions, the enforcement of judgments, in particular prohibitive injunctions, vis-à-vis activities carried out on the Internet, will most probably continue to present thorny issues. The importance of this aspect should not be underestimated. This applies not least because the country in which the decision was handed down and the country where the judgment shall be enforced will often not be the same, with all the problems this could

[57] With a reservation to be made regarding violations of personal rights, including the *droit moral*. As was pointed out (*supra* note 42), applying a market impact rule with respect to these aspects would not be appropriate.

evoke as resulting from diverging public policies, and from lingering distrust regarding the ability and competence of foreign courts to adjudicate matters involving the use of signs on one's own national market.

Conflicts and International Copyright Litigation: The Role of International Norms

GRAEME B. DINWOODIE*

I. Introduction

Questions of private international law that arise in copyright disputes, and in particular the law applicable to claims of copyright infringement in multinational settings, typically implicate questions of *national* law. Indeed, even the international conventions that address copyright law rest firmly on the proposition that copyright law operates territorially. The creation of an original work gives rise to separate copyrights under the laws of each copyright-recognizing country. Multinational copyright disputes require courts to localize any allegedly infringing acts and measure them against the applicable national law.

Of course, the analysis required to perform such localization is not simple, and has been rendered more difficult still by the advent of the internet. Thus, several papers in this symposium have already addressed the different ways by which courts might determine the applicable law in copyright litigation (and in intellectual property litigation more generally). This paper will comment on many of the options that have been suggested, but will also approach the question from a slightly different angle, namely, by asking what should be the

---

* Thanks to Axel Metzger, Annette Kur and Josef Drexl for the invitation, and to all the participants at that event for comments and criticisms. I am grateful also to Brian Havel for comments on an earlier draft of the paper.

role of international norms in resolving these dilemmas?[1] From my analysis of that question, I will defend a proposition that I have previously advanced in some detail, namely, that national courts confronted with an international copyright dispute should consider using what the late Fritz Juenger called the substantive law method.

II. Some Comments on the Conventional Private International Law of Intellectual Property

Some of what I would like to suggest might seem heretical both to private international lawyers used to localizing international conduct so as to apply national law and to intellectual property lawyers in whom the principle of territoriality has been firmly ingrained (if perhaps without full contemplation of the different dimensions to that proposition).[2] Thus, in this part of the paper, I will engage with the conventional debate by commenting on the analysis offered in other papers, which I hope will also set the scene for my suggested approach.

1. The Central Issues in Copyright Law

A principal point of contention during the symposium discussion has been the extent to which any rules of private international law in this field must have horizontal effect. That is, should the approach to copyright law be the same as that adopted in the areas of industrial property, primarily patent and trademark, law? Catherine Kessedjian discussed this question in her paper under the rubric of dépeçage.[3]

---

[1] If international norms are to be found primarily in international conventions – a conventional premise, to be sure – I am really asking what use private international lawyers can make of public international law. But one of the most intriguing aspects of the internationalization of copyright norms that has occurred of late is that international norms arguably are being generated and embodied in a variety of instruments, some of which are neither public nor (formally) sources of law. *See* Graeme B. Dinwoodie, *Private Ordering and the Creation of International Copyright Norms: The Role of Public Structuring*, 160 Journal of Institutional and Theoretical Economics 161 (2004). Thus, while I concern myself primarily with public international laws, I do not mean to confine my use of the term "international norms."

[2] *See* Graeme B. Dinwoodie, *Trademarks and Territory: Detaching Trademark Law From the Nation-State*, 41 Hous. L. Rev. (2004) (forthcoming).

[3] *See* Catherine Kessedjian [in this volume p. 19 et seq.]. Professor Kessedjian appears to be using this term in its French sense of "dismembering" one part of the law from another. In U.S. conflicts parlance, the term has a slightly narrower meaning. There, the doctrine of dépeçage permits courts to apply the law of one state to one issue in a litigation before it and the law of another state to a separate issue in the same litigation. It thus recasts the choice of law exercise as an effort to select the law applicable to decide an issue rather than a case. *See* Willis Reese, *Dépeçage: A Common Phenomenon in Choice of Law*, 73 Colum. L. Rev. 58, 58

Why might we have a different focus, and different rules, for copyright law? Several commentators found this problematic, or at least demanded a persuasive rationale for departing from a more trans-substantive approach. And this is a fair demand. The subject matter of different intellectual property regimes is converging, and claims are often asserted based upon two or more intellectual property rights. Radically different approaches to the applicable law may substantially reduce the certainty necessary to encourage investment, and at the very least may threaten the consolidation gains that might otherwise be generated by the development of a common international approach to applicable law.

In rebutting the argument for consistency among the different intellectual property rights, however, I am reminded of Ralph Waldo Emerson's apothegm that "a foolish consistency is the hobgoblin of little minds."[4] That is, the rules should be different because the intellectual property rights are different in important respects. Most notably, many (though by no means all) industrial property rights are acquired by registration.[5] As a result, we might mitigate the conflicts dilemmas of territorial rights in a global market by constructing alternative acquisition or right-definition mechanisms. These may take the form of unitary supranational rights (such as the Community Trademark,[6] the proposed Community Patent,[7] or the Registered Community Design),[8] or cen-

(1973). The doctrine has been applied by U.S. courts in copyright cases. *See, e.g.,* Itar-Tass Russian News Agency v. Russian Kurier, Inc.,153 F.3d 82 (2d Cir. 1998) (applying Russian law to ownership question and U.S. law to infringement question); *see also* The Bridgeman Art Library Ltd. v. Corel Corp., 25 F.Supp.2d 421(S.D.N.Y. 1998), *aff'd on reconsideration*, 36 F.Supp.2d 191 (S.D.N.Y. 1999).

[4] *See* Ralph Waldo Emerson, Self-Reliance *in* Ralph Waldo Emerson, Essays: First and Second Series 35 (Vintage Press ed. 1990).

[5] At the symposium, Professor Joanne Schmidt suggested correctly that this line cannot be drawn too brightly given the existence of unregistered trademark rights and now, throughout the European Union, unregistered design rights. Unregistered trademark rights might be seen as akin to copyright in that the lack of registration mechanisms not only obviates problems for multinational adjudication (such as act of state claims) but also precludes the availability of opportunities to resolve territoriality problems through other means (such as international acquisition mechanisms). But separate treatment might still be warranted because, for example, the validity of unregistered trademark rights depends on consumer recognition (not assessment of creativity), which may be tied more closely to national adjudicators. *Cf.* American Law Institute Project on Principles Governing Jurisdiction, Choice of Law, and Judgments in Transnational Disputes (Prelim. Draft No. 2 Jan. 20, 2004, see below annex B) (hereinafter ALI Draft Principles) (treating unregistered trademark rights separately from copyright, though without articulating this rationale).

[6] *See* Council Regulation 40/94 of 20 December 1993 on The Community Trademark, 1994 O.J. (L 11), *reprinted in* Graeme B. Dinwoodie et al, International Intellectual Property Law and Policy, Documentary Supplement 209 (LexisNexis 2001).

[7] *See* Proposal for a Council Regulation on the Community Patent (Aug. 1, 2000), at <http://europa.eu.int/comm/internal_market/en/indprop/patent/412en.pdf>.

[8] *See* Council Regulation (EC) No. 6/2002 on Community Designs (Dec. 12, 2001), 2002 O.J. L 3/1, <http://oami.eu.int/en/design/pdf/reg2002_6.pdf>.

tralized mechanisms (such as the European Patent Convention,[9] the Patent Cooperation Treaty,[10] or the Madrid Protocol)[11] for granting, searching or examining applications. Although the latter maintain the basic premise of territorial rights, they tend to unify or at least cause the convergence of national definitions of the property right in question.

Instead, with copyright, which international law requires to come into being without condition of formalities,[12] all this work must occur in the courts, in the context of enforcement of rights. This, of course, has benefits (if one is a supporter of liberalized procedures for consolidation of national disputes) in that the grant of copyright is not (unlike registered rights) perceived as an "act of state". Thus, although copyright claims historically were not (for reasons discussed below) adjudicated in courts other than the courts of the country for which protection was sought, the act of state doctrine should not at least be a barrier to the adjudication of foreign copyright claims.[13]

Before addressing the adjudication of foreign copyright claims in greater detail, however, I shall briefly comment on another group of rationales that might support differential treatment. Copyrightable works possess a greater universality than trademark or patent rights. Although we adhere to the legal fiction that the single act of creation gives rise to numerous separate national copyrights, we are in fact talking about a single work. Trademark law (which depends on consumer understandings in different countries) and patent law (which depends on claims accepted by the patent office, partly a function of relevant prior art in each country) are more relative and thus more tied to national variables. At first blush, therefore, it would seem that the copyright's universality should lend itself more readily to international adjudication.

Contemporary copyright law may, however, alternatively be viewed merely as an instrument of national trade and investment policy, and thus no different than patent or trademark law. (Indeed, one might make that argument about

---

[9] *See* Convention on the Grant of European Patents (European Patent Convention), done at Munich Oct. 5, 1973, <http://www.european-patent-office.org/legal/epc/ma1.html#CVN>, *reprinted in* Dinwoodie et al, *supra* note 6, at 483.

[10] *See* Patent Cooperation Treaty (June 19, 1970), <http://www.wipo.int/pct/en/texts/pdf/pct.pdf>, *reprinted in* Dinwoodie et al, *supra* note 6, at 373.

[11] *See* Protocol Relating to the Madrid Agreement Concerning the International Registration of Marks (June 28, 1989), <http://www.wipo.int/madrid/en/legal_texts/madrid_protocol.htm>, *reprinted in* Dinwoodie et al, *supra* note 6, at 159.

[12] *See* Berne Convention for The Protection of Literary and Artistic Works (1971 Paris text), 1161 U.N.T.S. 31. *See generally* Sam Ricketson, The Berne Convention For the Protection of Literary and Artistic Works: 1886-1986 (1987).

[13] *See* London Film Prods. v. Intercontinental Comms., 580 F. Supp. 47, 49 (S.D.N.Y. 1984) ("But as Nimmer has noted, "[i]n adjudicating an infringement action under a foreign copyright law there is ... no need to pass upon the validity of acts of foreign government officials," since foreign copyright laws, by and large, do not incorporate administrative formalities which must be satisfied to create or perfect a copyright.").

copyright law historically as well.)[14] This is not to deny that the natural rights of authors are not an important justification, domestically and internationally, for the existence of copyright protection. Rather, particularly as the subject matter of copyright expands, one cannot ignore the instrumentalist rationale for protection: copyright protection for software, for example, exists for many of the same reasons as patent protection of software.[15]

Putting aside this (still important) question of whether copyright should be treated differently from other intellectual property rights, an important variable in the litigation of transnational copyright claims is whether national courts can and should adjudicate foreign copyright infringement actions. Although most courts historically declined to adjudicate these claims,[16] the arguments for such judicial self-abnegation have receded in the face of practical necessity. As I noted above, and as reflected in article 1(3) of the latest draft of the Hague Agreement on Jurisdiction and Judgments in Civil and Commercial Matters, the act of state doctrine has lesser relevance to the adjudication of foreign copyright claims than to patent or trademark claims.

Other historical objections, such as those rooted in the expertise necessary to decide copyright cases, have also faded.[17] The notion that copyright law is so specialized that only national experts could deal with its intricacies has finally and rightfully been found attributable solely to the arrogance of copyright scholars (and lawyers).[18] And the notion of copyright as a tool of national cultural and innovation policy – while undoubtedly true – has been tempered by the restricted ability of a nation state to effectuate such policies and by the

---

[14] *Cf.* Jane C. Ginsburg, *A Tale of Two Copyrights: Literary Property in Revolutionary France and America* in Of Authors and Origins: Essays on Copyright law 131 (Brad Sherman and Alain Strowel eds. 1994).

[15] The convergence of patentable, copyrightable and trademark subject-matter might be a practical counter argument against dépeçage, as we might wish all intellectual property claims on products to be litigated at once in the same court. This is a major criticism of the latest (post-symposium) draft of the Hague Convention on Jurisdiction, Recognition and Enforcement of Foreign Judgments in Civil and Commercial Matters, Work. Doc. No. 110E (Revised) (27 April 2004), at <www.hcch.net/doc/jdgm_wd110_e.pdf>, although the literal text of the latest draft would not appear to implement the stated aim of the most recent negotiations, namely, to exclude patent and trademark claims from the scope of the convention while including copyright.

[16] *See* Graeme W. Austin, *The Infringement of Foreign Intellectual Property Rights*, 113 Law Q. Rev. 321 (1997).

[17] To my mind, these arguments are of equally little merit in patent and trademark law. *See* Graeme B. Dinwoodie, *Private International Aspects of the Protection of Trademarks*, WIPO Doc. No. WIPO/PIL/01/4 (2001). But the expertise argument has proven more resilient in that context.

[18] The raw information necessary to develop expertise has been made more accessible by electronic retrieval systems, WIPO's collection of national laws, and the TRIPS Council's questionnaires on national laws. And if judges now converse among themselves in more significant ways, as is clearly the case among specialist intellectual property judges and perhaps the bench as a whole, the currency of that information and the understanding necessary to see its nuances will likewise increase.

realization that tort and contract law may lay equally as important a claim. Thus, in recent years, both U.S. and EU courts have increasingly permitted the adjudication of claims under foreign copyright law.[19]

More important than this development in and of itself, however, is the concomitant trend that adjudication of foreign copyright claims has facilitated, namely, the replacement of serial country-by-country litigation by consolidated litigation of numerous claims under different national laws. Must notable in this regard is perhaps the litigation between Boosey & Hawkes and Disney[20] in New York of claims under eighteen national laws; a global settlement of claims was reached as soon as the Court of Appeals for the Second Circuit permitted the case to proceed. Indeed, the consolidation of national litigation is one of the driving forces behind the ALI project[21] (although not so of the Hague negotiations, even when broader) and was apparently a leading sentiment underlying the AIPPI resolution on private international law at Lucerne.[22]

These recent developments have not, however, solved all the principal concerns of international copyright litigation. None of these developments resolves outstanding and troubling choice of law problems. Nor are plaintiffs *obliged* to consolidate their numerous national claims. Thus, in the battle over the legitimacy of peer-to-peer networks, the recording industry is simulta-

---

[19] *See, e.g.,* Boosey & Hawkes Music Pubs. v. The Walt Disney Co., 145 F.3d 481 (2d Cir. 1998); London Film Prods. v. Intercontinental Comms., 580 F. Supp. 47 (S.D.N.Y. 1984); Carrell v. The Shubert Organization Inc., 104 F.Supp.2d 236 (S.D.N.Y. 2000) (permitting claims based on foreign copyright laws to proceed notwithstanding the plaintiff's failure to specify in her complaint the particular countries under whose laws the claims were made); Armstrong v. Virgin Records, 91 F. Supp.2d 628, 637-38 (S.D.N.Y. 2000) (entertaining claims based on unspecified foreign copyright laws on the basis of diversity jurisdiction and pendent jurisdiction); Frink America, Inc., v. Champion Road Machinery, Ltd., 961 F. Supp. 398, 404 (N.D.N.Y. 1997) (declining to dismiss claim under Canadian copyright law). *Contra* ITSI T.V. Prods, Inc. v. California Authority of Racing Fairs, 785 F.Supp. 854 (N.D. Cal. 1992), *rev'd on other grounds,* 3 F.3d 1289 (9th Cir. 1993) (declining to enter the "bramble bush" of foreign copyright law). The English courts have recognized that certain foreign copyrights claim might be adjudicated before them. *See* Pearce v. Ove Arup Partnership, [1999] 1 All E.R. 769 (Ct. Appeal, 1999) (Eng.). This is a consequence of U.K. membership of the Brussels Convention on Jurisdiction and Enforcement of Judgments in Civil and Commercial Matters, *see* Convention on Jurisdiction and the Enforcement of Judgments in Civil and Commercial Matters, Sept. 27, 1968, 1972 O.J. (L 299) 32, reprinted in 8 I.L.M. 229 (1969), as amended by 1990 O.J. (C 189) 1, reprinted as amended in 29 I.L.M. 1413 (1990), the basic tenets of which have been repeated in the Brussels Regulation. *See* Council Regulation (EC) No. 44/2001 of 22 December 2000 on jurisdiction and the recognition and enforcement of judgments in civil and commercial matters, O.J. Jan. 16, 2001 (L 12/1). Unlike the EU, the U.S. courts have not been so inclined with patent and trademark law. The scope of cross-border jurisdiction in patent cases within the EU is, however, currently before the European Court of Justice. *See* Roche Nederland B.V. v. Primus and Goldenberg, Case C-593/03.

[20] Boosey & Hawkes Music Pubs. v. The Walt Disney Co., 145 F.3d 481 (2d Cir. 1998).

[21] ALI Draft Principles, *supra* note 5, at 19, 61 of the comments (not reprinted in annex B.)

[22] *See* AIPPI Resolution on Question 174, Jurisdiction and applicable law in the case of cross-border infringement (infringing acts) of intellectual property rights, recital (a) (Oct. 26, 2003).

neously pursuing copyright infringement claims (under U.S. law) in federal court in California and (under Australian law) in the Australian courts. Indeed, efforts by Kazaa to stay the Australian proceedings pending the U.S. decision have failed.[23]

Thus, in considering proposals to reform choice of law rules in copyright law or procedural rules regarding consolidated international litigation, one must make the proper comparison. The comparison is not to an ideal system, but to a system where parties in litigation are currently seeking to exploit for their advantage the weaknesses of an international system where there is an unstructured excess of adjudicatory and prescriptive authority – and this phenomenon is only likely to increase with the upsurge in internet-based claims.[24]

2. *Existing and Proposed Approaches to Choice of Law in Copyright Cases*

In fashioning a choice of law solution for copyright law, we are not working with a clean slate, however. Many scholars have suggested that Article 5 of the Berne Convention (and Article 5(2) in particular) mandates the *lex loci protectionis* as the applicable rule, at least for questions of infringement. Catherine Kessedjian has intimated that she does not feel bound by Article 5, but wanted instead to look at this question afresh. Neither do I feel bound by Article 5 to reach a particular choice of law rule. As the Second Circuit suggested in *Itar-Tass*, and as Mireille Van Echoud demonstrates in her superb book on choice of law in copyright,[25] it is by no means clear that Article 5 of the Berne Convention requires a particular choice of law rule. To be sure, the national treatment obligation of the Berne Convention suggests that foreign nationality should not result in lesser rights, and thus suggests that some notion of "place" (rather than nationality) should be controlling. But even if this hint were meant to operate as a choice of law rule, it is not clear which "place" is the most relevant.[26]

---

[23] *See* Universal Music Australia Pty Ltd. v. Sharman License Holdings Ltd [2004] FCA 183 (Fed Ct. Mar. 4, 2004) (Aus.). The problem is not unique to copyright law, of course. A similar phenomenon, with similar attachment to serial national litigation, can be seen in the ongoing dispute between Lindows and Microsoft regarding the trademark WINDOWS for software. After the U.S. court declined to issue an antisuit injunction against Microsoft pursuing its foreign litigation, *see* Microsoft Corp. v. Lindows.com, Inc., Case No. CO1-2115C, (W.D. Wash. Apr. 2, 2004) (copy of memorandum and order on file with author), and decisions in Europe favorable to Microsoft, Lindows decided to change its name (mostly only overseas, but with some effect in the United States).

[24] *See* Graeme B. Dinwoodie, *A New Copyright Order: Why National Courts Should Create Global Norms*, 149 U. Pa. L. Rev. 469, 536-37 (2000).

[25] *See* Mireille van Echoud, Choice of law in Copyright and related Rights: Alternatives to the Lex Loci Protectionis (2003).

[26] Indeed, the lack of clarity is such that, although Article 8(1) of the proposed Rome II Regulation comports with the conventional wisdom regarding choice of law in copyright law, it is not clear that Article 3(1) of the Rome II Regulation – the general provision governing tort liability – would, depending upon judicial interpretation, necessarily be inconsistent with the

Thus, relatively liberated from the constraints of international treaties, let me turn to possible choice of law rules. Before sketching the alternatives, however, let me suggest two ways in which *substantive* treaty law might in fact affect the equation. First, substantive rules (whether in treaties or joint recommendations of the WIPO and Paris Union Assemblies) might infuse and give content to conflicts rules. This is most evident in the context of trademark law. There, the restricted meaning of "use" operates as a subsidiary conflicts rule, modifying (or defining) the notion of territoriality.[27] So too, in copyright law, rules in the Berne Convention defining the "place of publication"[28] will confine our options if the place of publication is selected as the dominant connecting factor.[29] The definition of "act of communication to the public" promulgated in the Cable and Satellite Directive likewise operates as a choice of law rule.[30] Yet, these rules achieve effects comparable to rules contained in explicit choice of law provisions, such as proposals to limit the possible lex causae to places of "significant impact" (as in the draft ALI Principles rule on exceptions from territoriality)[31] or to the place of "effective use" (as proposed by Mireille van Echoud).[32]

A second way in which substantive international copyright law might be relevant is in the sense that, with growing harmonization of copyright laws, especially as (perhaps atypically) regards issues not yet fully vetted at the national level, there is what Jane Ginsburg has called an emerging "supra-national copyright code."[33] This "code" has greater potential to supply rules of decision than when the Berne Convention was limited to backwards codification of agreed-upon norms.[34]

So, what approaches should we take to choice of law in copyright cases? The starting point, historically, is the principle of territoriality that undergirds the Berne Convention and, indeed, all of international intellectual property law. The problem with territoriality as a dominant principle of international copy-

---

Berne Convention. *See* Proposal of the European Parliament and the Council on the Law Applicable to Non-contractual Obligations ("Rome II"), Doc. COM(2003) 427 final, 2003/0168 (COD) (July 22, 2003). That said, Article 8(1) makes EU compliance with Berne certain (even if the provision is bedeviled by the same uncertainty of meaning).

[27] *See* Dinwoodie, *supra* note 17, at 45-49; *see* Joint Recommendation Concerning the Protection of Marks, and Other Industrial Property Rights in Signs, on the Internet, adopted by the Assembly of the Paris Union and the General Assembly of WIPO, WIPO Doc. No. 845 (Sept. 2001) (commenting on the remedies in online trademark disputes).

[28] *See* Berne Convention, *supra* note 12, art. 5.

[29] *Cf. Itar-Tass*, 153 F.3d at 90-91.

[30] *See* Council Directive 93/83/EEC of 27 September 1993 on The Coordination of Certain Rules Concerning Copyright and Rights Related to Copyright Applicable to Satellite Broadcasting and Cable Retransmission, 1993 O.J. (L 248), art. 1(2).

[31] *See* Draft ALI Principles, *supra* note 5, at 109.

[32] *See* van Echoud, *supra* note 25, at 223.

[33] *See* Jane C. Ginsburg, *International Copyright: From a "Bundle" of National Copyright Laws to a Supranational Code*, 47 J. Copyr. Soc. 265 (2000).

[34] *See* Dinwoodie, *supra* note 24, at 494-501.

right law is that, especially in the online context, it offers an excess of prescriptive authority in resolving a multinational dispute. Thus, although the draft ALI Principles start by reaffirming territoriality and describing departures therefrom as the "exception," I was interested to hear Francois Dessemontet suggest that in practice those departures were not likely to be all that exceptional.

Thus, courts and scholars have sought different ways to apply a single law to a multinational dispute. Even in the face of territoriality one can conform to the basic principle of territoriality *and* effectuate the objective of applying a single law to a worldwide dispute by designating a single point as the relevant "place". That is, the localization sub-rule allows us to get the practical benefits of a single law without nominally departing from territoriality. In the United States, the application of a single law has been pursued both through localization devices and by an assortment of other pragmatic doctrinal devices that extrude a single (U.S.) law.

First, let's examine the alternatives for localization of international disputes through choice of law rules (with particular reference to online disputes, where these dilemmas are most acute). One option would be to choose the place of initiation or origination of the allegedly infringing copy. This would give a single law, but because this is easily manipulable in today's climate, this would likely lead infringers to copyright havens (technology permitting). Alternatively, one might consider localizing the infringing act in the place of receipt. This has the different problem of not providing a single law: there are too many places of receipt and indeed those locales may be quite fortuitous (a feature that conflicts rules typically wish to avoid in identifying the applicable law). The dispute can easily be localized in any place with jurisdiction, as the U.S. courts have done.[35]

An alternative rule, arguably favored by the U.S. courts, would involve applying the law of the most significant relationship to the parties and transaction.[36] This approach, favored also by Canadian courts in online copyright disputes,[37] has the benefit of flexibility. But because the policy analysis under-

---

[35] *See* National Football League v. TVRadioNow Corp., 53 U.S.P.Q.2d 1831, 1834-35 (E.D. Pa. 2000) (holding that where defendants originated the streaming of copyrighted programming over the internet from a web site in Canada, public performances occurred in the United States because users in the United States could access the web site and receive and view the defendants' streaming of the copyrighted material).

[36] In *Itar-Tass*, the Court of Appeals for the Second Circuit applied the law of the place of infringement, the *lex loci delicti* to determine the question of infringement, but it was unclear whether the court was articulating a strict First Restatement-based rule of *lex loci delicti,* or was intimating that, as a matter of interest analysis more typical of the Second Restatement, the law of the most significant relationship would result in the application of the law of the place of infringement.

[37] *See* Society of Composers, Authors and Music Publishers of Canada v. Canadian Association of Internet Providers (Tariff 22), 2002 FCA 166 (Federal Court of Appeal 2002) (Canada) (holding that Canadian copyright law could be applied to any communications that

lying that approach strongly (almost presumptively) favors the *lex loci delicti*, it suffers in the internet context from the same problem as the place of receipt – too many loci delicti (places of publication). These approaches suffer from a common flaw, in that they seek to identify a single "place" rather than a single "law".

Before elaborating on possible choice of law rules, however, an alternative set of devices used by U.S. courts to extrude U.S. law globally is worth noting. First, several U.S. courts have suggested that they will exercise jurisdiction over acts abroad where there exists a "predicate act" in the United States that facilitates infringement abroad (and, implicitly, apply U.S. law to determine the legality of those acts).[38] Second, if an act abroad is alleged to have contributed towards an infringement in the United States, the U.S. courts will exercise jurisdiction over the foreign acts.[39] Finally, in some (but not all) courts, the authorization in the United states of allegedly infringing acts abroad will be sufficient to give rise to a cause of action under U.S. law.[40]

---

had a "real and substantial connection" with Canada and was not restricted to communications from a host server located in Canada). The Canadian Supreme Court recently handed down its opinion in the *Tariff 22* appeal and does not depart radically from the lower court's approach to choice of law. *See* Canadian Association of Internet Providers v. Society of Composers, Authors and Music Publishers of Canada (Tariff 22), 2004 SSC 45 (Supreme Court of Canada) (June 30, 2004). The majority endorsed the proposition that Canadian law could apply where there was a "real and substantial connection", *see id* at ¶¶ 54-78, regardless of where the host server was located, and identified several factors (situs of the content provider, host server, intermediaries and end users) that would be relevant connecting factors. *See id.* at ¶ 61. The Court did however conduct a separate analysis of whether the Canadian Parliament had exercised this prescriptive authority in the relevant statutory enactment.

[38] *See, e.g.,* Los Angeles News Serv. v. Reuters T.V. Int'l Limited, 149 F.3d 987 (9th Cir. 1998) (unauthorized transmission and copy of work made in the United States and then further transmitted to Europe and Africa); Update Art, Inc. v. Modiin Publishing, Ltd., 843 F. 2d 67, 72-73 (2d Cir. 1988) (unauthorized copy of plaintiff's poster made in the United States and then further copied and distributed in Israel); Sheldon v. Metro-Goldwyn Pictures Corp., 106 F.2d 45, 52 (2d Cir.1939) (awarding plaintiff profits from both U.S. and Canadian exhibition of infringing motion picture where a copy of the motion picture had been made in the United States and then shipped to Canada for exhibition), *aff'd*, 309 U.S. 390 (1940).

[39] *See, e.g.,* GB Mktg. USA Inc. v. Gerolsteiner Brunnen GmbH & CO., 782 F. Supp. 763 (W.D.N.Y. 1991 (contributory infringement)); Armstrong v. Virgin Records, 91 F. Supp.2d 628, 635-36 (S.D.N.Y. 2000) (finding that jurisdiction may exist over defendant's foreign acts to the extent that the defendants could be liable contributory or vicariously for subsequent infringement within the United States); Blue Ribbon Pet Prods., Inc., v. Rolf C. Hagen (USA) Corp., 66 F. Supp.2d 454, 461-63 (E.D.N.Y. 1999); ITSI T.V. Prods, Inc. v. California Authority of Racing Fairs, 785 F.Supp. 854, 864 (E.D. Cal. 1992), *rev'd on other grounds,* 3 F.3d 1289 (9th Cir. 1993); *see also* Metzke v. The May Department Stores Company, 878 F. Supp. 756 (W.D. Pa. 1995) (defendant can be liable where it supplied copy of design to copier in Taiwan if it knew or should have known that unauthorized copies made in Taiwan would be distributed in the United States).

[40] *See* Expediters Int'l of Wash., Inc. v. Direct Line Cargo Mgt. Servs., Inc., 995 F.Supp. 468, 477 (D.N.J.1998) and Curb v. MCA Records, Inc. 898 F. Supp. 586 (M.D. Tenn. 1995). *Contra* Subafilms, Ltd. v. MGM-Pathe Comms. Co., 24 F.3d 1088, 1095 (9th Cir. 1994) (en banc) (mere authorization in the United States of foreign infringing conduct cannot be

These devices might be seen (favorably) as driven by the same efficiency and security objectives that drive consolidation efforts. Indeed they avoid some of the problems of consolidation, such as how to try cases under eighteen foreign copyright laws (which may weaken claims of efficiency in preference to serial national litigation).[41] But they might also be seen as efforts by U.S. courts to extrude their laws extraterritorially. If I may paraphrase Paul Torremans, the U.S. courts have moved not so much from dodging the bullets to biting them, but onward still to actively seeking them.[42]

III. The Role/Demise of Territoriality in Choice of Law

In looking for other alternatives, it is worth having a clear view of national claims of prescriptive authority in the online environment. First, let me emphasize that I am not what Jack Goldsmith called a "regulation skeptic";[43] online conduct clearly affects national interests offline and nation states have a claim to prescribe conduct notwithstanding its online character.[44] By the same token, because online conduct is likely to affect any number of other claimants, that authority must be seen as diluted or shared.[45]

In that light, it is therefore useful to re-assess our focus on territoriality. The resort to the principle of territoriality in the Berne Convention has to be seen as progress when viewed in its historical context. It was a departure from anti-foreigner discrimination that characterized pre-1886 copyright relations, and a vehicle for the harmonization and development of authors' rights on an international scale. We are now at a different historical point in time, where it might be advisable to rethink territoriality as the defining feature of international

---

actionable under U.S. copyright law because the direct act of infringement abroad was not actionable in the United States); Fun-Damental Too v. Gemmy Indus., 41 U.S.P.Q.2d 1427 (S.D.N.Y. 1996) (following *Subafilms*) and Armstrong v. Virgin Records, 91 F. Supp.2d 628, 634 (S.D.N.Y. 2000).

41 This may not be quite as significant a hurdle as it might first appear. In practice, in an era characterized by numerous harmonization pressures, most national laws can be grouped together under a relatively small number of different approaches. Thus, the trial may involve the application of several paradigmatic rules. Indeed, one concern of critics who support consolidation for (inter alia) its efficiency gains but fear universal rules for other normative reasons, *see* Graeme W. Austin, *Domestic Laws and Foreign Rights: Choice of Law in Transnational Copyright Infringement Litigation*, 23 Colum.-VLA J. L. & Arts 1 (1999), might be that the application of a single law (most likely, the forum law) might effectively occur as courts, in the setting of a trial that appears to involve a single work, subconsciously pursue the convenience of a smaller number of rules.

42 *See* Paul Torremans, *Jurisdiction and Choice of Law issues in United States Intellectual Property Cases: From Dodging the Bullet to Biting It*, 3 I.P.Q. 372 (1999).

43 *See* Jack L. Goldsmith, *The Internet and the Abiding Significance of Territorial Sovereignty*, 5 Ind. J. Global Legal Stud. 475, 484-85 (1998).

44 *See* Dinwoodie, *supra* note 24, at 541 n.224.

45 *See id.* at 551 n.252.

copyright law. "Place" may not be as appealing a sole connecting factor pragmatically when "place" is not so fixed, nor so normatively compelling if place is less central to the ability of the citizenry to participate in the democratic process and less tied to the felt obligations of a community.

The arguments for such a radical departure from prevailing approaches can be grounded in conflicts concerns or in broader questions about the potential of the substantive law method to contribute to international lawmaking. I first argued for using the substantive law method in international copyright litigation because of what I saw as advantages for the international copyright system.[46] For present purposes, I focus on conflicts rationales, and thus turn to the different ways in which public international copyright norms might be relevant to conflicts.

IV. The Role of International Norms in National Choice of Law Analyses

The conventional view of public international norms, as embodied in treaties, was that they stood as an *alternative* to conflicts methodology. That is, if we effected substantial harmonization then conflicts would be minimized. For a variety of obvious reasons I won't detail here, harmonization will not avoid the need for rules of private international law (even if it might lessen them).

A second use for international norms is in *identifying* acceptable *lex causae*. In Jane Ginsburg's early work, she used the notion of "TRIPS-compliant laws" to exclude certain information havens from potentially supplying the applicable law.[47] Indeed, the current ALI draft Principles would, when they depart from territoriality in Section 302 to find a single law applicable to a multi-territorial dispute, might have regard to TRIPS (and other international norms) in identifying that law.[48]

A third – and presently speculative – use for international norms would be in *constituting* the applicable substantive rule. That is, some scholars, reprising efforts made in the development of the initial Berne Convention in 1886, have suggested the development of a supranational copyright code.[49] Of course, supranational codes have been used successfully to resolve the difficulties of

---

[46] *See id.* at 569.

[47] Jane C. Ginsburg, *Private International Law Aspects of the Protection of Works and Objects of Related Rights Transmitted Through Digital Networks*, WIPO Doc. GCPIC/2 (Nov. 30, 1998) at 18-19; Jane C. Ginsburg, *Private International Law Aspects of the Protection of Works and Objects of Related Rights Transmitted Through Digital Networks, 2000 Update*, WIPO Doc. No. PIL/01/02 (2000), available at <http://wipo.int/pil-forum/en/documents/pdf/pil_01_2.pdf>.

[48] *See* ALI Draft Principles, *supra* note 5, § 302(2)(b). Even without express reference this consideration might have come to be relevant via the "public policy" safety-valve to traditional choice of law analysis.

[49] *See* Adrian Sterling, *International Copyright Protection System*, at <www.qmipri.org/icps.html>.

private international law in the industrial property arena. Notable examples include the Uniform Domain Name Dispute Resolution Policy (UDRP)[50] and the Community Trademark Law (CTM). Yet, neither of these supranational codes wholly obviates the need to have regard to national laws, and thus to involve (albeit less extensively) questions of conflicts of law.[51]

Moreover, these models are less likely to have application in the copyright *infringement* context, where rights are not (like the CTM) dependent on a centralized acquisition procedure and are not easily sent to quasi-arbitration (like the UDRP).[52] Moreover, even if such supranational systems were successfully installed, this might simply shift the focus of choice of law dilemmas to "vertical" choice of law, choices between international and national norms rather than two competing national rules.[53]

Finally, there is the use of international norms to *contribute* to the development of the applicable substantive law. What do I mean by that?[54] The basic approach would require that when confronted by an international copyright dispute, a court would consider whether the international dimension implicated policies of other states or the international copyright system,[55] and develop (and apply) a substantive rule of copyright law that best effectuated this range of

---

[50] *See* Uniform Domain Name Dispute Resolution Policy (Oct. 24, 1999), *at* <http://www.icann.org/udrp/udrp-policy-24oct99.htm> [hereinafter UDRP]; *see also* Rules for Uniform Domain Name Dispute Resolution Policy (Oct. 24, 1999), *at* <http://www.icann.org/udrp/udrp-rules- 24oct99.htm>.

[51] *See* Winfried Tilmann [this volume]; Dinwoodie, *supra* note 17, at ¶¶ 117-126; *see also* Graeme B. Dinwoodie, *International Intellectual Property Litigation: A Vehicle for Resurgent Comparativist Thought?*, 49 Am. J. Comp. L. 429, 444-45 (2001).

[52] *See* Dinwoodie, *supra* note 24, at 522-528. Larry Helfer and I have tried to suggest a system whereby, through ISP contracts, a copyright parallel to the UDRP might be developed, but such a system is presently unlikely in the context of widespread copyright owner satisfaction with ISP notice and take own procedures. *See* Laurence R. Helfer and Graeme B. Dinwoodie, *Designing Non-National Systems: The Case of the Uniform Domain Name Dispute Resolution Policy*, 43 Wm. & Mary L. Rev.141 (2001); *see also* Dinwoodie, *supra* note 1, at 170-74 (discussing the ways in which ISP practices might create international norms); Mark A. Lemley and R. Anthony Reese, *Reducing Digital Copyright Infringement Without Restricting Innovation,* 56 Stan. L. Rev. 1345, 1410-1422 (2004) (discussing adaptation of the UDRP to copyright).

[53] *See* Dinwoodie, *Resurgent Comparativist Thought, supra* note 51 at 445, 449, 451-52.

[54] For a much fuller elaboration, see Dinwoodie, *supra* note 24; *see also* Graeme B. Dinwoodie, *The Development and Incorporation of International Norms in the Formation of Copyright Law*, 62 Ohio St. L. J. 733 (2001).

[55] Reference to public international copyright lawmaking in adjudicating copyright cases by U.S. courts have largely been made to support deference to treaty negotiations by the executive branch and thus to limit litigation of international copyright questions. *See, e.g.*, Creative Technology, Ltd. v. Aztech System, Ltd, 61 F.3d 696, 701 (9th Cir. 1995) (referencing Berne and Universal Copyright Convention in justifying dismissal of international copyright claim on grounds of forum non conveniens); Subafilms, Ltd. v. MGM-Pathe Comms. Co., 24 F.3d 1088, 1098 n.16 (9th Cir. 1994) (en banc) (noting deleterious effect of applying U.S. copyright law to domestic authorization of allegedly unauthorized acts abroad in light of Berne accession and TRIPS negotiations).

policies. The approach is not without historical antecedent (although not in copyright law). In Roman law, starting around 242 B.C., this was the method by which the *praetor peregrinus* developed the *ius gentium*, applied to the increasingly frequent disputes involving non-Roman citizens that occurred with the expansion of Empire.[56] Importantly, the *ius gentium* came eventually to inform the development of law applicable to disputes between citizens. More recently, this is essentially a description of the *lex mercatoria*, which is frequently used in international commercial arbitration. And, in rare cases, national courts have resorted to analogous methods to resolve multistate disputes.[57]

Modern scholarly support for such an approach to transnational disputes, most particularly that found in the writings of Arthur von Mehren, was grounded in the perceived capacity of the approach to reconcile the objectives of multilateral and unilateral conflicts methodology.[58] But, thirty years after von Mehren articulated the rationale behind *his* support of the substantive law method, and in light of the challenges currently facing international copyright law, additional justifications grounded both in pragmatism and principle can be advanced. Pragmatically, the substantive law method represents an alternative avenue to the development of international norms at a time when little progress is being made in the arena of public international copyright law. And, as a matter of principle,

> a method that draws its applicable rule in international cases from an amalgam of national and international norms reflects the complex and interwoven forces that govern citizens' conduct in a global society. Existing choice of law methodology fails to recognize these interacting forces by compelling courts to localize matters that are not local and to judge disputes according to a single norm where citizens do not act (or expect to be judged) according to that norm alone. A substantive law method would seek to reflect rather than to deny that reality of modern life.[59]

Nor is the approach conceptually novel. In a domestic context, where no single previously announced substantive rule of decision provides an answer, a court will often articulate a new rule, likely drawing upon the extent to which the new set of facts mirrors and implicates the same concerns as existing rules. Why should courts be more constrained when the new variable is the multistate nature of the transaction?

---

[56] *See* Friedrich K. Juenger, Choice of Law and Multistate Justice 8-10 (1993).

[57] *See* In re Agent Orange Product Liability Litigation, 580 F. Supp. 690 (E.D.N.Y. 1984) (developing "national consensus law" on manufacturer's liability in multistate product liability class action).

[58] *See* Arthur T. von Mehren, *Special Substantive Rules for Multistate Problems: Their Role and Significance in Contemporary Choice of Law Methodology*, 88 Harv. L. Rev. 347 (1974); *see also* Arthur T. von Mehren, *Choice of Law and the Problem of Justice*, 41 Law & Contemp. Probs. 27 (1977).

[59] Dinwoodie, *supra* note 24, at 550.

In my 2000 article, advocating this method, I argued, "[i]f plaintiff would be awarded $800,000 under the law of State X, and recover nothing under the law of State Y, might a cause of action implicating both State X and State Y entitle the plaintiff to recover $400,000 (or some other intermediate amount) that reflects the interests of both states?"[60] In fact, a recent German decision reflects in a similar way the need to balance the interests of competing states. In *Sender Felsberg,*[61] the defendant, a radio station situated in Germany 300 meters from the French border, transmitted French radio programs in the direction of French territory. There was no evidence of a substantial number of German listeners. The radio station was established as a subsidiary of a Paris-based parent that produced all programs and sent them to the German subsidiary for re-transmission. The plaintiff, the German collecting society for performing artists, sued for damages after the defendant stopped paying royalties in Germany in response to an action brought by the French collecting society in France. The German plaintiff held only the neighboring right in Germany. The Bundesgerichtshof created a new legal rule to solve the problem. It applied German law, but addressed the possible double payments to different right holders by limiting the amount of compensation available to the plaintiff so that it recovered for only the damage that occurred in Germany.[62]

There are some limits to the creative anarchy that the substantive law method might appear to portend. I am not suggesting that in international copyright cases there will not be cases where the prescriptive claim of a single states so dominates that the law of that state should apply. Rather, I am simply suggesting that in many cases that historical assumption may not pertain. No single national law will apply. When that is so, and the problem is truly *international* in nature, a court should look to a variety of sources: treaties, relevant national laws that will constrain the range of choices, and the norms of post-national groupings (just as commercial customs inform the lex mercatoria).

Such an approach is not, of course, without costs. In particular, this approach might appear to undervalue the certainty necessary to ensure a climate in which there is adequate investment in the development of creative products. But one must ask the proper question: is the level of certainty in such an approach, especially over the long-term, any less than that engendered by the current system? Others might question the legitimacy of national judges making law, especially insofar as it purports to have international import. To this, I have two responses. First, judges make law. Second, any such law is not "international law" in any Benthamite sense. It is local law addressed to an international dispute. As such, it is subject to national political controls (and reform). Finally, this court-centric approach might appear to favor systems (such as the

[60] *See id.* at 548.

[61] Decision of the German Bundesgerichtshof (decision of 7 November 2002, GRUR Int. 2003, 470).

[62] I am greatly indebted to Josef Drexl for this English language summary of the case.

United States) where litigation is more prevalent. But courts are always dominant in the construction of private international law, and the extra-territorial effect of domestic decisions will in part be a function of its reception in enforcing countries.

V. Conclusion

So, you might ask, how does my proposal fit with the leading institutional projects we have been discussing in this symposium? My proposal was first advanced at a time when the U.S. courts had declared that they were obliged to create a new choice of law rule because neither treaties nor Congress had provided them with one. No copyright court has taken up my suggestion. And I doubt that the American Law Institute project will endorse the substantive law method as the approach to conflicts in copyright cases. If the current ALI draft is criticized, as it was by commentators at the symposium, as too heavy with detail in a "style typical of American lawmaking," then this proposed approach may lean too much in the other direction. For the same reason, I doubt that the European Commission is likely to adopt such a rule in any regulation or directive any time soon.

But discussion of the substantive law method will, I hope, focus our attention on a principle that I think we too readily ignore: that is, despite the efforts of private international lawyers (throughout most of our history) to take an international dispute and localize it in a single nation state, at some point it becomes inappropriate to judge conduct that takes place on an international level and affects the interests of many states as though it had occurred in one state alone. In our internationalized world, where the nation-state has lost some of its prominence as a source of prescriptive authority, we need to attend more directly to the possibility that international conduct be judged according to international norms.

Discussion: Non-contractual Obligations

FRIEDRICH WENZEL BULST and CHRISTIAN A. HEINZE

In the discussion of *Leistner*'s remarks on unfair competition law and Article 5 of the Rome II Proposal, the introduction of a criterion of foreseeability of the impact on the market in question was suggested, similar to the ALI draft. This would avoid holding producers to the law of a market that they could not expect their products to reach. Attention was drawn to the fact that a distinction may be difficult to establish between an attack exclusively directed at a single competitor and an attack that also has a market effect. It was also deplored that there was a divergence between the wording of Article 5 paragraph 2 of the Rome II Proposal and the accompanying explanatory memorandum. Given that this provision dealt with a tort, it should also refer to Article 3 paragraph 1 of the Rome II Proposal. In view of the ECJ case law on the requirements of Article 28 EC regarding national unfair competition law, Article 5 of the Rome II Proposal was expected to contribute rather little to substantive European private law in this area. It was submitted that the latter provision would be more important for trade with third states.

It was argued that, as far as slavish imitations are concerned, the law of unfair competition was now partially harmonized by Community law on designs. Another overlap was found to exist between the law of unfair competition and the law of copyright.

It was pointed out that, while in some areas of Community law the country of origin principle already exists (satellite broadcasting directive, e-commerce directive), different conflicts rules still prevail in other areas. Political discussion was needed to establish whether there should be a general country of origin approach.

A tension between a conflicts of laws approach in unfair competition and a unification approach in intellectual property law was noted. The question was raised of whether the stricter continental rules on unfair competition (vis-à-vis the English rules) were justifiable barriers to trade.

The question was raised as to why the Commission did not follow the suggestion advanced by the Hamburg Group to extend Article 5 of the Rome II Proposal to antitrust law. It transpired that the reason for this decision was a reluctance of the Council to include Article 5 in the first place, let alone to extend its scope.

Regarding *Tilmann's* presentation, the impulse of intellectual property law for European private law unification was welcomed, and its potential for establishing a common core regarding the law of damages was considered.

Regarding a possible reformulation of Article 8 paragraph 2 of the Rome II Proposal, it was argued that its aim to override referrals in specific Community instruments to the private international law of a Member State was sufficiently clearly expressed in its current form. However, a replacement of "for any question that is not governed by that instrument" by "for any question that is not governed by the substantive provisions of that instrument" might be advantageous. Furthermore, the suggestion was made to specify "act of infringement" in Article 8 paragraph 2 of the Rome II Proposal as "initial act of infringement."

Regarding the establishment of a Community court for trademarks and designs, concerns as to subsidiarity and federalism were raised.

With respect to *Dinwoodie's* proposal, the development of substantive law for international cases was considered not to obviate the need for conflict rules. Furthermore, the doctrinal differences regarding the moral rights in copyright were regarded as unbridgeable by judge-made law. In response, it was argued that while there may be irreconcilable values in some areas, they were often of little impact on the result of a specific case and that a certain convergence could be achieved. The UNIDROIT principles and the WIPO domain name dispute resolution scheme were used as evidence of such convergence in the past. Arbitration and other alternative dispute resolution case law would help national courts to develop international substantive rules. An example of how one could facilitate the application of soft law in judicial proceedings could be found in section 101 paragraph 2 of the ALI draft, which provides that the court must determine whether a case comes within the scope of international principles either *sua sponte* or by request of a party.

Regarding *Pertegás'* comments on patent litigation, the question was raised as to whether there was a need for central litigation on the European patent after the introduction of the Community patent. It was suggested that cross-border enforcement of patents should be centralized in a single place no matter whether in a national or in a European court. It was also pointed out that cross-border patent litigation might be rendered more complicated in view of a request for a preliminary ruling by the Oberlandesgericht Düsseldorf regarding the effect of the nullity defense on the rules of jurisdiction. It is at issue whether raising the nullity defense triggers exclusive jurisdiction under Article 22 no. 4 of the Brussels Regulation. In this context, a Swiss decision (ATF 129 III 295) was referred to. The Swiss court held that it was consistent with Article 16 no. 4 of the Lugano Convention to seek a declaration of non-infringement regarding a patent registered outside Switzerland as such a declaration was not a question of nullity.

In response to *Kur's* presentation on trademark conflicts on the Internet, the soundness of an application of the WIPO market impact test to rights other than trademarks, in particular to copyright, was discussed and affirmed with reference to the ALI draft. On the other hand, an obstacle would arise if the action for infringement was regarded as one in property rather than one in tort as some French authors suggest. However, the market impact approach was expected to avoid difficulties that beset the country of origin principle, such as the existence of copyright havens and a lack of harmonization on the global level. The market impact rule was also seen as compatible with the most recent European approach to emphasize the place of the result of a tort. At the same time, the helpfulness of the distinction between *act* and *result* for intellectual property law infringements was questioned, and a reconceptualization into two separate acts of infringement was advocated. In addition, the inclusion of the market impact rule into jurisdiction rules was proposed, in particular in Article 5 paragraph 3 Brussels Regulation.

Attention was also drawn to the fact that trademark law could be regarded as forming part of unfair competition law, and that Article 5 paragraph 1 of the Rome II Proposal might therefore have a spillover effect on trademark questions.

Annexes

Annex 1

COMMISSION OF THE EUROPEAN COMMUNITIES

Brussels, 22.7.2003
COM(2003) 427 final

2003/0168 (COD)

Proposal for a

REGULATION OF THE EUROPEAN PARLIAMENT AND THE COUNCIL

ON THE LAW APPLICABLE TO NON-CONTRACTUAL OBLIGATIONS ("ROME II")

(presented by the Commission)

2003/0168 (COD)

Proposal for a

REGULATION OF THE EUROPEAN PARLIAMENT AND THE COUNCIL

ON THE LAW APPLICABLE TO NON-CONTRACTUAL OBLIGATIONS ("ROME II")

THE EUROPEAN PARLIAMENT AND THE COUNCIL OF THE EUROPEAN UNION,

Having regard to the Treaty establishing the European Community, and in Article 61(c) thereof,
Having regard to the proposal from the Commission,[1]
Having regard to the opinion of the European Economic and Social Committee,[2]
Acting in accordance with the procedure laid down in Article 251 of the Treaty,[3]
Whereas:

(1) The Union has set itself the objective of establishing an area of freedom, security and justice. To that end the Community must adopt measures relating to judicial cooperation in civil matters with a cross-border impact to the extent necessary for the proper functioning of the internal market, including measures promoting the compatibility of the rules applicable in the Member States concerning the conflict of laws and of jurisdiction.

(2) For the purposes of effectively implementing the relevant provisions of the Amsterdam Treaty, the Council (Justice and Home Affairs) on 3 December 1998 adopted a plan of action specifying that the preparation of a legal instrument on the law applicable to non-contractual obligations is among the measures to be taken within two years following the entry into force of the Amsterdam Treaty.[4]

(3) The Tampere European Council on 15 and 16 October 1999[5] approved the principle of mutual recognition of judgments as a priority matter in the establishment of a European law-enforcement area. The Mutual Recognition Programme[6] states that measures relating to harmonisation of conflict-of-law rules are measures that "actually do help facilitate the implementation of the principle".

– 2 –

[1] OJ C [...], [...] , p. [...] .
[2] OJ C [...], [...] , p. [...] .
[3] Opinion of the European Parliament of [...] (OJ C [...], [...] , p. [...] .
[4] Action Plan of the Council and the Commission on how best to implement the provisions of the Treaty of Amsterdam on an area of freedom, security and justice: OJ C 19, 23.1.1999.
[5] Presidency conclusions of 16 October 1999, points 28 to 39.
[6] OJ C 12, 15.1.2001, p. 1.

(4) The proper functioning of the internal market creates a need, in order to improve the predictability of the outcome of litigation, certainty as to the law and the free movement of judgments, for the rules of conflict of laws in the Member States to designate the same national law irrespective of the country of the court in which an action is brought.

(5) The scope of the Regulation must be determined in such a way as to be consistent with Regulation (EC) No 44/2001[7] and the Rome Convention of 1980.[8]

(6) Only uniform rules applied irrespective of the law they designate can avert the risk of distortions of competition between Community litigants.

(7) The principle of the lex loci delicti commissi is the basic solution for non-contractual obligations in virtually all the Member States, but the practical application of the principle where the component factors of the case are spread over several countries is handled differently. This situation engenders uncertainty in the law.

(8) The uniform rule must serve to improve the foreseeability of court decisions and ensure a reasonable balance between the interests of the person claimed to be liable and the person who has sustained damage. A connection with the country where the direct damage occurred (lex loci delicti commissi) strikes a fair balance between the interests of the person causing the damage and the person sustaining the damage, and also reflects the modern approach to civil liability and the development of systems of strict liability.

(9) Specific rules should be laid down for special torts/delicts where the general rule does not allow a reasonable balance to be struck between the interests at stake.

(10) Regarding product liability, the conflict rule must meet the objectives of fairly spreading the risks inherent in a modern high-technology society, protecting consumers' health, stimulating innovation, securing undistorted competition and facilitating trade. Connection to the law of the place where the person sustaining the damage has his habitual residence, together with a foreseeability clause, is a balanced solution in regard to these objectives.

(11) In matters of unfair competition, the conflict rule must protect competitors, consumers and the general public and ensure that the market economy functions properly. The connection to the law of the relevant market generally satisfies these objectives, though in specific circumstances other rules might be appropriate.

(12) In view of the Charter of Fundamental Rights of the European Union and the Council of Europe Convention for the Protection of Human Rights and Fundamental Freedoms, the conflict must strike a reasonable balance as regards violations of privacy and rights in the personality. Respect for the fundamental principles that apply in the Member States as regards freedom of the press must be secured by a specific safeguard clause.

– 3 –

[7] OJ L 12, 16.1.2001, p. 1.

[8] The consolidated text of the Convention as amended by the various Conventions of Accession, and the declarations and protocols annexed to it, is published in OJ C 27, 26.1.1998, p. 34.

(13) Regarding violations of the environment, Article 174 of the Treaty, which provides that there must a high level of protection based on the precautionary principle and the principle that preventive action must be taken, the principle of priority for corrective action at source and the principle that the polluter pays, fully justifies the use of the principle of discriminating in favour of the person sustaining the damage.

(14) Regarding violations of intellectual property rights, the universally acknowledged principle of the *lex loci protectionis* should be preserved. For the purposes of the present Regulatio, the term intellectual property rights means copyright, related rights, sui generis right for the protection of databases and industrial property rights.

(15) Similar rules should be provided for where damage is caused by an act other than a tort or delict, such as unjust enrichment and agency without authority.

(16) To preserve their freedom of will, the parties should be allowed to determine the law applicable to a non-contractual obligation. Protection should be given to weaker parties by imposing certain conditions on the choice.

(17) Considerations of the public interest warrant giving the courts of the Member States the possibility, in exceptional circumstances, of applying exceptions based on public policy and overriding mandatory rules.

(18) The concern to strike a reasonable balance between the parties means that account must be taken of the rules of safety and conduct in operation in the country in which the harmful act was committed, even where the non-contractual obligations is governed by another law.

(19) The concern for consistency in Community law requires that this Regulation be without prejudice to provisions relating to or having an effect on the applicable law, contained in the treaties or instruments of secondary legislation other than this Regulation, such as the conflict rules in specific matters, overriding mandatory rules of Community origin, the Community public policy exception and the specific principles of the internal market. Furthermore, this regulation is not intended to create, nor shall its application lead to obstacles to the proper functioning of the internal market, in particular free movement of goods and services.

(20) Respect for international commitments entered into by the Member States means that this Regulation should not affect conventions relating to specific matters to which the Member States are parties. To make the rules easier to read, the Commission will publish the list of the relevant conventions in the *Official Journal of the European Union* on the basis of information supplied by the Member States.

(21) Since the objective of the proposed action, namely better foreseeability of court judgments requiring genuinely uniform rules determined by a mandatory and directly applicable Community legal instrument, cannot be adequately attained by the Member States, who cannot lay down uniform Community rules, and can therefore, by reason of its effects throughout the Community, be better achieved at Community level, the Community can take measures, in accordance with the subsidiarity principle set out in Article 5 of the Treaty. In accordance with the proportionality principle set out in that Article, a Regulation, which increases certainty in the law without requiring harmonisation of the substantive rules of domestic law, does not go beyond what is necessary to attain that objective.

(22) [In accordance with Article 3 of the Protocol on the position of the United Kingdom and Ireland, annexed to the Treaty on European Union and the Treaty establishing the European Community, these Member States have stated their intention of participating in the adoption and application of this Regulation. / In accordance with Articles 1 and 2 of the Protocol on the position of the United Kingdom and Ireland, annexed to the Treaty on European Union and the Treaty establishing the European Community, these Member States are not participating in the adoption of this Regulation, which will accordingly not be binding on those Member States.]

(23) In accordance with Articles 1 and 2 of the Protocol on the position of Denmark, annexed to the Treaty on European Union and the Treaty establishing the European Community, that Member State is not participating in the adoption of this Regulation, which will accordingly not be binding on that Member State,

HAVE ADOPTED THIS REGULATION:

Chapter I - Scope

Article 1 - Material scope

1. This Regulation shall apply, in situations involving a conflict of laws, to non-contractual obligations in civil and commercial matters.

It shall not apply to revenue, customs or administrative matters.

2. The following are excluded from the scope of this Regulation:

a) non-contractual obligations arising out of family relationships and relationships deemed to be equivalent, including maintenance obligations;

b) non-contractual obligations arising out of matrimonial property regimes and successions;

c) obligations arising under bills of exchange, cheques and promissory notes and other negotiable instruments to the extent that the obligations under such other negotiable instruments arise out of their negotiable character;

d) the personal legal liability of officers and members as such for the debts of a company or firm or other body corporate or incorporate, and the personal legal liability of persons responsible for carrying out the statutory audits of accounting documents;

e) non-contractual obligations among the settlers, trustees and beneficiaries of a trust;

f) non-contractual obligations arising out of nuclear damage.

3. For the purposes of this Regulation, "Member State" means any Member State other than [the United Kingdom, Ireland or] Denmark.

Article 2 – Universal application

Any law specified by this Regulation shall be applied whether or not it is the law of a Member State.

Chapter II - Uniform rules

SECTION 1
RULES APPLICABLE TO NON-CONTRACTUAL OBLIGATIONS ARISING OUT OF A TORT OR DELICT

Article 3 – General rule

1. The law applicable to a non-contractual obligation shall be the law of the country in which the damage arises or is likely to arise, irrespective of the country in which the event giving rise to the damage occurred and irrespective of the country or countries in which the indirect consequences of that event arise.

2. However, where the person claimed to be liable and the person sustaining damage both have their habitual residence in the same country when the damage occurs, the non-contractual obligation shall be governed by the law of that country.

3. Notwithstanding paragraphs 1 and 2, where it is clear from all the circumstances of the case that the non-contractual obligation is manifestly more closely connected with another country, the law of that other country shall apply. A manifestly closer connection with another country may be based in particular on a pre-existing relationship between the parties, such as a contract that is closely connected with the non-contractual obligation in question.

Article 4 – Product liability

Without prejudice to Article 3(2) and (3), the law applicable to a non-contractual obligation arising out of damage or a risk of damage caused by a defective product shall be that of the country in which the person sustaining the damage is habitually resident, unless the person claimed to be liable can show that the product was marketed in that country without his consent, in which case the applicable law shall be that of the country in which the person claimed to be liable is habitually resident.

Article 5 – Unfair competition

1. The law applicable to a non-contractual obligation arising out of an act of unfair competition shall be the law of the country where competitive relations or the collective interests of consumers are or are likely to be directly and substantially affected.

2. Where an act of unfair competition affects exclusively the interests of a specific competitor, Article 3(2) and (3) shall apply.

Article 6 – Violations of privacy and rights relating to the personality

1. The law applicable to a non-contractual obligation arising out of a violation of privacy or rights relating to the personality shall be the law of the forum where the application of the law designated by Article 3 would be contrary to the fundamental principles of the forum as regards freedom of expression and information.

2. The law applicable to the right of reply or equivalent measures shall be the law of the country in which the broadcaster or publisher has its habitual residence.

Article 7 – Violation of the environment

The law applicable to a non-contractual obligation arising out of a violation of the environment shall be the law determined by the application of Article 3(1), unless the person sustaining damage prefers to base his claim on the law of the country in which the event giving rise to the damage occurred.

Article 8 – Infringement of intellectual property rights

1. The law applicable to a non-contractual obligation arising from an infringement of a intellectual property right shall be the law of the country for which protection is sought.

2. In the case of a non-contractual obligation arising from an infringement of a unitary Community industrial property right, the relevant Community instrument shall apply. For any question that is not governed by that instrument, the applicable law shall be the law of the Member State in which the act of infringement is committed.

SECTION 2
RULES APPLICABLE TO NON-CONTRACTUAL OBLIGATIONS ARISING OUT OF AN ACT OTHER THAN A TORT OR DELICT

Article 9 – Determination of the applicable law

1. If a non-contractual obligation arising out of an act other than a tort or delict concerns a relationship previously existing between the parties, such as a contract closely connected with the non-contractual obligation, it shall be governed by the law that governs that relationship.

2. Without prejudice to paragraph 1, where the parties have their habitual residence in the same country when the event giving rise to the damage occurs, the law applicable to the non-contractual obligation shall be the law of that country.

3. Without prejudice to paragraphs 1 and 2, a non-contractual obligation arising out of unjust enrichment shall be governed by the law of the country in which the enrichment takes place.

4. Without prejudice to paragraphs 1 and 2, the law applicable to a non-contractual obligation arising out of actions performed without due authority in connection with the affairs of another person shall be the law of the country in which the beneficiary has his

habitual residence at the time of the unauthorised action. However, where a non-contractual obligation arising out of actions performed without due authority in connection with the affairs of another person relates to the physical protection of a person or of specific tangible property, the law applicable shall be the law of the country in which the beneficiary or property was situated at the time of the unauthorised action.

5. Notwithstanding paragraphs 1, 2, 3 and 4, where it is clear from all the circumstances of the case that the non-contractual obligation is manifestly more closely connected with another country, the law of that other country shall apply.

6. Nowithstanding the present Article, all non-contractual obligations in the field of intellectual property shall be governed by Article 8.

SECTION 3
COMMON RULES APPLICABLE TO NON-CONTRACTUAL OBLIGATIONS ARISING OUT OF A TORT OR DELICT AND OUT OF AN ACT OTHER THAN A TORT OR DELICT

Article 10 – Freedom of choice

1. The parties may agree, by an agreement entered into after their dispute arose, to submit non-contractual obligations other than the obligations to which Article 8 applies to the law of their choice. The choice must be expressed or demonstrated with reasonable certainty by the circumstances of the case. It may not affect the rights of third parties.

2. If all the other elements of the situation at the time when the loss is sustained are located in a country other than the country whose law has been chosen, the choice of the parties shall be without prejudice to the application of rules of the law of that country which cannot be derogated from by contract.

3. The parties' choice of the applicable law shall not debar the application of provisions of Community law where the other elements of the situation were located in one of the Member States of the European Community at the time when the loss was sustained.

Article 11 – Scope of the law applicable to non-contractual obligations

The law applicable to non-contractual obligations under Articles 3 to 10 of this Regulation shall govern in particular:

a) the conditions and extent of liability, including the determination of persons who are liable for acts performed by them;

b) the grounds for exemption from liability, any limitation of liability and any division of liability;

c) the existence and kinds of injury or damage for which compensation may be due;

d) within the limits of its powers, the measures which a court has power to take under its procedural law to prevent or terminate injury or damage or to ensure the provision of compensation;

e) the assessment of the damage in so far as prescribed by law;

f) the question whether a right to compensation may be assigned or inherited;

g) persons entitled to compensation for damage sustained personally;

h) liability for the acts of another person;

i) the manners in which an obligation may be extinguished and rules of prescription and limitation, including rules relating to the commencement of a period of prescription or limitation and the interruption and suspension of the period.

Article 12 – Overriding mandatory rules

1. Where the law of a specific third country is applicable by virtue of this Regulation, effect may be given to the mandatory rules of another country with which the situation is closely connected, if and in so far as, under the law of the latter country, those rules must be applied whatever the law applicable to the non-contractual obligation. In considering whether to give effect to these mandatory rules, regard shall be had to their nature and purpose and to the consequences of their application or non-application.

2. Nothing in this Regulation shall restrict the application of the rules of the law of the forum in a situation where they are mandatory irrespective of the law otherwise applicable to the non-contractual obligation.

Article 13 – Rules of safety and conduct

Whatever may be the applicable law, in determining liability account shall be taken of the rules of safety and conduct which were in force at the place and time of the event giving rise to the damage.

Article 14 – Direct action against the insurer of the person liable

The right of persons who have suffered damage to take direct action against the insurer of the person claimed to be liable shall be governed by the law applicable to the non-contractual obligation unless the person who has suffered damage prefers to base his claims on the law applicable to the insurance contract.

Article 15 – Subrogation and multiple liability

1. Where a person ("the creditor") has a non-contractual claim upon another ("the debtor"), and a third person has a duty to satisfy the creditor, or has in fact satisfied the creditor in discharge of that duty, the law which governs the third person's duty to satisfy the creditor shall determine whether the third person is entitled to exercise against the debtor the rights which the creditor had against the debtor under the law governing their relationship in whole or in part.

2. The same rule shall apply where several persons are subject to the same claim and one of them has satisfied the creditor.

Article 16 – Formal validity

A unilateral act intended to have legal effect and relating to a non-contractual obligation is formally valid if it satisfies the formal requirements of the law which governs the non-contractual obligation in question or the law of the country in which this act is done.

Article 17 – Burden of proof

1. The law governing a non-contractual obligation under this Regulation applies to the extent that, in matters of non-contractual obligations, it contains rules which raise presumptions of law or determine the burden of proof.

2. Acts intended to have legal effect may be proved by any mode of proof recognised by the law of the forum or by any of the laws referred to in Article 16 under which that act is formally valid, provided that such mode of proof can be administered by the forum.

Chapter III – Other provisions

Article 18 – Assimilation to the territory of a State

For the purposes of this Regulation, the following shall be treated as being the territory of a State:

a) installations and other facilities for the exploration and exploitation of natural resources in, on or below the part of the seabed situated outside the State' s territorial waters if the State, under international law, enjoys sovereign rights to explore and exploit natural resources there;

b) a ship on the high seas which is registered in the State or bears lettres de mer or a comparable document issued by it or on its behalf, or which, not being registered or bearing lettres de mer or a comparable document, is owned by a national of the State;

c) an aircraft in the airspace, which is registered in or on behalf of the State or entered in its register of nationality, or which, not being registered or entered in the register of nationality, is owned by a national of the State.

Article 19 – Assimilation to habitual residence

1. For companies or firms and other bodies or incorporate or unincorporate, the principal establishment shall be considered to be the habitual residence. However, where the event giving rise to the damage occurs or the damage arises in the course of operation of a subsidiary, a branch or any other establishment, the establishment shall take the place of the habitual residence.

2. Where the event giving rise to the damage occurs or the damage arises in the course of the business activity of a natural person, that natural person's establishment shall take the place of the habitual residence.

3. For the purpose of Article 6 (2), the place where the broadcaster is established within the meaning of the directive 89/552/EEC, as amended by the directive 97/36/EC, shall take the place of the habitual residence.

Article 20 – Exclusion of renvoi

The application of the law of any country specified by this Regulation means the application of the rules of law in force in that country other than its rules of private international law.

Article 21 – States with more than one legal system

1. Where a State comprises several territorial units, each of which has its own rules of law in respect of non-contractual obligations, each territorial unit shall be considered as a country for the purposes of identifying the law applicable under this Regulation.

2. A State within which different territorial units have their own rules of law in respect of non-contractual obligations shall not be bound to apply this Regulation to conflicts solely between the laws of such units.

Article 22 – Public policy of the forum

The application of a rule of the law of any country specified by this Regulation may be refused only if such application is manifestly incompatible with the public policy ("*ordre public*") of the forum.

Article 23 – Relationship with other provisions of Community law

1. This Regulation shall not prejudice the application of provisions contained in the Treaties establishing the European Communities or in acts of the institutions of the European Communities which:

- in relation to particular matters, lay down choice-of-law rules relating to non-contractual obligations; or
- lay down rules which apply irrespective of the national law governing the non-contractual obligation in question by virtue of this Regulation; or
- prevent application of a provision or provisions of the law of the forum or of the law designated by this Regulation.

2. This regulation shall not prejudice the application of Community instruments which, in relation to particular matters and in areas coordinated by such instruments, subject the supply of services or goods to the laws of the Member State where the service-provider is established and, in the area coordinated, allow restrictions on freedom to provide services or goods originating in another Member State only in limited circumstances.

Article 24 – Non-compensatory damages

The application of a provision of the law designated by this Regulation which has the effect of causing non-compensatory damages, such as exemplary or punitive damages, to be awarded shall be contrary to Community public policy.

Article 25 – Relationship with existing international conventions

This Regulation shall not prejudice the application of international conventions to which the Member States are parties when this Regulation is adopted and which, in relation to particular matters, lay down conflict-of-law rules relating to non-contractual obligations.

Chapter IV – Final provisions

Article 26 – List of conventions referred to in Article 25

1. The Member States shall notify the Commission, no later than 30 June 2004, of the list of conventions referred to in Article 25. After that date, the Member States shall notify the Commission of all denunciations of such conventions.

2. The Commission shall publish the list of conventions referred to in paragraph 1 in the *Official Journal of the European Union* within six months of receiving the full list.

Article 27 – Entry into force and application in time

This Regulation shall enter into force on 1 January 2005.

It shall apply to non-contractual obligations arising out of acts occurring after its entry into force.

This Regulation shall be binding in its entirety and directly applicable in all Member States in accordance with the Treaty establishing the European Community.

Done at Brussels, […].

For the European Parliament
The President

For the Council
The President

Annex 2

This document, as of the date it was printed, had not been considered by the Council or membership of The American Law Institute, and therefore does not represent the position of the Institute on any of the issues with which it deals.

The American Law Institute

INTELLECTUAL PROPERTY: **PRINCIPLES GOVERNING JURISDICTION, CHOICE OF LAW, AND JUDGMENTS IN TRANSNATIONAL DISPUTES**

Preliminary Draft No. 2

(January 20, 2004)

Subjects Covered:

Intellectual Property: Principles Governing Jurisdiction, Choice of Law, and Judgments in Transnational Disputes

REPORTERS

FRANÇOIS DESSEMONTET, Lausanne University, Law School, Lausanne, Switzerland
ROCHELLE C. DREYFUSS, New York University School of Law, New York, New York
JANE C. GINSBURG, Columbia University School of Law, New York, New York

ADVISERS

GRAEME W. AUSTIN, The University of Arizona, James E. Rogers College of Law, Tucson, Arizona
IAN C. BALLON, Palo Alto, California
DANIEL R. BERESKIN, Toronto, Ontario
PAULA ELAINE BOGGS, Seattle, Washington
GRAEME B. DINWOODIE, Chicago-Kent College of Law, Illinois Institute of Technology, Chicago, Illinois
RICHARD FENTIMAN, Queens' College, University of Cambridge, Cambridge, England
RICHARD GARNETT, Melbourne Law School, University of Melbourne, Victoria, Australia [from 2003]
MICHAEL A. GEIST University of Ottawa Law School, Ottawa, Ontario
PAUL GOLDSTEIN, Stanford Law School, Stanford, California
ROBIN JACOB, High Court and Patents Court of England and Wales, London, England
CATHERINE KESSEDJIAN, University of Pantheon-Assas (Paris II), Paris, France
TOSHIYUKI KONO, Kyushu University Faculty of Law, Fukuoka, Japan
ANNETTE KUR, Max-Planck-Institute for Intellectual Property, Competition and Tax Law, Munich, Germany
ANDRE LUCAS, University of Nantes, Nantes, France
M. MARGARET McKEOWN, United States Court of Appeals for the Ninth Circuit, San Diego, California
SAMUEL K. MURUMBA, Brooklyn Law School, Brooklyn, New York
DAVID NIMMER, Los Angeles, California
DAVID C.L. PERKINS, London, England
HARVEY S. PERLMAN, University of Nebraska, Lincoln, Nebraska
SHIRA PERLMUTTER, New York, New York
PAMELA SAMUELSON, University of California at Berkeley School of Law and School of Information Management and Systems, Berkeley, California
HERBERT F. SCHWARTZ, New York, New York
LINDA J. SILBERMAN, New York University School of Law, New York, New York
COENRAAD JOHANNES VISSER, University of South Africa, Pretoria, South Africa

LIAISONS

JEFFREY D. KOVAR, Washington, District of Columbia, for the United States Department of State
JULE L. SIGALL, Washington, District of Columbia, for the United States Copyright Office
ELAINE WU, Washington, District of Columbia, for the United States Patent and Trademark Office
JOHANNES CHRISTIAN WICHARD, for the World Intellectual Property Organization (WIPO), Geneva, Switzerland

EX OFFICIO

ROSWELL B. PERKINS, New York, New York — *Chair of the Council, The American Law Institute*
MICHAEL TRAYNOR, San Francisco, California — *President, The American Law Institute*
LANGE LIEBMAN, New York, New York — *Director, The American Law Institute*

TABLE OF CONTENTS

INTELLECTUAL PROPERTY:
PRINCIPLES GOVERNING JURISDICTION, CHOICE OF LAW,
AND JUDGMENTS IN TRANSNATIONAL DISPUTES
(without commentary)

INTELLECTUAL PROPERTY: PRINCIPLES GOVERNING JURISDICTION, CHOICE OF LAW, AND JUDGMENTS IN TRANSNATIONAL DISPUTES (without commentary)

Part I - SCOPE OF THE PRINCIPLES

§ 101 Substantive Application

(1) These Principles apply to copyright, neighboring rights, patents, trade secrets, trademarks, domain names, other intellectual property rights, and unfair competition.

(2) A court whose adjudication of an intellectual property dispute is sought should as soon as requested by a party determine if the case comes within the Principles. If the court so determines, it shall declare the Principles applicable. A court may also declare the Principles applicable sua sponte, if that is consistent with its authority under forum law.

§ 102 Distinction between judicial and legislative competence

As a rule, the choice of forum does not imply a choice of law.

Part II – JURISDICTION

Chapter One: Bases of Jurisdiction

§ 201 Defendant's Forum

(1) A defendant may be sued in the courts of the State where that defendant is habitually resident.

(2) For the purposes of these Principles, an entity or person other than a natural person shall be considered to be habitually resident in the State -

(a) where it has its statutory seat,

(b) under whose law it was incorporated or formed,

(c) where it has its central administration, or

(d) where it has its principal place of business.

§ 202 Agreements Pertaining to Choice of Court

(1) If the parties have agreed that a court or courts shall have jurisdiction to settle any dispute which has arisen or may arise in connection with a particular legal relationship, that court or those courts shall have jurisdiction, and its jurisdiction shall be exclusive unless the parties have agreed otherwise.

(2) An agreement within the meaning of paragraph 1 shall be valid as to form, if it was entered into or confirmed -

(a) in writing;

(b) by any other means of communication which renders information accessible so as to be usable for subsequent reference;

(c) in accordance with practices established between the parties; or

(d) in accordance with a usage of which the Parties were or ought to have been aware and which is regularly observed by parties to contracts of the same nature in the particular trade or commerce concerned.

(3) An agreement within the meaning of paragraph 1 shall be valid as to substance, if it is valid under the law of the forum designated, unless the parties have chosen a different substantive law.

(4) In non negotiated contracts, an agreement within the meaning of paragraph 1 shall be valid if the designated forum is reasonable in light of -

(a) the interests of the parties, including the location, resources and sophistication of the weaker party or parties.

(b) the interests of the states, including the substantiality of the connection between the designated forum, and the parties or the substance of the dispute; whether the designated forum would have had jurisdiction over the weaker party in the absence of a forum-selection clause; and the policies of the state of the weaker party.

(c) the availability of online dispute resolution or other forms of virtual representation.

(d) whether the terms of the agreement were sufficiently apparent with respect to accessibility, typographic readability, and national language so as not to cause surprise.

(e) whether the designated forum was established by the State to foster expertise in adjudicating disputes of this type.

(5) If the designated forum is not reasonable under paragraph (4), then the forum selection clause should be disregarded in determining jurisdiction, and the forum should be determined according to the other jurisdictional provisions of these Principles.

§ 203 Appearance by the Defendant

(1) A court has jurisdiction over the defendant if the defendant proceeds on the merits without contesting jurisdiction.

(2) The defendant has the right to contest jurisdiction no later than at the time of the first defense on the merits.

(3) If defendant does not appear, the court may enter judgment. However, if local rules so permit, it must satisfy itself that the plaintiff's assertions of the bases of jurisdiction are well-founded.

§ 204 Infringement Actions

(1) A plaintiff may bring an infringement action in the courts of -

> (a) any State where defendant substantially acted (including preparatory acts), or threatened to act, in furtherance of the alleged infringement, or
>
> (b) any State to which the alleged infringement was directed, including those States for which defendant took no reasonable steps to avoid acting in or directing activity to that State

(2) If an action is brought in the courts of a State only on the basis of the direction of the alleged infringement to that State, then those courts shall have jurisdiction only in respect of the injury arising out of unauthorized use occurring in that State unless the injured person has his habitual residence or principal place of business in that State.

§ 205 Agreements Pertaining to Intellectual Property Fights

(1) An action to enforce an agreement pertaining to intellectual property may be brought in any country whose rights are substantially at issue in the dispute.

(2) In non negotiated contracts, the court should also consider the factors listed in § 202(4).

§ 206 Prohibited Grounds of Jurisdiction

(1) Jurisdiction shall not be exercised by the courts of a State on the basis solely of any of the following:

(a) the presence or the seizure in that State of tangible property belonging to the defendant, except where the dispute is directly related to that property;

(b) the presence or the seizure in that State of intellectual property belonging to the defendant, except where the dispute is directly related to that intellectual property;

(c) the nationality of the plaintiff;

(d) the nationality of the defendant;

(e) the domicile, habitual or temporary residence, or presence of the plaintiff in that State;

(f) the carrying an of commercial or other activities by the defendant in that State, except where the dispute is directly related to those activities;

(g) the service of a writ upon the defendant in that State;

(h) the temporary residence or presence of the defendant in that State;

(i) the signing in that State of the contract from which the dispute arises.

Chapter Two: Simplification of Multiterritorial Actions

§ 220 Counterclaims and Supplemental Claims

(1) A court that has jurisdiction to determine a claim under the Principles also has jurisdiction to determine all claims between the parties arising out of the transaction or series of transactions or occurrences on which the original claim is based, irrespective of the territorial source of the rights at issue, and irrespective of which party asserts them.

(2) A court may decline to exercise jurisdiction over a supplemental claim unrelated to intellectual property rights if it substantially predominates over the claims properly within the scope of the Principles.

§ 221 Multiple Defendants

(1) A plaintiff bringing an action against a defendant in a court of the State in which that defendant is habitually resident may also proceed in that court against other defendants not habitually resident in that State if the claims against the defendant habitually resident in that State and the other defendants are so closely connected that they should be adjudicated together to avoid a risk of inconsistent judgments, and

(a) as to each defendant not habitually resident in that State, there is a substantial connection between that State's intellectual property rights at issue and to the dispute involving the habitually resident defendant, or

(b) as between the States in which the other defendants are habitually resident, and the forum, the forum is the most closely related to the entire dispute.

(2) Paragraph (1) shall not apply to a codefendant invoking an exclusive choice of court clause agreed with the plaintiff and conforming with § 202.

§ 222 Third Party Claims

(1) A court that has jurisdiction to determine a claim under, the Principles shall also have jurisdiction to determine a claim by a defendant against a third party for indemnity or contribution in respect of the claim against that defendant to the extent that such an action is permitted by the law of the forum, provided that there is a substantial connection between that State's intellectual property rights and the dispute involving that third party.

(2) Paragraph 1 shall not apply to a third party invoking an exclusive choice of court clause agreed with the defendant and conforming with § 202.

§ 223 Declaratory Judgments

(1) Actions for a declaration of rights may be brought on the same terms as an action seeking substantive relief.

(2) In proceedings which have as their sole object the obtaining of a declaration of the invalidity or nullity of registered rights, and if

(a) the declaration is sought with respect to the validity of registration in one State, the courts of the State in which deposit or registration has been applied for, has taken place or, under the terms of an international Convention, is deemed to have taken place, have jurisdiction to the exclusion of the courts of third countries; or if

(b) the declaration is sought with respect to the validity of registration in more than one State, the courts of the State in which the defendant has its principal place of business shall have jurisdiction to the exclusion of the courts of third countries.

(3) The issue of invalidity of registered rights granted under the laws of another country may be adjudicated in an infringement action brought pursuant to these Principles.

(4) However, lis pendens under § 224 (1) will not apply with respect to an action seeking declarations of non liability.

§ 224 Lis Pendens

(1) Subject to § 225, when the same parties are engaged in proceedings in courts of different States, the court first seized has primary authority over the case, and shall retain the case. Accordingly, the second seized shall suspend the proceedings if the court first seized has jurisdiction and is expected to render a judgment capable of being recognized under the Principles in the State of the court second seized, irrespective of the relief sought, when:

(a) the claims arise from a single territory's intellectual property rights, or

(b) the claims arise out of the same transaction or series of transactions or occurrences.

(2) Paragraph 1 does not apply if the court second seized has exclusive jurisdiction under § 202.

(3) The court second seized shall decline jurisdiction as soon as it is presented with a judgment rendered by the court first seized that complies with the requirements for recognition or enforcement under the Principles.

(4) Upon application of a party, the court second seized may proceed with the case if the plaintiff in the court first seized has failed to take the necessary steps to bring the proceedings to a decision an the merits or if that court has not rendered such a decision, or cannot be expected to render a decision, within a reasonable time.

(5) If in the action before the court first seized, the plaintiff seeks a determination that it has no obligation to the defendant, and if an action seeking substantive relief is brought in the court second seized -

(a) the provisions of paragraphs 1-4 above shall not apply to the court second seized, unless the declaratory judgment plaintiff has advanced its claim as part of an action initiated before the court first seized by the declaratory judgment defendant, and

(b) the court first seized shall suspend the proceedings at the request of a party if the court second seized is expected to render a decision capable of being recognized under the Principles.

(6) A court shall be deemed to be seized -

(a) at the time when the document instituting the proceedings or an equivalent document is lodged with the court, provided that the plaintiff has not subsequently failed to take the steps he was required to take to have service effected an the defendant, or

(b) if the document has to be served before being lodged with the court, at the time when it is received by the authority responsible for service, provided that the plaintiff has not subsequently failed to take the steps he was required to take to have the document lodged with the court.

(7) If a separate action is not made subject to the lis pendens provision, then the, judgement in one action shall not be preclusive of the other.

§ 225 Consolidation of Territorial Claims

(1) Upon the motion of an interested party, or sua sponte, the court first seized, as determined by § 224(6), should consider consolidation of related pending actions and claims in a single forum in order to achieve worldwide resolution of a dispute among multiple litigants.

(2) For the purposes of this section, actions are deemed to be related where, irrespective of the territorial source of the rights and the relief sought, the claims arise out of the same transaction or series of transactions or occurrences.

(3) In deciding whether to consolidate the actions and claims, the court should consider:

(a) in general, whether consolidating would promote efficiency and conserve judicial resources and the resources of the parties,

(b) whether or not inconsistent judgments could result if multiple courts adjudicated the related claims;

(4) If the court determines that the actions and claims should be consolidated, the court should next consider whether it should retain jurisdiction over the consolidated action, or should instead suspend proceedings in favor of another court. Considerations to take into account in reaching this determination include:

(a) where the center of gravity of the dispute lies;

(b) whether the court first seized has jurisdiction over as many parties as another court, including courts in which related claims are pending;

(c) whether the court has, relative to another court, including courts seized with related causes of action, the subject matter authority to adjudicate all of its territorial rights put into issue;

(d) the difficulty of managing the litigation, including whether the Court first seized would be obliged to consider novel or complex questions of foreign law;

(e) whether the court first seized would be required to decide factual issues requiring procedures unavailable in that jurisdiction

(f) in disputes over contract rights, whether the court first seized has the most significant relationship to the contract. In particular, the court may take into account:

(i) the existence, if any, of a forum selection clause in the contracts;

(ii) the residence of the parties;

(iii) the country in which the rights which are the object of the contract are to be exercised

(iv) the country of initial title to the intellectual property subject matter, as defined in § 311-312;

(5) A case should not be consolidated in a court of a state that is not a member of the World Trade Organization.

(6) The issue of consolidation must be raised no later than at the time of the first defense on the merits.

(7) If there is no consolidation of related actions, the judgment in one action shall not be preclusive of the other.

§ 226 Exceptional Circumstances for Declining Jurisdiction

(1) In exceptional circumstances, when the jurisdiction of the court seized is not founded on an exclusive choice of court agreement valid under § 202, or on a declaration of nonliability under § 223, the court may, on application by a party, suspend its proceedings if in that case a court of another State has jurisdiction and is clearly more appropriate to resolve the dispute. Such application must be made no later than at the time of the first defense on the merits.

(2) Exceptional circumstances may lie, in -

(a) the claims are subject to consolidation in another court, pursuant to these Principles;

(b) any inconvenience to the parties in view of their habitual residence;

(c) the nature and location of the evidence, including documents and witnesses, and the procedures for obtaining such evidence;

(d) applicable limitation or prescription periods;

(e) the possibility of obtaining recognition and enforcement of any decision on the merits;

(f) whether the state in which the court seized is located has the most significant relationship to the parties or the claims;

(g) in patent cases, the expertise of the judicial system of the state in which the court seized is located.

(h) A court shall not dismiss or suspend the proceedings on the sole ground that the case raises questions of foreign law.

(3) If the court decides to suspend its proceedings under paragraph 1, it may order the defendant to provide' security sufficient to satisfy any decision of the other court an the merits.

(4) When the court has suspended its proceedings under paragraph 1,

(a) it shall decline to exercise jurisdiction if the court of the other State exercises jurisdiction, or if the plaintiff does not bring the proceedings in that State within the time specified by the court, or

(b) it shall proceed with the case if the court of the other State decides not to exercise jurisdiction.

§ 227 Provisional and Protective Measures

(1) A court having jurisdiction over a defendant under §§ 201-205 of these Principles has jurisdiction to order any provisional or protective measures, including trans-border injunctions.

(2) The courts of a State in which intellectual or tangible property is located have jurisdiction to order any provisional or protective measures in respect of that property. The measure must be limited to the territory of that State.

Part III - APPLICABLE LAW

Chapter One: Territoriality

§ 301 Existence and scope of rights and remedies

(1) As a general rule, with respect to rights that arise out of registration, the law applicable to determine the existence, validity and scope of those rights and remedies for their infringement is the law of each country of registration.

(2) With respect to other intellectual property rights, the law applicable to determine the existence, validity and scope of the intellectual property rights and remedies for their

infringement is the law of any country where the alleged infringing act has or will significantly impact the market for the work or subject matter at issue.

(3) With respect to personal rights, the law applicable to determine the existence, validity and scope of the rights and remedies for their violation is the law of the country where the damage occurred.

§ 302 Scope of rights and remedies in exceptional cases

(1) Except as to claims relating to the validity of registered rights, the rule of territoriality does not apply in whole or in part in the following exceptional circumstances:

(a) it is clear from all the circumstances of the case that it is more closely connected to the law of another country;

(b) the court determines that its ruling will potentially impact territories outside the borders of its jurisdiction, and that it is unduly burdensome to decide an the basis of all the laws of the territories involved; or

(c) there is a preexisting relationship between the parties that is closely connected with the claims in issue, or

(d) the content of the applicable substantive law cannot be ascertained.

(2) The factors to take into account in choosing which law or laws to apply in exceptional cases include:

(a) The law of the country with the closest connection to the dispute as evidenced by:

(i) the center of gravity of the alleged infringer's business undertaking, as measured as objective factors;

(ii) the extent of the activities and the investment of the right holder;

(b) the degree to which the desirability of such regulation is generally accepted as evidenced by the TRIPS and successive international laws.

(3) If these norms do not supply a rule, or if the rule cannot be ascertained, the law of the forum applies.

Chapter Two: Title to and Transfer of Rights

§ 311 Initial title to registered rights

(1) Except as otherwise provided, with respect to rights that arise out of registration, the law applicable to determine the initial ownership of those rights is the law of each country of registration.

(2) In the case where the subject matter of the registered right was created pursuant to a contractual relationship, initial title is governed by the law that governs the contract.

§ 312 Initial title to non registered trademark rights

(1) With respect to an unregistered trademark or trade dress, the law applicable to determine the initial ownership of those rights is the law of each country in which the trademark or trade dress identifies and distinguishes the source of the goods or the services, except as provided in (b);

(2) When there is a contractual or other pre-existing relationship among the claimants, the law applicable to that contract or relationship will govern.

§ 313 Initial title to other rights

(1) Initial title to rights, such as copyright, which do not arise out of registration, is determined by:

(a) for works of authorship, the country in or from which the work has ferst been made available to the public;

(b) for other subject matter, or if the country designated by (a) lacks a significant relationship to the creation of the work, then the country of the creator's residence or principal place of business at the time of the work's creation.

(c) in the case where the work or subject matter derives from a commission or employment contract, initial title is governed by the law of this contract.

(d) in non negotiated contracts other than collective bargaining agreements, the applicable law designated in the contract should be applied if it is reasonable in light of.

(i) the substantiality of the connection between the designated national law, and the parties or the substance of the agreement, and;

(ii) the location of the weaker party

(iii) the sophistication of the parties, in particular, of the weaker party;

(iv) whether the terms of the agreement were sufficiently apparent with respect to accessibility, typographic readability, and national language so as not to cause surprise;

(v) whether the terms intrude an the fundamental policies of the law of the country of residence or the principal place of business of the weaker party

(vi) if the designated law is unreasonable, the law of the weaker party shall apply.

(2) For the purpose of those Principles, the "creator" of the work is:

(a) in the case of a work of authorship, the author;

(b) in the case of rights of performers, the performer;

(c) in the case of a rights of producers of phonogram, the phonogram producer;

(d) in the case of rights of broadcasting, the broadcasting entity;

(e) in the case of unregistered rights for the semi conductor topography, the developer;

(f) in the case of a plant variety, the breeder;

(g) in the case of rights an unregistered design or a model, the designer;

(h) in the case of a trade secret, the developer;

(i) in the case of a geographical indication, the first group of producers;

(j) in the case of the right of publicity, the person whose name and likeness is appropriated;

(k) in the case of a right an a non-original database, the producer.

(3) If the work has more than one creator, the country whose law determines initial title is the law of one creator's residence, as designated by contract between the co-creators, or, in the absence of such an agreement, the country with the most significant relationship to the work's creation and first exploitation.

(4) Where the law designated by the previous paragraphs does not provide a solution, then initial title is determined by the law of the place where the right is first exploited.

§ 314 Transferability of Intellectual Property Rights

Alternative A.

The transferability of rights is determined by the laws of each for which rights are transferred.

Alternative B.

(1) With respect to rights arising out of registration, the transferability of rights is determined by the law of each country of registration.

(2) With respect to rights that do not arise out of registration, transferability of rights is determined by the law of the country of initial title.

§ 315 Transfers of title and grants of licenses

(1) Except for the transferability of rights and transfers by operation of law, the law applicable to a transfer of ownership in, or a grant of a license to use, intellectual property rights is the law designated by the parties to the contract.

(2) In the absence of a contractual choice of law clause, the applicable law is that of the country with the closest connection to the contract. It shall be presumed that the contract is most closely connected to the country where the assignor or the licensor has its habitual residence or its main business establishment.

(3) In non negotiated contracts other than collective bargaining agreements, the applicable law designated in the contract should be applied if it is reasonable in light of:

(a) the substantiality of the connection between the designated national law, and the parties or the substance of the agreement, and;

(b) the location of the weaker party

(c) the sophistication of the parties, in particular, of the weaker party;

(d) whether the terms of the agreement were sufficiently apparent with respect to accessibility, typographic readability, and national language so as not to cause surprise;

(e) whether the terms intrude on the fundamental policies of the law of the country of residence or the principal place of business of the weaker party

(f) If the designated law is unreasonable, the law of the weaker party shall apply.

(4) Except as provided in subsection (3), choice of law clauses are valid under the same conditions as choice of court clauses are valid under §§ 202(2) and (3).

§ 316 Transfers by operation of law

(1) For registered rights, the law of the country of registration governs transfers by operation of law.

(2) For unregistered rights, transfer by operation of law is determined by the law of the country for which protection is sought.

(3) These Principles do not apply to transfers by operation of laws other than intellectual property law, such as marital, estate, and competition law.

Chapter Three: general principles regarding choice of law

§ 321 Proof of applicable law

The party requesting the application of a foreign substantive law under these Principles should prove its content. A court may also apply the foreign law sua sponte, if that is consistent with its authority under the forum law.

§ 322 Exclusion of the Renvoi

The application of the law of any country specified by these Principles means the application of the rules of law in force in that country other than its rules of private international law.

§ 323 Scope of the law of forum

(1) Except as otherwise provided, the law of the forum governs characterization, and the law of evidence and discovery.

(2) Where the parties have designated the law applicable to their contract, that law will also govern the applicable statute of limitations.

§ 324 Public Policy (ordre public)

The application of provisions of foreign law is excluded if such application leads to a result that is contrary to the public policy of the forum.

§ 325 Mandatory rules

Nothing in these Principles should restrict the application of the law of the forum or the law of third countries in a situation where rules under those laws are mandatory, irrespective of the otherwise law applicable.

Part IV: RECOGNITION AND ENFORCEMENT OF JUDGMENTS

Chapter One: In General

§ 401 Judgments to be Recognized or Enforced

(1) A court whose recognition and enforcement of a foreign judgment is sought should first determine whether the rendering court considered whether these Principles would be applicable.

(a) If the rendering court determined that the Principles were applicable, then the enforcing court should recognize or enforce the judgment pursuant to these Principles.

(b) If the rendering court determined that the Principles were not applicable, the enforcing court should determine recognition and enforcement pursuant to other applicable law.

(c) If the rendering court has not determined the application of these Principles, the enforcing court should determine for itself whether to apply the Principles.

(2) A judgment that is within a basis of jurisdiction provided for in these Principles should be recognized or enforced under this Chapter.

(a)In order to be recognized, a judgment referred to in paragraph 1 must be recognized in the rendering State.

(b) In order to be enforceable, a judgment referred to in paragraph 1 must be enforceable in the rendering State.

(c) However, recognition or enforcement may be postponed if the judgment is the subject of review in the rendering State or if the time limit for seeking a review has not expired.

(d) The preclusive effect of a judgment should be no greater than its effect in the rendering State.

§ 402 Verification of Jurisdiction

(1) Except in cases where the defendant has waived a challenge to jurisdiction by joining issue an the merits of the case in accordance with § 203(1), the court addressed should

verify the jurisdiction of the rendering court. In cases where objections to jurisdiction are waived through appearance, the court addressed should verify that issue was joined without contesting jurisdiction.

(2) In verifying the jurisdiction of the rendering court, the findings of fact on which the rendering court based its jurisdiction should be presumed correct. However, this presumption does not apply if the judgment was given by default.

(3) In verifying the jurisdiction of the rendering court when that court has rendered a default judgment, the court addressed must satisfy itself that the plaintiff's assertions of the bases of jurisdiction under these Principles and under the law of the State of the rendering court were well founded.

(4) Except as provided in § 403, recognition or enforcement of a judgment may not be refused on the ground that the court addressed considers that the rendering court should have declined jurisdiction in accordance with § 206.

§ 403 Judgments Not to be Recognized or Enforced

(1) A judgment based on a ground of jurisdiction which conflicts with §§ 201-204, 221 or 222, or whose application is prohibited by virtue of § 206, or which applied a law manifestly inconsistent with the rules set out in §§ 301-325 should not be recognized or enforced.

(a) The reviewing court should defer to the facts found by the rendering court in support of its designation of the applicable law.

(2) Recognition or enforcement of a judgment may also be refused if -

(a) proceedings between the same parties and having the Same subject matter are pending before a court of the State addressed, if first seized in accordance with § 223 or if consolidated in accordance with § 225 ;

(b) the judgment is inconsistent with the judgment of the court first seized, or if the actions were consolidated in accordance with § 225, the judgment is inconsistent with the judgment of the court of consolidation;

(c) the rendering court's jurisdiction was based on a non negotiated contract whose forum designation was unreasonable under § 202(4).

(d) the document which instituted the proceedings or an equivalent document, including the essential elements of the claim, was not notified to the defendant in sufficient time and in such a way as to enable the defendant to arrange for a defense;

(e) the judgment was obtained by fraud in connection with a matter of procedure;

(f) the judgment results from proceedings incompatible with fundamental principles of procedure of the State addressed, including the right of each party to be heard by an impartial and independent court;

(g) recognition or enforcement would be manifestly incompatible with the public policy of the State addressed.

(3) Without prejudice to such review as is necessary for the purpose of application of the provisions of this Chapter, there should be no review of the findings of fact or law relating to the merits of the judgment of the rendering court.

Chapter Two: Remedies

§ 410 Damages

(1) In so far as a judgment awards non-compensatory, including exemplary or punitive, damages, it should be recognized at least to the extent that similar or comparable damages could have been awarded in the State addressed. This rule does not apply to damages that are intended to compensate the plaintiff without requiring proof of actual damages.

(a) Where the debtor, after proceedings in which the creditor has the opportunity to be heard, satisfies the court addressed that in the circumstances, including those existing in the rendering State, grossly excessive damages have been awarded, recognition may be limited to a lesser amount.

(b) In no event should the court addressed recognize the judgment in an amount less than that which could have been awarded in the State addressed in the same circumstances, including those existing in the rendering State.

(2) In applying paragraphs 1 and 2, the court addressed should take into account whether and to what extent the damages awarded by the rendering court serve to cover costs and expenses relating to the proceedings, not otherwise covered by statutory provisions relating to the awards of attorneys fees.

§ 411 Injunctions

(1) In the ordinary course, injunctive relief is available; nonetheless courts may decline to enjoin activities within their territories if:

(a) health and safety are at issue, or;

(b) the judgment conflicts with fundamental cultural policies in the State where enforcement is sought.

(2) In cases where injunctive relief is denied, the court must award damages sufficient to afford an effective remedy for that territory.

Annex 3

HAGUE CONFERENCE ON PRIVATE INTERNATIONAL LAW

WORK. DOC. No 110 E
Revised*

Commission spéciale sur la compétence,
la reconnaissance et l'exécution des jugements
étrangers en matière civile et commerciale
(du 21 au 27 avril 2004)
Special Commission on Jurisdiction,
Recognition and Enforcement of Foreign Judgments
in Civil and Commercial Matters
(21 to 27 April 2004)

Distribution: May 2004

Proposal by the Drafting Committee

DRAFT ON EXCLUSIVE CHOICE OF COURT AGREEMENTS

The States signatory to the present Convention,

Desiring to promote international trade and investment through enhanced judicial cooperation,

Believing that such enhanced cooperation requires a secure international legal regime that ensures the effectiveness of exclusive choice of court agreements by parties to commercial transactions and that governs the recognition and enforcement of judgments resulting from proceedings based on such agreements,

Have resolved to conclude the following *Convention on Exclusive Choice of Court Agreements* and have agreed upon the following provisions -

CHAPTER I SCOPE AND DEFINITIONS

Article 1 *Scope*

1. The present Convention shall apply in international cases to exclusive choice of court agreements concluded in civil or commercial matters.

2. For the purposes of Chapter II, a case is international unless[at the time the agreement is concluded][and][at the time of commencement of the proceedings] the parties are resident in the Contracting State of the court seised and the relationship of the parties and all other elements relevant to the dispute, regardless of the location of the chosen court, are connected only with that State.

3. For the purposes of Chapter III, a case is international where recognition or enforcement of a foreign judgment is sought.

* This document reflects the changes made by the Drafting Committee at its meeting on 27 April 2004. Moreover, upon request of the Special Commission, the Permanent Bureau has aligned the English and French versions of this Document with the terminology traditionally used in Hague Conventions. Changes were made in agreement with the Chairman of the Drafting Committee. Reproduced with the Courtesy of the Hague Conference.

Article 2 *Exclusions from scope*

1. The Convention shall not apply to exclusive choice of court agreements -

   a) to which a natural person acting primarily for personal, family or household purposes (a consumer) is a party; or

   b) relating to contracts of employment, including collective agreements.

2. The Convention shall not apply to the following matters -

   a) the status and legal capacity of natural persons;

   b) maintenance obligations;

   c) other family law matters, including matrimonial property regimes and other rights or obligations arising out of marriage or similar relationships;

   d) wills and succession;

   e) insolvency, composition and analogous matters;

   f) contracts for the carriage of passengers or goods by sea[, and other admiralty or maritime matters];

   g) anti-trust (competition) matters;

   h) liability for nuclear damage;

   i) rights *in rem* in immovable property[and tenancies of immovable property];

   j) the validity, nullity, or dissolution of legal persons, and the validity of decisions of their organs;

   k) [intellectual property rights other than copyright or related rights, except in proceedings pursuant to a contract which licenses or assigns such intellectual property rights[including proceedings for infringement of the right to which the contract relates]];[1] or

   l) the validity of entries in public registers.

3. Notwithstanding paragraph 2, proceedings are not excluded from the scope of the Convention where a matter referred to in that paragraph arises merely as an incidental question and not as an object of the proceedings.

4. The Convention shall not apply to arbitration and related proceedings.

5. Proceedings are not excluded from the scope of the Convention by the mere fact that a government, a governmental agency or any person acting for a State is a party thereto.

6. Nothing in this Convention affects the privileges and immunities of sovereign States or of entities of sovereign States, or of international organisations.

Article 3 *Exclusive choice of court agreements*

For the purposes of this Convention,

   a) "exclusive choice of court agreement" means an agreement concluded by two or more parties that meets the requirements of paragraph c) and designates, for the purpose of deciding disputes which have arisen or may arise in connection with a particular legal relationship, the courts of one Contracting State or one or more specific courts in one Contracting State to the exclusion of the jurisdiction of any other courts;

[1] According to this draft, validity as a principal issue is excluded from the scope of the Convention.

b) a choice of court agreement which designates the courts of one Contracting State or one or more specific courts in one Contracting State shall be deemed to be exclusive unless the parties have expressly provided otherwise;

c) an exclusive choice of court agreement must be entered into or evidenced –

  i) in writing; or

  ii) by any other means of communication which renders information accessible so as to be usable for subsequent reference;

d) an exclusive choice of court agreement that forms part of a contract shall be treated as an agreement independent of the other terms of the contract. The validity of the exclusive choice of court agreement cannot be contested solely on the ground that the contract is not valid.

Article 4 *Other definitions*

1. In this Convention "judgment" means any decision on the merits given by a court, whatever it may be called, including a decree or order, and a determination of costs or expenses by the court (including an officer of the court), provided that such determination relates to a decision on the merits which may be recognised or enforced under this Convention. An interim measure of protection is not a judgment.

2. For the purposes of this Convention, an entity or person other than a natural person shall be considered to be resident in the State -

a) where it has its statutory seat;

b) under whose law it was incorporated or formed;

c) where it has its central administration; or

d) where it has its principal place of business.

CHAPTER II JURISDICTION

Article 5 *Jurisdiction of the chosen court*

1. The court or courts of a Contracting State designated in an exclusive choice of court agreement shall have jurisdiction to decide a dispute to which the agreement applies, unless the agreement is null and void under the law of that State.

2. A court that has jurisdiction under paragraph 1 shall not decline to exercise jurisdiction on the ground that the dispute should be decided in a court of another State.

3. The preceding paragraphs shall not affect rules -

a) on jurisdiction related to subject matter or to the value of the claim; or

b) on the internal allocation of jurisdiction among the courts of a Contracting State[unless the parties designated a specific court].[2]

[2] If the bracketed language in Article 5, paragraph 3 b) is not retained, the question of whether Articles 7 and 9 should apply where a case has been transferred by the chosen court to another court in the same Contracting State remains to be considered. See the bracketed language in Articles 7 e) and 9, paragraph 1 *bis*.

Article 6 *Stay of proceedings in the chosen court*

Nothing in this Convention shall prevent the chosen court from suspending or dismissing the proceedings before it, in particular in order to allow the courts of the State under the law of which an intellectual property right arose, to give a judgment on its validity, provided that such dismissal does not prevent the proceedings from being recommenced.]

Article 7 *Obligations of a court not chosen*

If the parties have entered into an exclusive choice of court agreement, any court in a Contracting State other than that of the chosen court shall suspend or dismiss the proceedings unless –

a) the agreement is null and void under the law of the State of the chosen court;[3]

b) a party lacked the capacity to enter into the agreement under the law of the State of the court seised;

c) giving effect to the agreement would lead to a very serious injustice or would be manifestly contrary to fundamental principles of public policy of the State of the court seised;[4]

d) for exceptional reasons, the agreement cannot reasonably be performed;[5] or

e) the chosen court has decided not to hear the case[, except where it has transferred the case to another court of the same State as permitted by Article 5, paragraph 3 b)][6].

Article 8 *Interim measures of protection*

Interim measures of protection are not governed by this Convention. This Convention neither requires nor precludes the grant of interim measures of protection by a Court of a Contracting State and does not affect whether or not a party may request or a court should grant such measures.

CHAPTER III RECOGNITION AND ENFORCEMENT

Article 9 *Recognition and enforcement*

1. A judgment given by a court of a Contracting State designated in an exclusive choice of court agreement shall be recognised and enforced in other Contracting States in accordance with this Chapter. Recognition or enforcement may be refused only on the following grounds[7] -

3 The policy issues related to this matter need further consideration. It has been proposed to delete the words "under the law of the State of the chosen court". It has also been proposed to add the words "on any ground, including incapacity".

4 The policy issues related to this matter need further consideration. The various options proposed are reflected in the following proposals:
i) giving effect to the agreement would lead to a very [delete: very] serious injustice or would[otherwise] be manifestly contrary to fundamental principles of public policy of the State of the court seised;
ii) under the mandatory rules on jurisdiction of the State of the court seised, the parties were unable to agree to exclude the jurisdiction of the courts of this State;
iii) giving effect to the agreement would be manifestly contrary to public policy of the State of the court seised.

5 It has been proposed to delete this provision; a decision on this proposal is linked to the final wording of paragraph (c).

6 This provision is linked to the policy decision to be taken on the bracketed part of Article 5, paragraph 3 and to the language in square brackets in Article 9, paragraph 1 *bis*.

7 Further consideration is required as to whether the matters covered by Article 7 c) and d) are adequately reflected in this paragraph.

a) the agreement was null and void under the law of the State of the chosen court[8], unless the chosen court has determined that the agreement is valid;

b) a party lacked the capacity to enter into the agreement under the law of the requested State;

c) the document which instituted the proceedings or an equivalent document, including the essential elements of the claim,

  i) was not notified to the defendant in sufficient time and in such a way as to enable him to arrange for his defence, unless the defendant entered an appearance and presented his case without contesting notification in the court of origin, provided that the law of the State of origin permitted notification to be contested, or

  ii) was notified to the defendant in the requested State in a manner that violated the public policy of that State;

d) the judgment was obtained by fraud in connection with a matter of procedure;

e) recognition or enforcement would be manifestly incompatible with the public policy of the requested State, including situations where the specific proceedings leading to the judgment were incompatible with fundamental principles of procedural fairness of that State; or

f) the judgment is inconsistent with a judgment given in a dispute between the same parties in the requested State, or it is inconsistent with an earlier judgment given in another State between the same parties and involving the same cause of action, provided that the earlier judgment fulfils the conditions necessary for its recognition in the requested State[under an international agreement], and provided that the inconsistent judgment was not given in contravention of this Convention.

[1bis. Paragraph 1 shall also apply to a judgment given by a court of a Contracting State pursuant to a transfer of the case from the chosen court in that Contracting State as permitted by Article 5, paragraph 3 b).][9]

2. Without prejudice to such review as is necessary for the application of the provisions of this Chapter, there shall be no review of the merits of the judgment rendered by the court of origin. The court addressed shall be bound by the findings of fact on which the court of origin based its jurisdiction, unless the judgment was given by default.

3. A judgment shall be recognised only if it has effect in the State of origin, and shall be enforced only if it is enforceable in the State of origin.

4. Recognition or enforcement may be postponed or refused if the judgment is the subject of review in the State of origin or if the time limit for seeking ordinary review has not expired. A refusal does not prevent a subsequent application for recognition or enforcement of the judgment.

Article 10 *Incidental questions*[10]

1. Where a matter referred to in Article 2, paragraph 2, arose as an incidental question, the ruling on that question shall not be recognised and enforced under this Convention.

– 5 –

8 It has been proposed to add the words "on any ground, including incapacity".

9 This provision is linked to the policy decision to be taken on the bracketed part of Article 5, paragraph 3 and to the language in square brackets in Article 7 e).

10 It was proposed to add a new paragraph 4 as follows: "The preceding paragraphs 2 and 3 shall apply *mutatis mutandis* to the matters provided for in Article 2, paragraph 2 to the extent that a judgment on such matters has effect not only as between the parties but also as regards all other persons."

[2. Where an incidental ruling on the validity of an intellectual property right other than copyright or related rights was necessary for the judgment of the court of origin, recognition or enforcement of the judgment may be refused to the extent that it is inconsistent with a judgment[11] on the validity of the intellectual property right rendered in the State under the law of which the intellectual property right arose.[12]]

[3. Where an incidental ruling on the validity of an intellectual property right other than copyright or related rights was necessary for the judgment of the court of origin, recognition or enforcement of the judgment may be postponed or refused at the request of one of the parties if proceedings on validity are pending in the State under the law of which the intellectual property right arose. A refusal does not prevent a subsequent application for recognition or enforcement of the judgment.]

[Article 11 Judgments in contravention of exclusive choice of court agreements

The provisions of Article 7 shall also apply to proceedings for recognition or enforcement of a judgment rendered in contravention of an exclusive choice of court agreement.[13]]

Article 12 Settlements

Settlements which a court of a Contracting State designated in an exclusive choice of court agreement has approved, or which have been concluded before that court in the course of proceedings, and which are enforceable in the same manner as a judgment in the State of origin, shall be enforced under this Convention in the same manner as a judgment.

Article 13 Documents to be produced

1. The party seeking recognition or applying for enforcement shall produce -

   a) a complete and certified copy of the judgment;
   b) the exclusive choice of court agreement, or evidence of its existence;
   c) if the judgment was rendered by default, the original or a certified copy of a document establishing that the document which instituted the proceedings or an equivalent document was notified to the defaulting party;
   d) all documents necessary to establish that the judgment has effect or, where applicable, is enforceable in the State of origin;
   e) in the case referred to in Article 12, a certificate of the court of origin that the settlement or a part of it is enforceable in the same manner as a judgment in the State of origin.

2. If the terms of the judgment do not permit the court addressed to verify whether the conditions of this Chapter have been complied with, that court may require any necessary documents.

3. An application for recognition or enforcement may be accompanied by a form recommended and published by the Hague Conference on Private International Law.

4. The court addressed may require a translation of any document referred to in this Article.

[11] It is recalled that the definition of "judgment" in Article 4, paragraph 1 includes a decision of a patent office or other authority exercising functions of a court.
[12] The relationship of this provision with Article 9, paragraph 1 f) requires further consideration.
[13] The intention of this provision is to prevent recognition or enforcement of judgments given in either Contracting or non-Contracting States in contravention of an exclusive choice of court agreement, save where the exceptions in Article 7 apply. The policy and the drafting require further consideration.

Article 14 *Procedure*

The procedure for recognition, declaration of enforceability or registration for enforcement, and the enforcement of the judgment, are governed by the law of the requested State unless this Convention provides otherwise. The court addressed shall act expeditiously.

Article 15 *Damages*

1. A judgment which awards non-compensatory damages, including exemplary or punitive damages, shall be recognised and enforced to the extent that a court in the requested State could have awarded similar or comparable damages. Nothing in this paragraph shall preclude the court addressed from recognising and enforcing the judgment under its law for an amount up to the full amount of the damages awarded by the court of origin.

2. a) Where the debtor, after proceedings in which the creditor has the opportunity to be heard, satisfies the court addressed that in the circumstances, including those existing in the State of origin, grossly excessive damages have been awarded, recognition and enforcement may be limited to a lesser amount.

   b) In no event shall the court addressed recognise or enforce the judgment for an amount less than that which could have been awarded in the requested State in the same circumstances, including those existing in the State of origin.[14]

3. In applying the preceding paragraphs, the court addressed shall take into account whether and to what extent the damages awarded by the court of origin serve to cover costs and expenses relating to the proceedings.

Article 16 *Severability*

Recognition or enforcement of a severable part of a judgment shall be granted where recognition or enforcement of that part is applied for, or only part of the judgment is capable of being recognised or enforced under this Convention.

CHAPTER IV GENERAL CLAUSES

Article 17 *No legalisation*

All documents forwarded or delivered under this Convention shall be exempt from legalisation[or *apostille*][or any analogous formality].

Article 18 *Limitation of jurisdiction*

Upon ratification, acceptance, approval or accession, a State may declare that its courts may refuse to determine disputes covered by an exclusive choice of court agreement if, except for the location of the chosen court, there is no connection between that State and the parties or the dispute.

[14] It was proposed that paragraph 2 be deleted.

Article 19 *Limitation of recognition and enforcement*

Upon ratification, acceptance, approval or accession, a State may declare that its courts may refuse to recognise or enforce a judgment of a court in another Contracting State if the parties are resident in the requested State, and the relationship of the parties and all other elements relevant to the dispute, other than the location of the chosen court, are connected only with the requested State, at the time the agreement is concluded.

Article 20 *Limitation with respect to asbestos related matters*

Upon ratification, acceptance, approval or accession, a State may declare that it will not apply the provisions of the Convention to exclusive choice of court agreements in asbestos related matters.[15]

Article 21 *Uniform interpretation*

In the interpretation of this Convention, regard shall be had to its international character and to the need to promote uniformity in its application.

Article 22 *Non-unified legal system*

1. In relation to a Contracting State in which two or more systems of law apply in different territorial units with regard to any matter dealt with in this Convention –

a) any reference to the law or procedure of a State shall be construed as referring, where appropriate, to the law or procedure in force in the relevant territorial unit;

b) any reference to residence in a State shall be construed as referring, where appropriate, to residence in the relevant territorial unit;

c) any reference to the court or courts of a State shall be construed as referring, where appropriate, to the court or courts in the relevant territorial unit;

d) any reference to a connection with a State shall be construed as referring, where appropriate, to a connection with the relevant territorial unit.

2. Notwithstanding the preceding paragraph, a Contracting State with two or more territorial units in which different systems of law apply shall not be bound to apply this Convention to situations which, including the location of the chosen court,[16] involve solely such different territorial units.

3. A court in a territorial unit of a Contracting State with two or more territorial units in which different systems of law apply shall not be bound to recognise or enforce a judgment from another Contracting State solely because the judgment has been recognised or enforced by a court in another territorial unit of the same Contracting State under this Convention.

[15] Some delegations have proposed that further specific subject matters should be referred to in this provision, such as natural resources and joint ventures. These proposals are linked to issues that arise in relation to Articles 7 and 9.

[16] Where the chosen court is located in another Contracting State, Article 19 applies.

Article 23 Relationship with other international instruments

1. For the purposes of this Article, "international instrument" means an international treaty or rules made by an international organisation under an international treaty.

2. Subject to paragraphs 4 and 5, this Convention does not affect any international instrument to which Contracting States are parties and which contains provisions on matters governed by this Convention, unless a contrary declaration is made by the Contracting States bound by such instrument.

3. This Convention does not affect the ability of one or more Contracting States to enter into international instruments which contain provisions on matters governed by this Convention, provided that these instruments do not affect, in the relationship of such Contracting States with other Contracting States, the application of the provisions of this Convention.

4. Where a Contracting State is also a party to an international instrument which contains provisions on matters governed by this Convention, this Convention shall prevail in matters relating to jurisdiction except where -

a) the chosen court is situated in a State in which the instrument is applicable; and

b) all the parties are resident[only] either in a State in which the instrument is applicable or in a non-Contracting State.[17]

5. This Convention shall not restrict the application of an international instrument in force between the State of origin and the requested State for the purposes of obtaining recognition or enforcement of a judgment. [However the judgment shall not be recognised or enforced to a lesser extent than under this Convention.]

6. [Notwithstanding] [Subject to] paragraphs 4 and 5, this Convention does not affect the ability of one or more Contracting States to continue to apply or to enter into international instruments which, in relation to specific subject matters, govern jurisdiction or the recognition or enforcement of judgments, even if all States concerned are parties to this Convention.

CHAPTER V FINAL CLAUSES

Article 24 Signature, ratification, acceptance, approval or accession

1. The Convention is open for signature by all States.

2. The Convention is subject to ratification, acceptance or approval by the signatory States.

3. The Convention is open for accession by all States which are not signatory States as from the date it is open for signature.

4. Instruments of ratification, acceptance, approval and accession shall be deposited with the Ministry of Foreign Affairs of the Kingdom of the Netherlands, depositary of the Convention.

[17] The policy and drafting of this paragraph requires further discussion. One result of the present draft is that the Convention prevails where the chosen court is in a Contracting State in which the instrument is applicable, one party is resident in a Contracting State in which the instrument is not applicable, and the other party is resident in a non-Contracting State in which the instrument is applicable. It was proposed that the Convention should not seek to prevail over other instruments binding a Contracting State in its relations with non-Contracting States. An alternative approach would be to replace paragraph 4 b) with the following: "b) a party is resident in a non-Contracting State in which the instrument is applicable, or there is some other relevant connection between the parties or the dispute and such a State."

Article 25 *Non-unified legal system*

1. If a State has two or more territorial units in which different systems of law apply in relation to matters dealt with in this Convention, it may at the time of signature, ratification, acceptance, approval or accession declare that the Convention shall extend to all its territorial units or only to one or more of them and may modify this declaration by submitting another declaration at any time.

2. Any such declaration shall be notified to the depositary and shall state expressly the territorial units to which the Convention applies.

3. If a State makes no declaration under this Article, the Convention is to extend to all territorial units of that State.

Article 26 *Regional Economic Integration Organisations*

1. A Regional Economic Integration Organisation which is constituted by sovereign States and has competence over some or all of the matters governed by this Convention may equally sign, accept, approve or accede to this Convention. The Regional Economic Integration Organisation shall in that case have the rights and obligations of a Contracting State, to the extent that the Organisation has competence over matters governed by this Convention.

2. The Regional Economic Integration Organisation shall, at the time of signature, acceptance, approval or accession, notify the depositary in writing of the matters governed by this Convention in respect of which competence has been transferred to that Organisation by its Member States. The Organisation shall promptly notify the depositary in writing of any changes to its competence as specified in the most recent notice given under this paragraph.

3. For the purposes of the entry into force of this Convention, any instrument deposited by a Regional Economic Integration Organisation shall not be counted as additional to any instruments deposited by its Member States.

4. At the time of signature, acceptance, approval or accession, a Regional Economic Integration Organisation may declare that its Member States, by virtue of the law of the Organisation, are bound by this Convention. In this case, a reference to a Contracting State includes, where appropriate, a reference to the Member States of the Organisation[in accordance with Article 22].

5. A reference to a Contracting State in this Convention includes, where appropriate, a reference to a Regional Economic Integration Organisation that is a party to this Convention, with all necessary modifications. In particular, references to a Contracting State in Articles 1, paragraph 2, 18 and 19 shall be read as references to the Regional Economic Integration Organisation.

6. Article 9 shall not apply to the recognition and enforcement of judgments in cases where the State of origin and the requested State are Member States of a Regional Economic Integration Organisation that is a party to this Convention and has made a declaration under paragraph 4. [However the judgment shall not be recognised or enforced to a lesser extent than under this Convention.]

Article 27 *Entry into force*

1. This Convention shall enter into force on the first day of the month following the expiration of three months after the deposit of the [third][18] instrument of ratification, acceptance, approval or accession referred to in Article 24.

2. Thereafter this Convention shall enter into force –

a) for each State or Regional Economic Integration Organisation referred to in Article 26 subsequently ratifying, accepting, approving or acceding to it, on the first day of the month following the expiration of three months after the deposit of its instrument of ratification, acceptance, approval or accession;

b) for a territorial unit to which this Convention has been extended in accordance with Article 25, paragraph 1, on the first day of the month following the expiration of three months after the notification of the declaration referred to in that Article.

Article 28 *Reservations*

Article 29 *Declarations*

Article 30 *Denunciation*

1. A Contracting State may denounce this Convention by a notification in writing to the depositary. The denunciation may be limited to certain territorial units of a non-unified legal system to which this Convention applies.

2. The denunciation shall take effect on the first day of the month following the expiration of twelve months after the date on which the notification is received by the depositary. Where a longer period for the denunciation to take effect is specified in the notification, the denunciation shall take effect upon the expiration of such longer period after the date on which the notification is received by the depositary.

Article 31 *Notifications by the depositary*

The depositary shall notify the Members of the Hague Conference on Private International Law, and other States and Regional Economic Integration Organisations which have signed, ratified, accepted, approved or acceded in accordance with Articles 24 and 26, of the following –

a) the signatures and ratifications, acceptances, approvals and accessions referred to in Articles 24 and 26;

b) the date on which this Convention enters into force in accordance with Article 27;

c) the notifications, declarations and withdrawals of declarations referred to in Articles 18, 19, 20, 23, paragraph 2, 25, paragraph 1, and 26, paragraphs 2 and 4;

d) the denunciations referred to in Article 30.

[18] The required number of instruments deposited remains to be discussed, in particular with regard to Regional Economic Integration Organisations and their Member States.

RECOMMENDED FORM

(Sample form confirming the issuance and content of a judgment by the Court of Origin for the purposes of recognition and enforcement under the Convention on Exclusive Choice of Court Agreements (the "Convention"))

(THE COURT OF ORIGIN) ....

(ADDRESS OF THE COURT OF ORIGIN)...

(CONTACT PERSON AT THE COURT OF ORIGIN)...

(TEL./FAX/EMAIL OF THE COURT OF ORIGIN)...

CASE / DOCKET NUMBER: ....

_______________________________(PLAINTIFF)

v.

_______________________________(DEFENDANT)

(THE COURT OF ORIGIN) hereby confirms that it rendered a judgment in the above captioned matter on (DATE) in (CITY, STATE), which is a Contracting State to the Convention. Attached to this form is a complete and certified copy of the judgment rendered by (THE COURT OF ORIGIN).

1. This Court based its jurisdiction on an exclusive choice of court agreement:

YES________NO________

If so, the agreement was found in or evidenced by the following document(s):

....

....

....

2. This Court awarded the following payment of money *(Please indicate any relevant categories of damages included):*

....

....

....

....

....

3. This Court awarded interest as follows (*Please specify the rate of interest, the portion(s) of the award to which interest applies, and the date from which interest is computed*):

....

....

....

....

....

4. This Court included within the judgment the following court costs and expenses (including lawyers' fees) related to the proceedings *(Please specify the amounts of any such awards, including where applicable, any amount(s) within a monetary award intended to cover costs and expenses relating to the proceedings)*:

....

....

....

....

....

5. This Court awarded, in whole or in part, the following non-monetary remedy *(Please describe the nature of the remedy)*:

....

....

....

....

6. This judgment was rendered by default:

YES________ NO________

(If this judgment was rendered by default, please attach the original or a certified copy of the document verifying notice to the defendant of the proceedings.)

7. This judgment (or a part thereof) is currently the subject of review in (STATE OF THE COURT OF ORIGIN):

YES________ NO________

8. This judgment (or a part thereof) is enforceable in (STATE OF THE COURT OF ORIGIN):

YES________ NO________

List of documents annexed:

....

....

....

....

....

Dated this __________ day of ___________, 20__.

Signature and/or stamp by an officer of the Court

Index